The Appearance of Corruption

The Appearance of Corruption

Testing the Supreme Court's Assumptions about Campaign Finance Reform

DARON R. SHAW, BRIAN E. ROBERTS, AND MIJEONG BAEK

OXFORD
UNIVERSITY PRESS

OXFORD
UNIVERSITY PRESS

Oxford University Press is a department of the University of Oxford. It furthers the University's objective of excellence in research, scholarship, and education by publishing worldwide. Oxford is a registered trade mark of Oxford University Press in the UK and certain other countries.

Published in the United States of America by Oxford University Press
198 Madison Avenue, New York, NY 10016, United States of America.

Library of Congress Cataloging-in-Publication Data
Names: Shaw, Daron R., author. | Roberts, Brian E. (Professor), author. | Baek, Mijeong, author.
Title: The appearance of corruption : testing the Supreme Court's assumptions about
campaign finance reform / Daron R. Shaw, Brian E. Roberts, Mijeong Baek.
Description: New York, NY : Oxford University Press, 2021. |
Includes bibliographical references and index.
Identifiers: LCCN 2020028510 (print) | LCCN 2020028511 (ebook) |
ISBN 9780197548417 (hardback) | ISBN 9780197548431 (epub)
Subjects: LCSH: Campaign funds—Law and legislation—United States. |
Campaign funds—Corrupt practices—United States. | Elections—Corrupt practices—United States. |
Political corruption—United States. | United States. Supreme Court.
Classification: LCC KF4920 .S53 2021 (print) | LCC KF4920 (ebook) |
DDC 342.73/078—dc23
LC record available at https://lccn.loc.gov/2020028510
LC ebook record available at https://lccn.loc.gov/2020028511

1 3 5 7 9 8 6 4 2

DOI: 10.1093/oso/9780197548417.001.0001

Printed by Integrated Books International, United States of America

Contents

1

The Appearance of Corruption

An Introduction

What happens when the Supreme Court is wrong, when the foundation of decades of jurisprudence is simply not true? This book examines the empirical implications of the behavioral model adopted by the U.S. Supreme Court in its landmark 1976 *Buckley v. Valeo* (424 U.S. 1) decision—the bedrock of all extant campaign finance law. The behavioral model in question supports the anti-corruption arguments the Court uses to assert a compelling interest necessary to overcome significant First Amendment concerns presented by laws limiting the amount of money in politics.

Political corruption, even the appearance of corruption alone, threatens to so dishearten the American people, the Court argues, that they may simply walk away, eroding political participation to the point it jeopardizes the legitimacy of American democracy.[1] The Court's corruption teleology—the causal chain ultimately responsible for these existential fears—is testable. It involves a series of behavioral predictions that readily lend themselves to investigation. These predications start with the Court's precondition that campaign finance laws lower perceptions, if not the amount, of political corruption and then follow the Court's logic through to political participation.

The intrepid work of the handful of scholars who have broached the question consistently finds the Court's reasoning—what Adam Samaha calls part of "a judicial tradition of unflinching empirical claims" (Samaha, 2012: p. 1602)—suspect.[2] This book consolidates these findings and introduces new data and analysis to examine the full behavioral model undergirding the Supreme Court's willingness to limit money in politics. Reinforcing the compelling findings in Primo and Milyo (2020), even with the heightened awareness of campaign finance issues created in the wake of the 2010 *Citizens United v. Federal Election Commission* (558 U.S. 310) decision, there is limited empirical support for the Court's reasoning.

The Appearance of Corruption. Daron R. Shaw, Brian E. Roberts, and Mijeong Baek, Oxford University Press (2021).
 DOI: 10.1093/oso/9780197548417.003.0001

The policy implications of such limited support are significant. Most notably it was solely on the strength of its corruption logic that the Court looked past its constitutional misgivings over contribution limits, the most significant limit on money in politics upheld in the *Buckley* decision.[3] Absent a supporting behavioral model, the Court may find itself confronting a new breed of challenge to long-standing precedent.

* * *

Just shy of thirty-five miles south of Marfa, Texas, on Route 67 is the turnoff to Cibolo Creek Ranch, the secluded resort in the high desert of West Texas where Supreme Court Justice Antonin Scalia was discovered dead the morning of February 13, 2016. The untimely death of Justice Scalia occurred early in the presidential primary season and quickly became an outsized political story in its own right with the same-day announcement by Senate Majority Leader Mitch McConnell (R-KY) that the next president, not President Barack Obama, should fill the vacant Supreme Court seat.[4]

President Obama tested McConnell's mettle with his early April nomination of Merrick Garland to fill Scalia's seat. By all accounts, Garland was well qualified. More to the point, he was arguably as moderate a candidate as one could expect from a Democratic president. Following the Garland nomination, Senate Republicans embarked on a risky, politically charged, but ultimately successful strategy to keep the seat vacant. As vexing as this strategy was to Democrats, the conviction that Hillary Clinton would win the election and secure Scalia's replacement was both a source of ultimate comfort and reason to begin filling the legal pipeline with cases providing the context for undoing many of the Roberts Court decisions that had benefited from Justice Scalia's unwavering, occasionally caustic, conservative voice (Hasen, 2018). Prominent among those targeted for reversal was the 2010 *Citizens United v. FEC* decision, which for many came to symbolize all that is wrong about the influence of money in American politics.[5]

Against seemingly all odds, McConnell's Garland gambit paid off with Donald Trump's election victory. The new president wasted little time securing the appointment of Neil Gorsuch to fill the vacant Supreme Court seat, restoring and securing the ideological balance of the Roberts Court.[6] The consequences for campaign finance law could not be more significant, for it is the courts, not Congress, that have had the most to say about the contours of modern campaign finance law.

Buckley v. Valeo

Where Congress has dithered in addressing campaign finance over the years since the Supreme Court's *Buckley* decision—passing only one significant revision of the Federal Election Campaign Act (FECA), in 2002[7]—the courts have taken charge, issuing hundreds of related decisions.[8] Despite this concerted activity—and a complete turnover in Supreme Court justices—the per curiam 1976 *Buckley v. Valeo* opinion, which celebrated its fortieth anniversary in 2016, remains the touchstone of campaign finance law to this day.

That its basic tenets remain intact after decades of unrelenting litigation is less a signal of estimable legal reasoning than of an uneasy political truce between what election law authority Richard Hasen labels the forces of anti-corruption and anti-tyranny (Hasen, 2011a). The *Buckley* Court's reasoning with respect to political contributions, expenditures, disclosure, and public financing has proven remarkably resilient. This resilience is noteworthy not just for withstanding extraordinary changes in the scale and complexity of campaign finance over so many years but also because it was controversial—vilified by voices from across the political spectrum—from the day the opinion was published (Hasen, 2011b).

At the heart of the almost universal opprobrium directed at the opinion is the *Buckley* Court's decision to split the baby in its treatment of campaign contributions and expenditures, upholding strict limits on the former while eliminating all limits on the latter. While this continues to dominate scrutiny of *Buckley*, it is not the central concern of this book. Instead, the focus here is the Court's interest in corruption mitigation. To reach that issue it is essential that we account for the steps the Supreme Court took building the legal foundations for the regulation of campaign finance more generally in its landmark case.

Buckley v. Valeo (1976) challenged the constitutionality of the Federal Election Campaign Act Amendments of 1974, a series of amendments to the 1971 Federal Election Campaign Act that substantially rewrote federal campaign finance law.[9] A politically diverse set of plaintiffs mounted a broad attack on the law, arguing that key elements of the amendments violated the First Amendment (Winter, 1997).[10]

The *Buckley* opinion established, for the first time, foundational principles governing the constitutional limits of regulating money in politics. While these principles endured steadfastly, other aspects of the opinion proved contestable, broadening the scope of permissible campaign finance regulation, even while staying within the original *Buckley* framework. However, starting in 2007 with its *Wisconsin Right to Life* opinion,[11] the Supreme Court unremittingly charted a course back to *Buckley*, reawakening many of the earlier debates.[12] The ideas to which recent decisions returned emerged in a set of consequential steps the *Buckley* Court took before passing judgement upon specific provisions in the 1974 FECA Amendments.

Money, Speech, and the First Amendment

The single most important observation made by the *Buckley* Court was that political speech is expensive. Effective mass communication in federal elections, the Court argued, requires—not just benefits from—significant expenditures by and on behalf of candidates. In the Court's words:

> Virtually every means of communicating ideas in today's mass society requires the expenditure of money. The distribution of the humblest handbill or leaflet entails printing, paper, and circulation costs. Speeches and rallies generally necessitate hiring a hall and publicizing the event. The electorate's increasing dependence on television, radio, and other mass media for news and information has made these expensive modes of communication indispensable instruments of effective political speech. (P. 11)

The Court's observation about the financial realities of mass political communication stops well short of equating money and speech, the assertion of myriad critics of the *Buckley* decision notwithstanding.[13] The Court does not equate money and speech; it simply *observes* that political speech costs money.[14] Of course, this means that limiting money in politics effectively limits political speech, and that is problematic. As the Court notes:

> A restriction on the amount of money a person or group can spend on political communication during a campaign necessarily reduces the quantity of expression by restricting the number of issues discussed, the depth of their exploration, and the size of the audience reached. (P. 19)

Political speech, in a democracy, is special (Polsby, 1976). It is speech for which the First Amendment "affords the broadest protection" (p. 14). As the

Court notes, "discussion of public issues and debate on the qualifications of candidates are integral to the operation of the system of government established by our Constitution" (p. 14). Any limits on money in politics imperil the First Amendment.[15]

By linking—not equating—money and political speech, the Court forevermore established the principle that laws limiting money in politics infringe on the First Amendment.[16] The *Buckley* case was not the first venue in which First Amendment issues surfaced in the context of campaign finance, but it was the first to enshrine it.[17]

Having established in the opening paragraphs of its *Buckley* opinion the constitutional threat presented by limits on money in politics, the Court could have, as urged to by the appellants, summarily ended the discussion. The Court demurred, issuing instead a 144-page opinion establishing the modern framework for the regulation of money in politics. In order to do so, however, the Court had to offer a compelling reason why it would tolerate limits on political speech.

Compelling Interest

The Supreme Court does not lightly uphold laws it believes facially violate the Constitution, but it can and does.[18] Laws that intrude on a right explicitly protected by the U.S. Constitution are presumptively impermissible and, as a consequence, subject to the highest level of judicial review—strict scrutiny. A necessary condition for surviving such inspection is that the law advance a compelling state interest.[19]

The *Buckley* appellees offered a number of potentially compelling interests served by the FECA Amendments of 1974, but the two interests capturing the imagination of the Court most were equalization—leveling the financial (communications) playing field—and corruption mitigation. The *Buckley* Court divined equalization an important motivation of the authors of the 1974 amendments noting that

> although the Act does not focus on the ideas expressed by persons or groups subject to its regulations, it is aimed in part at equalizing the relative ability of all voters to affect electoral outcomes by placing a ceiling on expenditures for political expression by citizens and groups. (P. 17)

Although the U.S. Appeals Court accepted the equalization argument in upholding FECA contribution and expenditure limits, the Supreme Court, in perhaps the most infamous passage in its *Buckley* opinion, utterly dismisses the equalization interest, saying,

> the concept that government may restrict the speech of some elements of our society in order to enhance the relative voice of others is wholly foreign to the First Amendment, which was designed "to secure 'the widest possible dissemination of information from diverse and antagonistic sources,' and 'to assure unfettered interchange of ideas for the bringing about of political and social changes desired by the people.' *New York Times Co. v. Sullivan*, *supra*, at 266, 269, quoting *Associated Press v. United States*, 326 U.S. 1, 20 (1945), and *Roth v. United States*, 354 U.S., at 484. The First Amendment's protection against governmental abridgment of free expression cannot properly be made to depend on a person's financial ability to engage in public discussion. *Cf. Eastern R. Conf. v. Noerr Motors*, 365 U.S. 127, 139 (1961). 55 [424 U.S. 1, 50]. (P. 48–49)

Corruption mitigation was a different story. Political corruption, the Court argued, threatens to undermine "the integrity of our system of representative democracy." Threats to our very system of government posed by corruption were sufficiently grave to warrant consideration of campaign finance laws otherwise quickly dispatched for violating the First Amendment. Importantly, the threat comes not just from actual corruption but also the appearance thereof. In the words of the Court:

> Of almost equal concern as the danger of actual [corruption] is the impact of the appearance of corruption stemming from public awareness of the opportunities for abuse inherent in a regime of large individual financial contributions. . . . Congress could legitimately conclude that the avoidance of the appearance of improper influence "is also critical . . . if confidence in the system of representative Government is not to be eroded to a disastrous extent." [CSC v. Letter Carriers, 413 U.S. 548 (1973). 29] (P. 27)

This quote is of vital importance to this book, for it establishes the foundations of the Court's behavioral model, discussed at length later in the chapter.[20] For now, it is simply worth noting that the Court felt compelled to explain its extension of a compelling interest in mitigating corruption to include the appearance of corruption. The *Buckley* Court's efforts to explain the invocation of appearance, which it did not feel necessary in the apparently more self-evident case of actual corruption, suggests some recognition of the tenuousness of this interest.

Adding the *appearance* of corruption as a state interest was, as Persily and Lammie (2004) point out, unprecedented not only in campaign finance law but also in First Amendment jurisprudence more generally.[21] Somewhat cynically, they suggest the appearance criterion was a "fallback state interest," one that "has less to do with the importance of removing unsavory appearances and more to do with the difficulty of proving actual corruption."[22]

Samaha (2012) makes the important point that the *Buckley* Court effectively decoupled actual and perceived corruption, making no causal claims, in either direction, in reference to the two interests. Indeed, in the eyes of the Court, the two interests stand apart, separately sufficient to raise concern. On the other hand, Samaha suggests there is some implicit hierarchy, noting, "there seems to be no campaign finance decision holding that the regulatory interest in fighting corruption was insufficient but that the interest in combating corrupt appearance was strong enough."

Although the Court went to some trouble to explain why the appearance of corruption was a state interest, it stopped short of explaining what constitutes sufficient "appearance" to be compelling (Burke, 1997; Samaha, 2012).[23] The sufficiency condition applies to both quantity and quality, as the Court leaves unstated how much perceived corruption (and by whom) must exist before a law designed to mitigate perceived corruption no longer threatens First Amendment rights. This creates the unsettling possibility that we are in a Potter Stewart world, in which the perception of a majority of Supreme Court justices, who know it when they see it, is sufficient.[24]

In practice, courts have accepted evidence from public opinion surveys on the appearance of corruption, most notably over the course of the 2003 *McConnell v. FEC* (540 U.S. 93) litigation, in which both plaintiffs and defendants offered supporting data from polls (Shapiro, 2003; Mellman and Wirthlin, 2003; Primo, 2003).[25] The presentation of survey findings to the Court brought with it a wide array of measurement concerns, but the basic challenge of demonstrating broad public perceptions of corruption was easily overcome, as essentially any public opinion survey reveals that a large majority of Americans believe (perceive) that money corrupts politics.[26]

This basic fact of public opinion is critical. The ease of documenting broad perceptions of corruption ensures that essentially any proposed limit on money in politics meets the minimal necessary condition of establishing the existence of a compelling state interest established by the *Buckley* Court. Whether such perceptions create the "real harm" envisioned by the Court is a different question, one that this book seeks to answer.[27]

Defining Political Corruption

Interestingly, although the Court's decision to limit the scope of compelling state interests potentially served by limiting money in politics to mitigate corruption remains its guiding principle to this day, no such stability attends the Courts' operative definition of corruption. The contestability of corruption as a legal concept in the context of campaign finance begins with the *Buckley* decision itself (Weintraub, 2004).[28]

The *Buckley* Court offers a seemingly straightforward definition, to wit acts done "to secure a political quid pro quo from current and potential office holders." To the extent money or anything else of value is used to secure "improper commitments" from candidates or elected officials, it is being used for corrupt purposes. The opinion repeats the "quid pro quo" phrase five times, leaving little doubt to what the Court referred. The *Buckley* opinion, however, clouds the issue when comparing its conception of political corruption to bribery, for which strict laws already exist (see note 31, this chapter), when it notes that

> laws making criminal the giving and taking of bribes deal with only the most blatant and specific attempts of those with money to influence governmental action. (P. 28)

The Court strongly suggests here that there are less blatant quid pro quo arrangements that limits on money in politics—in this instance the Court was referring to contribution limits—account for but fall short of those covered under bribery statutes. Unfortunately, the Court offers no guidance to its thinking, effectively making the operative definition of corruption contestable. And so it proved (Burke, 1997).

The Supreme Court's opinion in *Austin v. Michigan Chamber of Commerce*, 494 U.S. 652 (1990) introduced the broadest corruption definition invoked in campaign finance jurisprudence. The *Austin* Court, in upholding a Michigan law banning corporate independent expenditures, advanced an anti-distortion argument, finding that voters' exposure to advocacy paid for by amassed corporate wealth could distort (corrupt) political preferences.[29] By including not just politicians but also voters among the potentially corrupted, the court fundamentally transformed the corruption argument in *Buckley* and signaled the potential for unlimited creativity along these lines by future courts.

Future courts did indeed revisit the operative definition of corruption. Starting with *Citizens United v. FEC* (2010), and then reemphasized in *McCutcheon v. FEC,* 572 U.S. 185 (2014), the Supreme Court emphatically returns to the quid pro quo corruption of *Buckley*, saying in no uncertain terms that "the only type of corruption that Congress may target is quid pro quo corruption."[30] Seemingly aware that the *Buckley* opinion left considerable room for interpretation, the *McCutcheon* Court offered more specific guidance, with a concluding admonition, citing *FEC v. Wisconsin Right to Life*, that "the Court must 'err on the side of protecting political speech rather than suppressing it.' "[31] With such clarifications and admonitions in place, it is fair to say that the Court now operates with a far stricter notion of corruption than it first articulated in *Buckley*, much to the potential relief of Rod Blagojevich (among others). This is also why the drama that unfolded in the wake of Justice Scalia's death was so consequential for campaign finance; history has shown the creativity—some would say mischief—engendered by the plasticity of political corruption.

The fiercely contested definition of corruption over the years speaks, ironically, to the durability of the corruption paradigm created by *Buckley*. The creativity of reformers, plaintiffs, and judges in their promotion and use of different notions of corruption marks more than just tacit acceptance of the *Buckley* Court's adoption of corruption as the lone compelling state interest potentially advanced by limits on money in politics. Although there have been any number of suggestions for expanding the set of state interests met by regulating campaign finance, none has been seriously entertained by the courts.[32] It is well understood that regardless of any underlying motive for limiting money in politics—whether it be safeguarding electoral integrity, equalizing voices, or ensuring more competitive elections—any proposed legislation or regulation must use the vocabulary of corruption if it is to have any chance of surviving constitutional review. The elasticity accepted by the courts over the years in defining corruption accommodated a wide range of motives.

The contestability of the corruption definition not only creates a fascinating legal history but also presents a measurement challenge for any related empirical work, particularly when measuring corruption, or the appearance thereof, over time. Researchers have employed a variety of measures of both actual and perceived corruption.[33] In the chapters to follow, where we focus on the appearance of corruption, we allow for a generous range of interpretation of the meaning of political corruption; it is our strong suspicion that careful attention to Supreme Court semantics is not likely to drive public perceptions of corruption.

The Distinct (and Curious) Treatment of Contributions and Expenditures

It is only after establishing its corruption paradigm that the *Buckley* Court weighed in on the actual complaints targeting the FECA Amendments of 1974, most notably the proposed limits on both campaign contributions and expenditures, by both candidates and independently by individuals.[34] The Court upheld limits on contributions but overturned all expenditure limits.

The focal point of most *Buckley* opinion criticism is the differential treatment of laws limiting contributions and expenditures. The 1974 amendments to FECA passed by Congress in the wake of egregious campaign finance practices uncovered by Watergate investigations included stringent limits on both contributions and expenditures. Although the Court of Appeals for the District of Columbia Circuit upheld both limits, the Supreme Court split the baby, upholding limits on contributions but finding limits on independent expenditures to be unconstitutional. To many this seemed a politically expedient solution, giving something to both those who clamored for across-the-board limits and those believing any limits posed an intolerable assault on the First Amendment (Issacharoff, 2010). Neither side was the least bit pleased with the Court's decision or the reasoning behind it. And yet, it endures.[35]

Definition of Expenditures

The *Buckley* Court took issue with the statutory language in the 1974 FECA Amendments defining independent expenditures as anything spent "relative to a clearly identified candidate." The Court found this too vague and went to some pains to offer a very clear definition of an independent expenditure, to wit, "an expenditure for a communication that expressly advocates the election or defeat of a clearly identified candidate" or, "precisely to that spending that is unambiguously related to the campaign of a particular federal candidate."[36]

Unlike with corruption, the *Buckley* Court's definition of independent expenditure (aka, express advocacy) has remained surprisingly steadfast, even prompting the addition of a closely related term—"the functional equivalent of express advocacy"—to the campaign finance lexicon in *McConnell v. FEC* (2003), so as not to tamper with, or invite the contestability of, its original definition. The difference in both precision and resoluteness in the Court's treatment of two vital campaign finance concepts—corruption and expenditures—is notable.

Treatment of Disclosure

The *Buckley* opinion also weighed in on the constitutionality of disclosure requirements.[37] The Court acknowledged and carefully weighed the plaintiffs' argument that enhanced disclosure requirements have a chilling effect on speech—curtailing speech by those concerned for their safety and property following the disclosure of their names. The Court agreed that disclosure requirements implicate the First Amendment but that, in general, compelling state interests render them permissible.[38]

> We long have recognized that significant encroachments on First Amendment rights of the sort that compelled disclosure imposes cannot be justified by a mere showing of some legitimate governmental interest. (P. 64)

Interestingly, unlike in the context of campaign contribution and expenditure limits, where corruption mitigation was the lone state interest entertained by the Court, in the case of disclosure requirements the Court offered three (!) state interests, and corruption mitigation was listed second, upstaged by the value of disclosed information to a voter's ability to both

> place each candidate in the political spectrum more precisely than is often possible solely on the basis of party labels and campaign speeches

and,

> alert the voter to the interests to which a candidate is most likely to be responsive and thus facilitate predictions of future performance in office. (P. 67)

The first of the voter information arguments—allow for better candidate placement on the political spectrum—seems utterly novel (with a strange nod to spatial voting; see Enelow and Hinich, 1984) and unrelated to the rest of the *Buckley* opinion.[39] The second information argument is more closely aligned with an accountability argument and, oddly, undermines the upholding of contribution limits, which censor the potential interests otherwise illuminated by unlimited contributions.

The Court also notes a corruption mitigation interest and an enforcement enhancement interest as reasons to accept the acknowledged chilling effects of disclosure laws. For the purposes of this book, the disclosure interests open up an additional set of behavioral predictions—for example, how voters use campaign finance information to inform their understanding of candidates and how to place them ideologically—beyond those implied by the corruption arguments that otherwise dominate the *Buckley* opinion. We take up this additional challenge in Chapter 6.

Contribution Limits

The Court's corruption logic gained its most significant purchase in the decision to uphold contribution limits; as noted in the *Buckley* decision:

> It is unnecessary to look beyond the Act's primary purpose—to limit the actuality and appearance of corruption resulting from large individual financial contributions—in order to find a constitutionally sufficient justification for the $1,000 contribution limitation. (P. 26)

For the Court, no provision of the 1974 FECA Amendments more closely fit "the weighty interests" captured by its quid pro quo definition of corruption given "the opportunity for abuse inherent in the process of raising large monetary contributions" (p. 30).

Interestingly, the Court went to some effort to distance contribution limits from its speech rights concerns, describing the limits as having "only a marginal restriction upon the contributor's ability to engage in free communication" (pp. 20–21), suggesting that

> the quantity of communication by the contributor does not increase perceptibly with the size of his contribution, since the expression rests solely on the undifferentiated, symbolic act of contributing. (P. 21)

All of these arguments allowed the Court to use a lower standard of scrutiny when evaluating the constitutionality of contribution limits and, ultimately, decided that such limits did not sufficiently infringe on speech rights. This conclusion could not be reached without the Court's acceptance of the quid pro quo corruption interest and its supporting logic.

* * *

In sum, the Supreme Court's corruption teleology implies a behavioral model, the contours of which are detailed in this chapter along with its testable implications. In pursuing these implications, this book thus offers the Court empirical insights to its theoretical claims. It is an open question, however, how such insights will be received.

Social Science and the Courts

When Chief Justice John Roberts declared measures of partisan gerrymandering proffered by academic researchers as "sociological gobbledygook,"[40] he was not the first to question the usefulness of social science in the courtroom.[41] Starting with what is often cited as the first Supreme Court case explicitly to invoke social science research in its decision—*Brown v. Board of Education of Topeka*, 347 U.S. 483 (1954)—there has been a healthy debate about the usefulness of social science as a guide to legal reasoning.[42] The debate aside, there is no question that one of the hallmarks of American jurisprudence has been the extensive use of social science by the courts. The ascendency of social science grew out of the emergence of the legal realism school at the turn of the last century, a movement very much aligned with the growing faith in expertise associated with Progressive Era (Fuller, 1934).[43]

In an influential 1942 article, administrative law scholar Kenneth Culp Davis described two ways in which social science research enters the legal realm. The first as a source of "adjudicative facts," which bear narrowly on the outcome of a specific case. More impactful is the use of social science in the establishment of "legislative facts," which Davis characterizes as applying more broadly in courts' interpretations of law or policy rather than to any particular dispute.[44] Although a relatively common addition to court records, and relied upon as important foundations for legal rulings, these so-called legislative facts generally lie outside standard evidentiary rules, as they do not bear directly on decisions at hand in any particular case.[45] It is precisely in such context—providing an overarching empirical foundation for behavioral assumptions about political actors—that social science research can enlighten courts wrestling with the regulation of money in politics.

Starting in 1978, with the debut of the Federal Election Commission's *Reports of Financial Activity*—the first accessible comprehensive data on federal campaign contributions and expenditures—social scientists launched an industrial-scale empirical research program to expose the role of money in American politics. Of immediate (and enduring) interest were such questions as whether money influences (determines?) election outcomes (Jacobson, 1978; Abramowitz, 1988; Green and Krasno, 1988; Levitt, 1994) and, particularly germane to the corruption concerns at the heart of the Court's campaign finance doctrine, whether campaign contributions influence legislative voting (Welch, 1982; Wright, 1985; Frendreis and Waterman, 1985; Stratmann, 1991; Bronars and Lott, 1997). The latter research has been vexingly inconclusive, as the object of interest in all such studies are contributions made by corporate political action committees (PACs), presumably advancing the rational, profit-maximizing interests of their patron corporations.[46]

The dearth of systematic evidence that political investments by bottom-line-driven corporate interests yield policy benefits—a phenomenon economist Fred McChesney describes as "money for nothing" (McChesney, 1997)—undermines a key quid pro quo corruption argument; if campaign contributions do not advance corporate interests, why should we expect *any* contributions to yield quid pro quo benefits?[47] This body of evidence, however, has not found its way to the courts, in the main because the corruption doctrine has, other than in uncountable law journal articles, never been seriously challenged.

The failure of such a comprehensive body of research to inform the foundational assumptions of the Court could well have something to do with the circumstances and conclusions of the *Buckley* Court. In 1976, at the time of its seminal *Buckley* decision, there was little academic research—and certainly no systematic studies—bearing on the veracity of the Court's behavioral model.[48] Absent any related findings, the Court understandably turned to anecdotes and its own intuition.

In the articulation of its campaign finance doctrine, the Supreme Court advanced a well-formed and inherently testable behavioral model.

The Behavioral Model

Persily and Lammie (2004) rightly note that the *Buckley* decision ventured into seldom explored territory by ceding authority to public opinion (or at least somebody's opinion or belief) when the Court found that the appearance of corruption, not just actual corruption, provided a compelling state interest for limiting money in politics.[49] The Court, however, did not make this judgement casually or arbitrarily. Rather, the justices went to some length explaining their reasoning. In doing so, the Court advanced nothing less than a plausible, sophisticated, multistep behavioral model of how and why members of the American public would respond to laws limiting money in politics.

Drawing on language from its 1973 decision in *United States Civil Service Commission v. National Association of Letter Carriers* (413 U.S. 548), the *Buckley* Court links the appearance of corruption to erosion of trust in government:

> Congress could legitimately conclude that the avoidance of the appearance of improper influence "is also critical . . . if confidence in the system of representative Government is not to be eroded to a disastrous extent." [CSC v. Letter Carriers] 413 U.S., at 565. (424 U.S. 1, 27)

The dire consequence of this lost trust is the threat it represents to "the integrity of the electoral process," an argument the Court reiterates and refines in its 2000 *Nixon v. Shrink Missouri Government PAC* (528 U.S. 377) decision where it establishes a linkage between trust and political participation:

> Leave the perception of impropriety unanswered, and the cynical assumption that large donors call the tune could jeopardize the willingness of voters to take part in democratic governance. Democracy works "only if the people have faith in those who govern, and that faith is bound to be shattered when high officials and their appointees engage in activities which arouse suspicions of malfeasance and corruption." United States v. Mississippi Valley Generating Co., 364 U. S. 520, 562 (1961).

Federal Election Comm'n v. National Right to Work Comm., 459 U. S. 197, 208 (1982) (noting that Government interests in preventing corruption or the appearance of corruption "directly implicate 'the integrity of our electoral process, and, not less, the responsibility of the individual citizen for the successful functioning of that process.'" (P. 390)

The ultimate behavioral concern of the *Buckley* Court—the foundation of its corruption teleology—was the threat corruption posed to political participation. To the extent that laws limiting money in politics affect participation, they affect the legitimacy of democratic political institutions; political participation is both the cornerstone and a barometer of democratic rule. Mediating this behavioral response are crucial links to perceptions of corruption and trust in government. This model, what Adam Samaha calls "a causal path from perceived official misconduct to citizen demoralization and loss of confidence in government," (2012: p. 1599) has stood the test of time; at least to the extent the logic has remained largely unchallenged, legally.[50]

For the social scientist, the Court lays out a well-crafted, clear set of seemingly irresistible testable hypotheses. Yet, as a percentage of the scholarly effort devoted to examining *Buckley* and its progeny, efforts examining this behavioral model empirically are vanishingly small. They do, however, challenge almost every link of the logic chain.

The Effect of Campaign Finance Laws on Corruption

> *If [campaign finance] regulation does not positively influence how outsiders perceive the political system, there will be only costs, without an effective response to the potentially demoralizing perceptions of corruption.* (Samaha, 2012: p. 1606)

The central prescription of the *Buckley* Court, which has unwaveringly guided courts to this day, is that only those campaign finance laws sustaining the promise of mitigating corruption, actual or perceived, are eligible for upholding.[51] Related federal law, therefore, ought to exhibit such effects; that is, observably limit actual corruption or the appearance thereof. Uncovering empirical evidence of this effect by examining reactions to changes in federal campaign finance law presents something of a challenge, however, because there have been so few significant changes in the law. Since the 1976 *Buckley* decision, which took issue with parts of the 1974 FECA Amendments, there has been but one noteworthy change in federal campaign finance law: The 2002 Bipartisan Campaign Reform Act (BCRA) (Pub.L. 107–155, 116 Stat. 81). That said, any number of significant court rulings in the wake of the *Buckley* decision led, if not to Congressional (statutory) responses, to many changes in campaign finance practices effected through changes in Federal Election Commission regulations, advisory opinions, and enforcement.

Given the importance attached by the Court to the relationship between campaign finance laws and corruption mitigation there is surprisingly little research either supporting or refuting it at the federal level. Those researchers focused on changes in federal law discern no effect of limiting money in politics on perceptions of corruption.[52] Persily and Lammie (2004) use a chart (Fig. 2, p. 149) to show what appears to be a strong *negative* relationship between soft money—a source of potentially unlimited contributions to national political parties reaching in the neighborhood of $500 million dollars in 2000 removed almost entirely by the 2002 Bipartisan Campaign Reform Act[53]—and public perceptions of corruption. Notably there is a sharp *rise* in the percentage of survey respondents concerned with the influence of special interests *after* the BCRA soft money ban.[54]

Researchers have not fully exploited significant court decisions related to campaign finance, of which there have been considerably more than laws passed by Congress, as demarcations of potentially observable changes in corruption behavior or perceptions. The 2010 *Citizens United* decision has emerged as a notable exception.[55]

The paucity of new federal campaign finance laws led researchers to employ state-level data, where significant variation in campaign finance laws, across both time and space, can be leveraged to explore the effects of campaign finance laws on a number of political outcomes, including perceptions of corruption. Rosenson (2009) finds no ameliorative effect of campaign finance laws on state political reporters' perceptions of corruption. Similarly, Cordis and Milyo (2013) find no effect of state campaign finance laws on actual corruption.

Unfortunately, the exploitation of variation in state campaign finance laws has long been be plagued by variation in state disclosure rules (and assiduous of their enforcement), which limited data availability and introduced potentially serious selection bias in the data that were available.[56] Ironically, just as data quantity and quality have dramatically improved, recent Supreme Court decisions have reduced the variation researchers so value.[57]

The Effect of Corruption on Trust in Government

The academic literature is replete with research linking corruption to trust in government, but primarily in the context of comparative politics (Anderson and Tverdova, 2003; Chang and Chu, 2006; Morris and Klesner, 2010). In the United States, however, models explaining trust rarely focus on corruption, finding empirical purchase elsewhere, such as presidential approval and the president's personal characteristics (Citrin, 1974; Citrin and Green, 1986; Hetherington, 1998), Thus, existing research suggests that perceptions of corruption have at best an incidental effect, which is no doubt related to relatively lower levels of measurable corruption in U.S. politics.

This is not to say that there has not been substantial scholarly interest in the question of trust in government in the United States. Responding to declining trust in government in the 1960s, political scientists initially found little relationship between this fact and public policy or other aspects of public opinion (Citrin, 1974; Citrin and Green, 1986). More recent research, though, has demonstrated that trust indeed "matters" for both public opinion and policy. Most notably, Hetherington (2006) contends that trust has significant policy implications, with declining trust coinciding with decreased support for liberal domestic policy programs. After the 9/11 attacks and the subsequent wars in Afghanistan and Iraq, some argued that trust in government became more connected with foreign policy such that increased trust correlated with greater support for the war efforts that were mostly associated with the conservative (Republican) party (Hetherington and Husser, 2012). A less obvious aspect of this argument is the notion that news media attention is important in shaping citizens' trust in government. Put simply, the news media prime people to focus on and use certain evaluative criteria when assessing how much they trust the government; the media can emphasize the government's handling of domestic issues, race, foreign policy, and defense, or even corruption when presenting the news, and this emphasis connects assessments of government performance on these issues to the broader attitude of trust in government.

What is important for our purposes is that there is little evidence that the American news media prime voters to evaluate the federal government or state governments based on their honesty and integrity (i.e., their lack of corruption). There are, to be sure, news stories of politicians who take kickbacks or bribes. Moreover, there are occasionally deeper stories such as Teapot

Dome, Watergate, the Keating Five, Jack Abramoff, or the House Post-Office and Banking scandals. But, news media interest in these tends to be ephemeral, and the related scholarly assumption is that trust in government attitudes are more powerfully correlated with other factors.

It is worth noting, though, that there is scant scholarly research on the relationship between perceptions of corruption and political trust. Assuming there is a relationship, there has also been precious little theorizing about the causal relationship between attitudes about corruption and trust in government. Is it that people see (or don't see) corruption and this influences their broader attitudes about the efficacy of government? Or is it that this broader trust (or lack of trust) in government informs their perceptions of whether the government is corrupt?

The Effect of Trust in Government on Political Participation

If political scientists have mostly ignored perceptions of corruption in their explorations of political trust, they have been much more diligent in estimating the link between political trust and participation. This should come as no surprise. As noted, political participation has long been deemed a cornerstone of a healthy, functioning democracy, and scholarly interest reflects the centrality of the concept. Different manifestations of political participation in the United States—running for office, going to a meeting, protesting or marching, volunteering or donating money to a candidate or campaign, writing a letter to a representative, simply discussing politics, and (of course) voting in elections—have been enumerated, measured empirically, and correlated with demographic and attitudinal variables. Political science studies suggest that an array of institutional factors (constitutional context, registration and voting laws, etc.) and some demographic characteristics (socioeconomic status) affect participation (in general) and turnout (in particular). Conversely, this extensive literature suggests a weak relationship between trust and participation (Citrin, 1974; Rosenstone and Hansen, 1993; Chanley, Rudolph, and Rahn, 2000).[58]

One reason for the lack of a strong and consistent relationship between political trust and participation is that a lack of trust does not logically lead one to abstain from political acts. In fact, cynicism about the government could conceivably cause someone to *become* involved in politics. Change requires involvement. Conversely, satisfaction with the status quo could lull someone into complacency and abstention.

Still, the absence of a connection between political trust and participation is contrary to the Court's behavioral model and merits a more detailed look with more recent data. Indeed, the absence of a correlation is quite curious given that, as with the relationship between perceptions of corruption and political trust, the causal relationship between political trust and participation might run in either (or both) directions. That is, someone who is more trusting of government might be more likely to participate in politics while (at the same time) someone who participates in politics might be more likely to trust the political system. The possibility that one of these does not affect the other is important both for our immediate interest and for the wider question of why citizens participate.

The Direct Effect of Corruption on Political Participation

The "real harm" of perceived corruption envisioned by the *Buckley* Court was to political participation, the heart of "our system of government." Corruption has been linked to a number of democratic ills (Rose-Ackerman, 1999; Montinola and Jackman, 2002; Warren, 2013).[59] As Olsson (2014) notes, however, "research on how corruption perceptions shape our political behaviour is scarce." What little there is offers mixed results, with some finding a positive correlation between corruption and participation, suggesting that voters are motivated to participate to address problems rather than disengage (Johnston, 1983; Stockemer and Calca, 2013; Blass, Roberts, and Shaw, 2012; Kelly, 2016). Others, perhaps more conventionally, and certainly as the *Buckley* Court believed, find a negative relationship (Stockemer et al., 2013; Stockemer, 2013; Simpser, 2005; Kostadinova, 2009; McCann and Dominguez, 1998). Olsson (2014), coming closest to capturing the Court's behavioral model, also finds a negative relationship between perceptions of corruption and political participation, mediated through political efficacy.[60]

Most of the research examining the corruption-participation relationship uses comparative data, which tend to encompass more extreme levels of corruption, and more commonly find a negative relationship (i.e., higher corruption is associated with lower participation). Conversely, studies using U.S. corruption data find a positive relationship (Johnson, 1983; Blass, Roberts, and Shaw, 2012; Kelly, 2016).[61] Speculatively, the positive relationship between corruption and participation found in the U.S.-based studies may reflect the existence of a corruption threshold beyond which its relationship to participation turns negative.

Once again, what empirical research we have calls into question the seemingly plausible assumptions of the Court about basic relationships. The limited extant research focused on the effect of corruption on political participation—particularly when limited to perceptions of corruption in the United States (Blass, Roberts, and Shaw, 2012; Kelly, 2016)—does not support the Court's behavioral model. Furthermore, much of this research is of recent vintage—so while focused and updated analyses are welcome, there appears less chance here that the fundamental relationships have changed in a post-*Citizens United* world.

The Direct Effect of Campaign Finance Laws on Political Participation

A larger concern drives the Supreme Court's interest in corruption mitigation, to wit the effect laws limiting corruption have on political participation. The integrity of our electoral system, our representative democracy, hinges crucially on citizen participation. Although people can choose, as free riders, not to participate because they are perfectly happy with the collective choices made by others, participation lowered by disenchantment born of perceived corruption is an existential threat to our democratic institutions. The ultimate reason the Court is willing to uphold the constitutionality of any campaign finance laws is because the Court assumes that these laws increase the likelihood that individuals will choose to participate in politics. More distantly, these laws should, *ceteris paribus*, increase the aggregate turnout levels wherever they are adopted.

Again, there is extremely limited related research. Milyo, Primo, and Jacobsmeier (2011) examine the effects of state-level public funding initiatives, which are designed both to achieve funding equality and to limit candidates' campaign expenditures, on voter turnout. They find no relationship between state-level public financing programs and turnout. At the local level, Kraus (2006) examines New York City's fifteen years of experience with the public financing of political campaigns, which heralded, but ultimately failed to deliver, several normative improvements, including higher turnout.[62]

The conclusion we draw is that that the salutary effects of campaign finance reform laws on political participation are questionable, at best. There is, however, a clear need for additional (and updated) research on this component of the Court's assumed behavioral model.

The Effect of Money in Politics on Trust in Government

Even in a field where many key relationships remain understudied, there is a crying need for analyses of how campaign finance laws and regulations affect political trust, the latter attitude being the proximate variable driving participation in the Court's behavioral model. Rather than examine the effects of laws and regulation on trust, however, researchers have examined campaign expenditures (variation in which may well be partially a function of laws and regulation). Leveraging state-level variation in campaign expenditures, Coleman and Mana (2000) explore the relationship between money in politics and a number of potential effects—trust, efficacy, involvement, and attention, along with knowledge of and affect toward candidates—it might have on voters. While there is some evidence of a positive impact on candidate knowledge and affect, they find no effect of campaign spending on trust or efficacy.

Likewise, at the federal level Primo (2002) finds no link between campaign spending and trust in government. Subsequent to the Watergate scandal, when good campaign finance data became accessible, there is no evidence of a correlation between spending and trust. Noting the historically low levels of trust in the United States following the unrest of the 1960s and early 1970s, Primo concludes, "The cynicism toward politics is clearly rooted in something far deeper than campaign contributions."

The Effect of Money in Politics on Corruption

Again, while ideally we would like to know whether campaign finance laws affect perceptions of corruption, political scientists have been more interested in the connection between campaign spending and corruption. This is understandable. The public's perception of the corrupting influence of money in politics is a maxim of survey research (Primo, 2002), and it is also the case that there have been notable cases of flagrant campaign finance abuse; the campaign finance abuses associated with Nixon's 1972 re-election (Watergate) being of particular note and relevance. The amount of money in politics, however, cannot explain perceptions of corruption (Persily and Lammie, 2004). Studies of (actual) political corruption list campaign-related corruption as a relatively small percentage (Peters and Welch, 1980; Welch and Hibbing, 1997).

It is also important to note that while many lament the amount of money in politics, this was not the stated concern of the *Buckley* Court. The Court's concern was the corruption potential of large individual contributions to individual candidates (quid pro quo), not the total amount of money in politics. At best this is an implicit concern of the Court. The *Buckley* Court did uphold aggregate and per candidate limits on individual contributions, but the argument made by the Court with respect to aggregate limits was restricted to concern that individuals would be able to circumvent limits on candidate contributions by giving money to others knowing it would be channeled to those they support.

The Effect of Money in Politics on Participation

Political advertising is by far the largest campaign expenditure category (Ansolabehere and Gerber, 1994) and is the most direct way by which money affects voter behavior. People might thus reasonably base their perceptions of corruption, and thereby their enthusiasm to participate, in American politics on their exposure to political advertising. Research on the effects of political advertising on political participation offer mixed results, but none that suggests the overall effect is negative (Freedman, Franz, and Goldstein, 2004; Huber and Arceneaux, 2007).[63]

* * *

As discussed, the behavioral model advanced by the Supreme Court in *Buckley v. Valeo* has numerous testable implications. Some of these hypotheses—for example, the relationship between trust and participation—do not relate directly to money in politics and are well studied in the broader voting behavior literature. The intersection of money and behavior is far less well understood, even decades after the *Buckley* opinion, in which that relationship stood center stage.

Policy Consequences

The most consequential implication of an unsupported behavioral model is the threat posed to contribution limits, the most significant provision of the 1974 FECA Amendments upheld by the *Buckley* Court. If there is no empirical evidence that campaign contribution limits increase the percentage of the public that believes politicians are honest and trustworthy or improve trust in government or result in higher turnout, then it is difficult to see how the upside to such limitations warrants the reduction in speech. At the very least, it seems the Court would have to rely on other grounds to justify the restriction on a fundamental freedom.

The Plan

The following chapters systematically explore the empirical support for the behavioral model posited by the U.S. Supreme Court in its 1976 *Buckley v. Valeo* decision. At its core, this model links individuals' perceptions of corruption to their decisions to participate politically, hypothesizing that the greater an individual's perception of corruption the less likely that person is to participate in the political process (e.g., vote) because of an erosion of trust in government.

But there is a temporal element to our analysis that is worth highlighting. Prior to testing the Court's model explicitly, we evaluate the impact of the 2010 *Citizens United* decision on campaign-finance-driven perceptions of corruption. It is no secret (nor much of a revelation) that prior to the Court's decision a significant percentage of American survey respondents believed that money corrupts politicians (Primo, 2002). It will come as little surprise that *Citizens United* did nothing to diminish those beliefs.

The *Citizens United* decision, which found laws banning corporate independent expenditures to be unconstitutional, arguably raised the political salience of campaign finance issues in the United States to levels not seen since the Watergate era and, thereby, might reasonably have changed not only public perceptions of corruption but also any number of other well-established beliefs about money and politics. It is also possible—indeed, probable given the logic of the Court's behavioral model—that trust in government and participation have declined in this new era of unfettered opportunities for campaign spending.

The unshakable truths—the folklore—of pre-*Citizens United* public opinion are the following:

1. There is too much money in politics, and it corrupts our elected officials.
2. Campaign finance regulation is ineffective, but we need more of it (!).
3. Campaign finance is *not* one of the most important issues facing the country.
4. Knowledge of campaign finance laws and practices is very low.

Given the attention garnered by *Citizens United*, both in its immediate wake and as a perennial campaign talking point, it is worth revisiting these "truths" to examine the extent to which the decision altered the public opinion landscape with respect to campaign finance. [64] Interestingly, we find surprisingly little change from the pre-*Citizens United* tenets. While aspects of this may give pause to some campaign strategists, the principal finding of unflagging perceptions of corruption does sustain the Supreme Court's precondition for laws limiting money in politics, to wit that there exists a (more than) sufficient level of perceived corruption for such laws to target for mitigation.

The approach pursued in this analysis is straightforward. In Chapter 2, we establish a baseline by reviewing public opinion concerning money and politics, pre- and post-*Citizens United*. Our focus is on what Americans know about money in politics and campaign spending. Given that citizens are typically not well informed about politics, it should come as no surprise that they do not know all that much about candidate spending or campaign finance. On the other hand, the public is not completely off base with respect to its sense of money in politics, and this basic intuition is perhaps even sharper in the post-*Citizens United* era.

Chapter 3 aims to gauge both the reality of, as well as public opinion on, the central issue of corruption. What do we know about corruption among elected officials? How do we measure this? More important for our purposes, what does the public think about political corruption? How common is it? How does it supposedly occur and what is its perceived source? Finally, drawing from the Court's assumptions, is it endemic or can it be mitigated (or cured) by laws and regulations? The data strongly suggest that people think corruption is rampant despite limited evidence that quid pro quo corruption is anything more than a minor problem. This fundamental attitude has not changed much in the wake of the *Citizens United* decision. Furthermore, they believe the problem is mostly intractable and that most of the commonly proposed reforms of the campaign finance system will not work. Nevertheless, they still support these reforms.

Moving from simple descriptive data to more associational analyses, that chapter also explores the effect of campaign finance laws on campaign spending, and then the effect of both on corruption attitudes. The results are not what the Court would have expected.

Chapter 4 examines the relationship between perceptions of corruption and trust in government. The analysis begins by reviewing variation in levels of trust over time and proceeds to an estimation of the relationship between perceptions of corruption and trust, as posited by the Court. The issue of causality, while intriguing, is not the focus here; rather, we are primarily concerned with the extent to which corruption and trust attitudes move together. As with the previous chapter, the focus then shifts to the influence of election spending and campaign finance reforms and regulations on political trust. Is it the case that states with stricter campaign finance laws and/or lower election spending also have higher levels of political trust? Support for the Court's model is, once again, mixed or absent.

In Chapter 5 the focus shifts to the final—and perhaps most important—element of the Court's behavioral model: political participation. Adopting a broad and comprehensive scale of political participation, we first estimate the relationships between attitudes toward corruption and trust on participation. We find little support for the notion that those who see (perceive) more corruption and those who are less trusting of government are *less* likely to participate. Emboldened by these results the analysis is extended beyond campaign contributions to consider the influence of campaign finance reforms and regulation and election spending—a measure of the overall amount of money in politics that commonly finds its way into press accounts—on turnout and other political acts and find that increased spending is associated with *greater* participation.

Chapter 6 considers the effects of campaign finance information on partisan (candidate) vote choice. This takes place in the context of a separate behavioral model proffered by the *Buckley* Court in rationalizing its acceptance of disclosure provisions in the 1974 FECA Amendments. This model asserts that voters can use disclosed campaign finance to perfect their understanding of candidate ideology, allowing them to make better informed vote choices. In that chapter, survey-based experiments are used to ascertain the impact of information about the amount of money raised by a candidate for office, as well as the source of that money, on a respondent's likelihood of casting a ballot for that candidate. This gets at the possibility that disclosure constitutes an avenue by which voters can acquire information that allows them to more accurately fix where the candidates stand on relevant evaluative criteria. The data indicate that the amount raised by a candidate matters much less than where that money comes from.

As with the previous empirical chapters, the analysis leverages surveys and other data from pre- and post-*Citizens United*. The analysis in Chapter 6 reaffirms the finding that the fundamental dynamics animating basic perceptions of government functioning and subsequent political behavior are largely unchanged over the past decade.

The concluding Chapter 7 offers a discussion of the main results and a consideration of the political and jurisprudential implications of the study. We are particularly interested in what happens in instances like this—when the Supreme Court fosters the construction of an entire edifice of laws and regulations that limit a fundamental right (free speech) based on an erroneous set of assumptions about political opinion and behavior.

2
What Do Americans Know about Campaign Finance?

As noted in the introductory chapter, in *Buckley v. Valeo* the Supreme Court posits a set of relationships between citizens' attitudes and their attendant behaviors. On its face, this behavioral model is plausible. But, as we also noted, it has never been fully tested nor have key elements of the model been examined in the aftermath of the transformative *Citizens United* decision. Underlying the specific relationships posited in the Court's behavioral model is a more general assumption: the model assumes that Americans are politically engaged and knowledgeable. That is, citizens presumably know (at least in rough terms) how much money is flowing from donors into candidates' campaigns. Perhaps more to the point, their attitudes about corruption and government are influenced by this knowledge. More money, and especially more money from disreputable sources, should induce higher levels of perceived corruption and lower levels of trust.

But is this true? How much knowledge *do* most Americans have about money and politics? More particularly, how much money do voters think candidates raise and spend in federal election campaigns? Numerous scholars have explored political knowledge, but relatively fewer scholars have provided evidence on what voters know about campaign finance (e.g., Ansolabehere, Snowberg, and Snyder, 2005; Primo, 2002, 2003). The sum of this research suggests that voters know little about campaign finance but have strong biases with respect to what they think they know. Some studies find that voters think candidate campaigns raise and spend more money than they in fact do, and voters overrate the relative contribution of outside interests to overall campaign finances (Ansolabehere, Snowberg, and Snyder, 2005). Our task here is to re-examine how much voters know and to ascertain whether knowledge has increased in the wake of *Citizens United*.

This chapter presents an extensive array of data on what Americans know about campaign spending and campaign finance laws. In addition to some descriptive results available from public polls, we relied on detailed

The Appearance of Corruption. Daron R. Shaw, Brian E. Roberts, and Mijeong Baek, Oxford University Press (2021).
 DOI: 10.1093/oso/9780197548417.003.0002

and specific original data from several nationally representative surveys conducted between 2009 and 2016. Once again, getting a handle on this is critical. A more informed and current understanding of campaign finance knowledge is important for our broader assessment of the Court's reasoning in *Buckley*. Beyond its stand-alone theoretical significance, it will be brought to bear in Chapter 3, as we estimate the effects of this knowledge, along with actual campaign finance regulations and campaign spending, on perceptions of corruption.

Empirical Estimation Strategy

As detailed in Chapter 1, our exploration of the Court's behavioral model and the underlying assumptions are based on simple statistical analyses of nationally representative surveys. For historical information, we often refer to the American National Election Study (ANES) surveys, which have been conducted for every presidential election (and many midterm elections) from 1952 through 2016. The ANES surveys consist of panel studies with pre- and post-election interviews. The interviews are conducted face-to-face, and the overall sample size averages around 2,000.[1]

In addition to the ANES's historical data, we also relied extensively on unique and original nationally representative surveys conducted online by YouGov in 2009, 2012, 2013, and 2016.[2] The 2009 survey was officially titled the "University of Texas' Money and Politics Poll" and was subsidized by an award from the Lyndon Baines Johnson School of Public Affairs. It was conducted in October 2009 and consisted of interviews with 2,100 registered voters. In the aftermath of the *Citizens United* case, we designed the 2013 survey as a companion poll; it was conducted during October 2013 and consisted of 2,000 interviews with registered voters. Many of the 2009 items were repeated, while additional instrumentation was added. To supplement these, in both 2012 and 2016 the University of Texas purchased "modules" on the Cooperative Congressional Election Study (CCES). In 2012, the corruption, campaign finance, and participation questions made up only a small portion of the overall instrument for the survey of 1,000 registered voters. In 2016, there were two surveys conducted simultaneously, both of which contained a significant number of items on corruption, campaign finance, and participation. A small set of items were included on both 2016 surveys, yielding a total sample size of 2,000 registered voters. Most questions, however, were asked on one or the other poll, yielding a total sample of 1,000 registered voters. The 2012 and 2016 CCES survey modules were part of a panel design, with pre-election interviews in October and post-election interviews in November. The most common approach in both 2012 and 2016 was to ask items once, either in the pre- or post-election survey, and not to ask the same item across both waves of the panel.

On several occasions, we supplemented survey data with contextual information on election spending and campaign finance regulation from the respondent's state. For example, for a 2016 respondent from Florida, we added information on federal election spending in 2016 and relevant state campaign finance regulation information to facilitate the estimation of the effect of these higher level variables on perceptions of corruption, trust in government, and participation. Notice that we are making an important theoretical assumption here: by using state-level information about campaign spending and the regulatory environment of elections, we assume that voters' attitudes about corruption are (potentially) influenced by what is happening in their home state. Since the most prominent U.S. elections occur at the state level (presidential, senatorial, and gubernatorial), this strikes us as reasonable. We did not include measures of either national or local campaign spending or campaign finance regulation.[3]

Knowledge of Campaign Spending, Regulation, and Reform

To begin our exploration of the relationship between corruption, trust, and participation, these recent nationally representative surveys serve as the basis for the assessment of what people know about campaign finance. If citizens do not know very much, or if they are fundamentally misguided about the "facts," it is more difficult to accept the Court's assumption that shifts in objective circumstances (spending and laws and regulations) will influence their "downstream" attitudes and behaviors. The relationship between greater knowledge and distinct opinions is an important one here; the Court has occasionally referred to this relationship, but to our knowledge has never considered the possibility that better information about campaign contributions and expenditures could reduce perceived corruption. This possibility could shift the emphasis from limiting money in politics to greater disclosure (and perhaps more money!).

There is an extensive literature analyzing the American public's interest in, and knowledge of, politics. These works extend empirically a line of inquiry that goes back to the early days of the republic and the accounts of foreign observers like Alexis de Tocqueville. These early, observational accounts suggested that Americans were more interested, engaged, and knowledgeable about political affairs than their European counterparts. This perspective proved resilient up until public opinion polls by people like George Gallup, Lou Harris, and Emile Roper provided evidence that many Americans are not interested in politics and do not have much more than a basic sense of public affairs. A myriad of examples from recent polling data reinforce the broad contours of this pessimistic portrait of the American public. For example, according to a 2017 poll by the University of Pennsylvania's Annenberg School, 26 percent of people were able to name all three of the United States' branches of government—executive, legislative, and judicial. Thirty-three percent could not name *any* branch of government.[4] Only 25 percent knew that a U.S. senator's term stretches for six years. Even less, 20 percent, knew how many senators there were. Polls conducted for the Associated Press in 2001 showed that a majority of Americans were unable to name more than one of the protections guaranteed in the First Amendment of the Constitution—which include speech, assembly, religion, press, and "redress of grievance." Just one in 1,000 could name all five freedoms. However, 22 percent were able to come up with the name of every member of the Simpson family (Homer, Marge, Bart, Lisa, and Maggie). In 2011, a *Newsweek* poll found that 29 percent of Americans were unable to correctly identify the then-current vice president, Joe Biden, when asked to take a simple citizenship test. Although a relatively low 6 percent did not know when Independence Day was, a much, much higher percentage (73 percent) had no idea why we fought the Cold War.

Most of these "tests" rely on recall as opposed to recognition, though, and there are some who contend that America's political ignorance, while not inconsequential, is not as pervasive as is sometimes portrayed by sensationalistic reports of appalling survey results. With this critique in mind, a more systematic view of the American public's basic knowledge and engagement with respect to politics and campaigns can be seen in Figure 2.1, which shows some of these basic tendencies from the 1960s through the 2010s, relying on data from the ANES surveys.

The data indicate that basic political knowledge—as measured by the percent correctly identifying which party has the most members in Congress

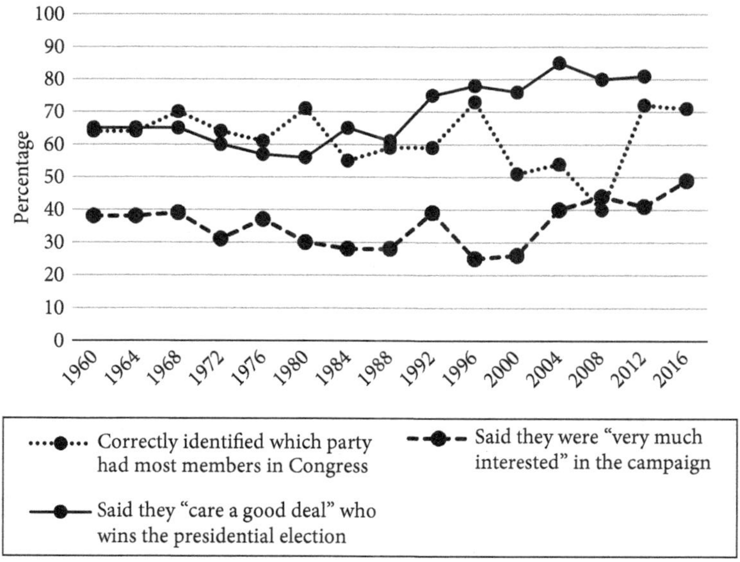

Figure 2.1 Measures of Knowledge and Engagement, 1960–2016
Source: American National Election Studies Cumulative Survey File, 1960–2016.

prior to the election—varies between 71 percent and 40 percent. There is a slight downward trend over the years, but this tendency is upset by upward spikes in 1996 and 2012 (it is perhaps notable that these were the first presidential elections after the Republicans captured the Congress in the preceding midterm elections of 1994 and 2010). Interest in the campaign has increased in recent years: the percent saying they are "very much interested" in the campaign averaged roughly 26 percent from 1980 to 2000 (1992 being a notable outlier); this improves to over 40 percent in the elections from 2004 to 2016. This general upward trend is also apparent in the percentage saying they "care very much" who wins the presidential election, which averaged over 80 percent from 2004 to 2012. Of course, this may reflect the intensity of politics and elections in a polarized era—as such, it may well be separate from any increase in general political knowledge.

These results jibe—more or less—with those from more extensive and exhaustive analyses of political knowledge and sophistication. Contrary to expectations, by many measures the surveys showed the level of ignorance of the American public remaining constant over time. In the 1990s, political scientists Michael X. Delli Carpini and Scott Keeter concluded that there was statistically little difference between the knowledge of the parents of the Silent Generation of the 1950s, the parents of the Baby Boomers of the 1960s, and American parents of the Gen Xers of the 1980s (Delli Carpini and Keeter, 1997.

But what about the "specific" knowledge Americans may or may not have on campaign spending and campaign finance? Our work here extends the analysis of Ansolabehere, Snowberg, and Synder (2005), who established that voters in the 1990s and early 2000s were systematically likely to overestimate the amount of money in political campaigns, especially if they paid attention to the news media. But given the substantial increases in federal and state campaign contributions, as well as the proliferation of publicly available information about money and politics,[5] it is worth revisiting this relationship. In our 2016 surveys, we asked respondents a dozen questions probing their knowledge of money and politics in the United States. By comparison, in our 2009 survey, we asked nine questions. Two facts stand out: (1) people are not as *un*-informed about money and politics in the United States as we had expected, and (2) what people know about campaign finance (rather than how much they know) appears to be closely linked to whether one believes the system is corrupt (a notion explored more fully in Chapter 3).

Table 2.1 displays the summary data for campaign finance knowledge items from the 2016 surveys. The results show that between 70 and 80 percent of Americans are willing to offer a response when asked about some basic facts associated with money in U.S. politics. Furthermore, on the whole, from their responses they seem well informed. For example, we initially asked respondents how much money a person can contribute to candidates who run for federal office in a single election cycle. The median response was $2,500, while the mode was $1,000. This is, in fact, very close to the actual limit of approximately $2,700 (the mean answer was an astronomical $247 million, but this was driven by a handful of people who offered estimates in the range of a hundred million or billion dollars). The distribution of responses suggests a slight upward bias, but not as much as might have been expected. We followed this basic, fundamental item by asking respondents what percentage of Fortune 500 corporations form PACs. The average response was 53 percent, with a median and modal response of 50 percent. This is *less* than the actual percentage, which according to a 2011 study, is about 75 percent (Werner, 2011).

So, responses to our preliminary questions suggest people may know more about money in politics than we had assumed from the existing literature. We do not wish to overstate this fact, however. While respondents

Table 2.1 Estimating Knowledge of Money in Politics, 2016

General knowledge items	% Who offered a response	Mean	Median/ Mode
What is the individual contribution limit for federal election campaigns?	74	$246,938,254	$2,500/ $1,000
What percentage of Fortune 500 companies form PACs?	73	52.7%	50.0%/ 50.0%
What percentage of money in federal election campaigns comes from Super PACs?	73	54.0%	50.0%/ 50.0%
True or false knowledge items		**True**	**False**
True or false: Corporations are prohibited from giving money to candidates in federal election campaigns.	77	19%	81%
True or false: Corporations can spend unlimited amounts of money on television advertising for campaigns.	76	62%	38%
Yes or no: Knowledge items		**Yes**	**No**
Yes or no: Do you know what "dark money" is?	78	27%	73%
Yes or no: Candidates are required to disclose the identities of their contributors (over $200).	79	66%	34%
Yes or no: Parties are required to disclose the identities of their contributors (over $200).	79	50%	50%
Yes or no: PACs are required to disclose the identities of their contributors (over $200).	79	31%	69%
Yes or no: Super PACs are required to disclose the identities of their contributors (over $200).	79	26%	74%
Yes or no: 501(c)(4)s are required to disclose the identities of their contributors (over $200).	79	32%	68%

Source: University of Texas Modules for the 2016 Cooperative Congressional Election Study. *N* = 2,000.

did reasonably well when asked basic questions about how much money there is in election campaigns, they did less well when we posed a series of "true or false" questions to gauge the understanding people have of current laws. Specifically, we asked a battery of five questions about whether those receiving funds are required to disclose the identities of their major ($200 or greater) contributors, and the results were mixed. Forty-three percent, on average, gave the correct response, but this is inflated by the fact that we omitted the 23 percent from our calculations who said they "do not know." And, unlike the earlier knowledge measures, the errors for those offering a response to these items was systematic—respondents think that candidates and political parties are more likely to be required to disclose their contributors than PACs or 501(c)(4) groups.

The data also suggest that most Americans do not have much information when it comes to the complex distinctions among campaigns, parties, and the myriad of independent (and quasi-independent) interest groups and tend to assume the worst. For example, only 27 percent of people said they were familiar with the term, "dark money," whereas 73 percent admitted that they did not know what the term meant.[6] Similarly, only 19 percent know that corporations are prohibited from donating directly to candidates for federal office, whereas 62 percent (correctly) know that these same corporations can spend unlimited amounts of money on television advertising for campaigns.

Nor do they know much about where campaigns or independent actors get their money. Consider that when asked about how much Super PACs contribute to the total amount spent in federal election campaigns, the mean response is 54 percent with the median and mode resting at 50 percent. According to the Center for Responsive Politics, the total price tag for the 2016 federal election was $6.8 billion. Based on Federal Election Committee data, Super PACs spent less than $1.1 billion, which equates to roughly 16 percent of all spending. And while Super PACs cannot contribute to candidate committees, even the contributions of regular PACs to candidate committees are less than voters apparently think. In 2016 less than 3 percent of money in the presidential election campaign came from any sort of PAC. For U.S. House and Senate races, the figures are 34 percent and 18 percent, respectively.

This confusion persists when asked to guess where Super PAC money comes from. Forty-one percent say corporations, 39 percent wealthy individuals, 11 percent other interest groups, and 8 percent unions. In reality, according to a *Washington Post* report, 41 percent of all Super PAC money comes from just fifty mega-donors and their families (Matea and Narayanswamy, 2016). Thus, wealthy individuals dominate Super PAC contributions, but voters are just as likely to see corporations as the primary source of money.

But is it the case that Americans know more about campaign finance now than they did prior to the *Citizens United* decision? Although our survey data do not directly repeat the campaign finance knowledge items, it is clear that the 2016 results are consistent with those from 2009. Even prior to *Citizens United*, Americans knew some things about money and politics but were prone to upward biases when assessing how involved special interests were in federal election campaigns. In Table 2.2, we show the results from nine questions asked in our national survey in 2009. Most of the items differ from those asked in 2016—especially in that respondents in 2009 were given an explicit "don't know" option, which results in far fewer people offering an answer—but several are comparable.

As with the 2016 sample, the answers from our 2009 respondents seem fairly well informed. For example, we initially asked respondents how much money a person can contribute to candidates who run for federal office in a single election cycle. The median response was \$2,000, while the mode was \$2,000. This is, in fact, very close to the actual limit of approximately \$2,400 (similar to the 2016 poll, the mean answer was \$1.43 million, but this was driven by a handful of people who offered estimates of \$10 to \$100 million). Once again, the distribution of responses suggests a slight upward bias. In the survey, we followed the basic, fundamental question about contribution limits by asking respondents what percentage of Fortune 500 corporations form PACs. The average response was 59 percent, with a median and modal response of 60 and 50 percent, respectively. (The actual percentage in 2008 was 75 percent.)

Where respondents were off, in 2009 at least, was in their estimates of the percentage of campaign funds that come from special interest groups. In 2009 Americans said that between 60 and 70 percent of funding for presidential, Senate, and House election campaigns came from special interest groups. These estimates are more than double the percent that occurred in 2008, although the specifics of this overestimation depend upon the exact type of race and whether an incumbent was running. The tendency to believe that special interest groups are more important than they are is further demonstrated by the fact that respondents pegged the average PAC contributions to U.S. Senate and House candidate campaigns at \$50,000 and

Table 2.2 Estimating Knowledge of Money in Politics, 2009

	Among all respondents			Among those who initially said they "do not know"	
	% Responding	Mean	Median/ Mode	Mean	Median/ Mode
What is the per candidate contribution limit?	27	$1,433,901	$2,000/ $2,000	NA	NA
What percent of presidential campaign funds come from special interest groups?	29	62%	70%/ 75%	57%	60%/ 50%
What percent of Senate campaign funds come from special interest groups?	46	62%	70%/ 50%	53%	50%/ 50%
What percent of House campaign funds come from special interest groups?	46	60%	60%/ 50%	55%	50%/ 50%
What percentage of Fortune 500 companies form PACs?	31	74%	80%/ 100%	59%	60%/ 50%
What is the average PAC contribution to a Senate campaign?	27	$20,000,000	$50,000/ $100,000	$28,000,000	$57,973/ $100,000
What is the average cost of a Senate campaign?	38	$47,000,000	$5,000,000/ $10,000,000	$24,000,000	$2,000,000/ $5,000,000
What is the average PAC contribution to a House campaign?	26	$4,188,705	$12,572/ $100,000	$43,000,000	$10,930/ $50,000
What is the average cost of a House campaign?	35	$32,000,000	$2,000,000/ $1,000,000	$71,000,000	$2,000,000/ $10,000,000

Source: University of Texas Money in Politics Survey (Shaw and Roberts, 2009). $N = 2,100$.

$12,500, respectively, even though these contributions are capped at $5,000 per campaign.

The upshot from the data is a mixed bag. On the one hand, it seems that Americans have a sense of how much money is spent in federal election campaigns, as well how much they (as citizens) can spend in these races. On the other hand, they exaggerate both the absolute and relative amount of money coming from special interest groups. This occurred in both 2009 and 2016, which tells us that not much has changed in response to the dramatic increase in campaign spending from 2006 through 2016.

What Drives Campaign Finance Knowledge?

Baseline assessments of knowledge of campaign finance only tangentially speak to some of the larger questions we wish to consider here, most notably: (1) Do reforms and regulations increase citizen knowledge of campaign finance? (2) Does knowledge of campaign finance affect broader attitudes about political corruption? To assess these questions, we first developed an appropriate measure of campaign finance knowledge.

In doing this, however, we stumbled upon an interesting problem. In the 2016 survey, there were twelve distinct questions measuring knowledge of campaign finance reform (see Table 2.1): many correlate only modestly with one another, and a couple are negatively correlated with the battery as a whole. For example, the strongest positive correlation is between those who know the individual contribution limit and those who know what "dark money" is (the zero-order coefficient is 0.36). But there is a small negative correlation between knowing what "dark money" is and knowing that Super PACs must disclose their contributors (–0.03). Moreover, knowing that 501(c)(4)s do not have to disclose their contributors is negatively correlated to knowing that PACs and Super PACs are obliged to disclose their contributors.

This problem is revealed even more starkly when we regress the campaign finance knowledge items on our summary measure of political corruption. Nine of the twelve items have a positive coefficient, indicating that greater knowledge leads to increased perceptions of corruption (more on this shortly). Three of the items, however, have a negative coefficient, indicating that greater knowledge leads to decreased perceptions of corruption. These three items are knowledge of the percent of campaign money coming from Super PACs, knowledge that corporations are prohibited by law from contributing to candidate campaigns, and knowing that 501(c)(4)s are not required to disclose their contributors. In other words, not all campaign finance knowledge is the same. Contextual knowledge of how much money special interests contribute to campaigns and knowledge of the statutory limits that affect these groups is different—and potentially has a different effect—than knowledge of contributor limits or spending more generally.

What's particularly interesting is that these different knowledge effects reflect a post-*Citizens United* reality: Super PACs did not exist until 2010; corporations have been banned from making contributions since 1907, but one of the most common beliefs about *Citizens United* is that it allows for corporate contributions; and 501(c)(4)s only came to the fore in the wake of *Citizens United*. So, it seems that it is the people who really understood the *Citizens United* decision who perceive less corruption. That is quite striking.

As a result, we conducted a factor analysis on the 2016 items and confirmed our suspicion that the question battery taps into two distinct dimensions. As a result, we created two separate campaign finance knowledge variables for analysis. The first is an additive summary measure, made up of the nine items focusing on individual contribution limits, spending, and disclosure. These correlate reasonably well with each other and effectively define the first dimension of campaign finance knowledge. The second variable is also an additive summary measure, but it is made up of the three items discussed earlier. These correlate well with each other and define the second dimension. Focusing on these unique measures of campaign finance and campaign regulation knowledge, our initial analysis focused on whether people from states with more campaign finance reforms and regulations are more knowledgeable about money and politics. The answer is unambiguously "no."

This claim draws primarily on our analysis of the relationship between our summary measures of campaign finance knowledge (described earlier) and our measures of the regulatory environment for political campaigns in a voter's state. More specifically, we have three different (but related) variables gauging campaign finance laws and regulations in the fifty states from 2006–2016.[7] Initially, we had an updated version of the traditional tripartite "high-medium-low" variable gauging campaign finance regulatory environment. Second, we also had a simple binary variable capturing whether the state limits or prohibits independent expenditures from the general treasury. Third, and most uniquely, we developed a 0–7 summary variable based on the following: (1) Does the state have contribution limits for individuals, (2) for political parties, (3) for political action committees, (4) for corporations, and (5) for unions? For the first three items, states are scored either 0 (no limits) or 1 (limits). For the last two items, states are scored either

0 (no limits), 1 (limits), or 2 (prohibited). Factor analyses indicate that these items are connected by a single underlying dimension. Furthermore, while our new scaled variable performs best on validity tests, the correlations between our measure and the more traditional items are quite high (the zero-order correlation coefficients are 0.36 and 0.39), increasing our confidence in the new variable.[8] As noted, the theoretical assumption underlying these variables is that statewide regulatory environments affect how voters think about politicians, candidates, and elections.

In Figure 2.2a–b, we see that these state regulatory environments appear to be only weakly correlated with either of our measures of campaign finance knowledge. With respect to knowledge of campaign spending, the difference

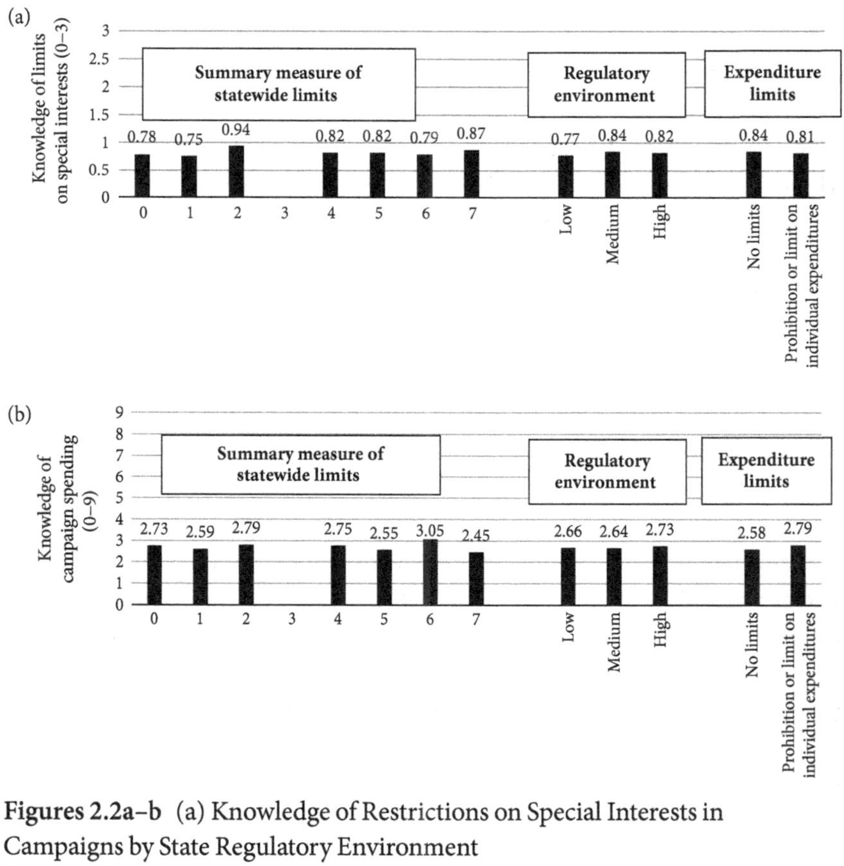

Figures 2.2a–b (a) Knowledge of Restrictions on Special Interests in Campaigns by State Regulatory Environment
(b) Knowledge of Campaign Spending by State Regulatory Environment
Source: University of Texas Modules for the 2016 Cooperative Congressional Election Study. $N = 2{,}000$.

between those in states with minimal campaign finance regulations (2.45) and those in states with maximal regulations (2.73) is 0.28 on a 10-point scale—negligible in statistical terms. If we instead refer to knowledge of restrictions on special interests in campaigns, the difference between those in states scoring 0 on campaign finance regulatory limits (0.78) and those in states scoring 7 (0.87) is 0.09 on a 4-point scale—again, negligible. This pattern—inconsistent and insignificant differences in campaign finance knowledge among those facing different regulatory environments—persists no matter how one measures these environments.

In Table 2.3, we present a more complete equation predicting the two main measures of campaign finance knowledge. Using a least squares (LS) estimator, the results for the 0–7 summary measure of campaign finance regulation are, *ceteris paribus*, statistically and substantively indistinguishable from 0. Campaign finance knowledge, whether defined as knowledge of campaign spending or as knowledge of interest group restrictions, is *not* predicted by statewide regulatory environment. Other versions of the campaign regulation/reform variable (not presented here) are similarly unrelated to knowledge.

The effects of contextual and experiential factors are more ambiguous. Take per-capita statewide spending, which is of specific relevance given the common expectation that campaign expenditures and knowledge are connected. The average statewide spending rate in federal election contests over the decade between 2006 and 2016 is *negatively* correlated with campaign spending knowledge. It is uncorrelated, however, with knowledge of special interest spending restrictions. Political interest is positively correlated with campaign finance knowledge, although the relationship is statistically significant only for knowledge of campaign spending. We also find that the influence of media exposure is (at best) inconsistent. Television usage is uncorrelated with campaign finance knowledge, while newspaper usage is positively correlated with knowledge of campaign spending limits but is negatively correlated with knowledge of restrictions on special interest spending (the latter effect is only marginally significant statistically). State population size does not seem to affect campaign finance knowledge.

In contrast, some specific demographic and attitudinal factors appear to matter. For example, increased levels of education seem to be associated with greater knowledge. Similarly, Americans who are 18–29 years of age and 65 years of age and older are relatively less knowledgeable. All other things being equal, Blacks and Latinos score slightly lower on campaign finance

Table 2.3 Campaign Finance Knowledge by State Regulatory Environment Regression Results

	Summary measure of knowledge of campaign spending			Summary measure of knowledge of restrictions on special interests in campaigns		
	Coeff.	S.E.	Prob = 0	Coeff.	S.E.	Prob = 0
Constant	2.079	0.256	0.000	0.808	0.104	0.000
Summary measure of limits on individuals, parties, PACs, corporations, unions	−0.003	0.022	0.886	0.002	0.009	0.867
Political interest	0.267	0.037	0.000	0.012	0.015	0.418
TV use	−0.095	0.098	0.333	0.055	0.040	0.168
News use	0.480	0.089	0.000	−0.049	0.036	0.171
Social media use	−0.061	0.095	0.520	−0.183	0.038	0.000
Average total candidate and committee expenditures per capita, 2006–2016	−0.018	0.010	0.072	0.003	0.004	0.461
Statewide population, 2016 (in millions)	−0.004	0.004	0.338	−0.002	0.002	0.200
Male	0.041	0.088	0.643	−0.087	0.036	0.016
African American	−0.412	0.143	0.004	−0.020	0.058	0.725
Latino	−0.651	0.148	0.000	−0.213	0.060	0.000
Under 30 years of age	−0.993	0.142	0.000	−0.222	0.057	0.000
65 years of age and over	0.339	0.151	0.024	0.013	0.061	0.837
College degree or more	0.175	0.113	0.120	0.087	0.046	0.057
High school degree or less	−0.653	0.101	0.000	−0.086	0.041	0.036
Democrat	0.137	0.126	0.274	0.095	0.051	0.062
Republican	0.063	0.127	0.620	0.072	0.052	0.165
Union household	0.142	0.144	0.323	0.199	0.042	0.001
Church attendance	−0.043	0.103	0.675	0.119	0.042	0.005
Catholic	−0.001	0.111	0.991	0.088	0.045	0.049
Jewish	0.672	0.272	0.014	0.380	0.110	0.001
Total cases (*N*)	1,995			1,995		
Standard error	1.882			0.764		
Adjusted R-Squared	0.159			0.061		

Note: Estimates derived from least squares estimator.

Source: University of Texas Modules for the 2016 Cooperative Congressional Election Study.

knowledge scales, whereas Jewish people score relatively higher. In addition, some relationships occur only for one or the other types of campaign finance knowledge. Most notably, being a church attender, a Catholic, or a union member is a significant predictor of greater knowledge of restrictions on special interest restrictions but not of greater knowledge of campaign spending.

Some caveats are in order. Most notably, given that we are using a LS estimator for a mixed-level model—recall that we offer state-level measures of campaign finance regulation, of campaign spending, and of statewide population—it is possible that our regression coefficients are biased and our standard errors too conservative. We re-estimated the equation using a fixed-effects model and calculated robust clustered standard errors; the results were virtually identical. In light of the similarity of the findings, we prefer to focus solely on the simple LS results due to the ease of interpretation.

Put simply, regulating campaign finance in a state does not improve the level of knowledge voters in that state have about money and politics. Of course, it doesn't hurt it any either. Regulation and reform, at least as they have been constituted in the states, are virtually unconnected with substantive knowledge of campaign finance.

Conclusion

We do not think it hyperbolic to suggest that the behavioral model advanced by the Supreme Court in the *Buckley* case seemingly hinges on the assumption that citizens have a basic understanding of what is going on in the conduct and regulation of American election campaigns. Otherwise, it would be almost impossible to influence or ameliorate perceptions of corruption (or anything else for that matter). In light of extensive survey research over the past seventy-five years, however, this assumption seems dubious. The data suggest that while Americans know a little bit about campaign finance, there is no systematic correlation between the regulatory environment of the state and how much people in that state know about campaign finance.

In fact, the nature of the data suggests another interpretation of the Court's thinking in *Buckley*: by including the appearance of the corruption condition in its ruling, the Court was tacitly admitting it really doesn't matter what people know, just what they believe, for our system of government to be threatened. The Court further assumes that people will respond to Congress passing a law—preferably one that suggests money in politics has been eliminated. Of much less concern to the Court is whether people (or members of Congress, for that matter) actually read and understand the law.

Toward the end of the chapter, the careful reader will no doubt recall that we posed two questions concerning campaign finance knowledge: The first asked about the connection between regulations and reform and campaign finance knowledge. The second asked about the connection between campaign finance knowledge and attitudes about corruption. Although we explored the first question, we dodged the second. But the influence of campaign finance knowledge, along with an array of other factors, on perceptions of corruption is the focal point of Chapter 3.

3

Gauging (Perceived) Corruption

In this chapter, we drill deeper in our exploration of the basic premises underlying the Supreme Court's decision to allow restrictions of political speech in federal elections. Most obviously, we take aim at perhaps the most important inference drawn from the Court's decision in *Buckley v. Valeo* (1976): the American people are likely to view large campaign contributions as leading to corrupt (quid pro quo) behavior on the part of our politicians.

Note that the focus here is on the *appearance* of corruption; that is, public opinion about the extent to which American politics is disproportionately or illegitimately influenced by money contributed by individuals and special interests. As Persily and Lammie (2004) note, and as we referenced in Chapter 1, this is one of the very few occasions in which the Supreme Court has allowed regulation of one of the fundamental freedoms based not on a fact but on the perception of that "fact." In other words, it is not that campaign finance regulation or reform decreases corruption or corrupt practices. Rather, it is that the Court thinks these laws cause people to perceive less corruption.

As we also mentioned in Chapter 1, the effect of campaign finance reform on perceptions of corruption has been investigated empirically by only a handful of scholars, including Alt and Lassen (2003), Rosenson (2009), Persily and Lammie (2004), and Primo and Milyo (2020). Alt and Lassen (2003) analyze the impact of state-level campaign finance laws on perceptions of corruption among journalists. They find a substantial relationship but do not address issues of causality. Rosenson (2009) also focuses on state campaign finance laws but specifies an instrumental variable model to account for potential endogeneity between reforms and perceived corruption. She finds that campaign finance reforms and regulations have virtually no impact on perceptions of corruption among the public.[1] Persily and Lammie (2004) draw on a range of survey data—including the American National Election Studies and the Eurobarometer—to offer a thorough and detailed assessment of corruption attitudes. They show that the American

The Appearance of Corruption. Daron R. Shaw, Brian E. Roberts, and Mijeong Baek, Oxford University Press (2021).
 DOI: 10.1093/oso/9780197548417.003.0003

public (a) thinks their political system is corrupt, (b) supports campaign finance reform, and (c) doubts these reforms will have much of an effect.

> In the end, we must admit that large shares of the American population distrust their government and believe the campaign finance system is a source of undue influence. However, as surveys from other countries indicate, Americans are not alone in their distrust of government, and countries with radically different campaign finance regimes also have populations registering a high level of government distrust. For those who would look to campaign finance reform to re-store "confidence in the system of representative government," they may be disappointed by the intractability and psychological roots of that lack of confidence. (Persily and Lammie, 2004, p. 174).

This perspective is updated by Primo and Milyo (2020), who reaffirm that while many individuals support the idea of reform, they are also skeptical that reform would successfully limit corruption, which Americans believe stains almost every fiber of the political system. They also contend that support for campaign finance restrictions is deeply divided along party lines. The bottom-line is that attitudes toward money in politics reflect larger fears about the health of American democracy, fears that will not be allayed by campaign finance reform.

Collectively, the gist of this research is that voters in jurisdictions that regulate campaign finance more aggressively do not necessarily perceive less corruption than do voters in jurisdictions with relatively less regulation. A legitimate concern is that this research—with the exception of the Primo and Milyo study—predates the 2010 *Citizens United* decision, which may well have changed the public's perception of the role of money in American politics. Furthermore, these studies look at measures of campaign finance that often focus on the letter of the law rather than how much regulation occurs in fact. We intend to update and expand on previous studies of the impact of campaign finance regulation on attitudes about political corruption. We leverage cross-sectional data from the different states to gauge the effects of distinct regulatory and campaign spending environments on opinions, as well as over-time data to gauge opinion changes between the pre– and post–*Citizens United* eras.

Although our main interest is in how campaign finance regulation affects attitudes toward corruption, our first order of business in this chapter is empirically establishing the extent to which voters believe the political system is corrupt. The rationale is simple: if we are to thoughtfully comment on restricting speech to limit the appearance of corruption, we clearly need to know what people think about their political system. Consequently, our initial line of inquiry focuses on the percentage of Americans who think politics is corrupt. Given existing research, the answer is almost certainly going to be a very high percentage. We then turn to beliefs about the sources of this corruption, with particular interest in the role of campaign finance.

We close this chapter by examining voters' attitudes toward campaign finance reforms. Setting aside whether actual reforms and regulations decrease perceptions of corruption, do voters support these reforms? What kinds of reforms are most popular? And do voters think that these reforms reduce corruption? Based on previous survey work, there is reason to think that Americans support proposals to reform campaign finance, but it is unclear whether they expect these reforms to positively impact the political system.[2] Obtaining information on these opinions—coupled with data on how reforms and regulations impact corruption attitudes—greatly enhances our ability to assess the efficacy of the Court's reasoning in *Buckley* and other more recent cases involving political and campaign speech.

It is worth reiterating at the outset of this chapter that we do not claim that the numerous opinion "linkages" posed by the Court have never been empirically considered. In fact, there has been excellent research on many of them. But most were conducted over a decade ago, and many focus on perceptions of corruption among journalists or other elites. Rather, this chapter offers a comprehensive look at a specific linkage—between corruption attitudes amongst the public and campaign finance reforms—over time with consistent, high-quality national survey data. We are especially interested in potential *changes* in opinion in the wake of the 2010 *Citizens United* decision. Consequently, we utilize and expand on the theoretical and empirical efforts of others. Let us begin by considering Americans' attitudes toward their political system.

Perceived Corruption: Levels and Trends

Although the Court in *Buckley* was mum on the question of whether the American public (at that time) perceived the system as corrupt, by almost any measure this sentiment was (and remains) pervasive.[3] Indeed, there is a long tradition in the United States of skepticism toward politics and government. This is manifest in the debates regarding the U.S. Constitution, where the opposition of the Anti-Federalists to the proposed new governing document draws on a suspicion of giving any central authority too much power. In *The Essential Anti-Federalist*, one key argument against the Constitution explicitly hinges on the ease with which corruption can take hold in a large country with a strong government: "The facility of corruption is increased in proportion as power tends by representation or delegation, to a concentration in the hands of the few" (p. 126). The tradition continues to this day in the form of reported skepticism toward major deliberations, such as those surrounding the Affordable Care Act (2010). Critics' suspicions of corruption peaked when policy "sweeteners" were added to the Senate version of the bill to obtain the support of recalcitrant members from Nebraska (the "cornhusker kickback"), Louisiana (the "Louisiana purchase"), and Florida ("gator-aid").[4]

The supposition that government officials are corrupt is given credence by the words of important political leaders throughout American history. Theodore Roosevelt, for example, once said: "When they call the roll in the Senate, the Senators do not know whether to answer 'Present' or 'Not Guilty.' " Barack Obama offered a subtler and more introspective take on the effect of money on politics in his 2006 book, *The Audacity of Hope*:

> I can't assume that the money chase didn't alter me in some ways . . . I know that as a consequence of my fund-raising I became more like the wealthy donors I met, in the very particular sense that I spent more and more of my time above the fray, outside the world of immediate hunger, disappointment, fear, irrationality, and frequent hardship of the other 99 percent of the population—that is, the people that I'd entered public life to serve. And in one fashion or another, I suspect this is true for every senator: The longer you are a senator, the narrower the scope of your interactions. You may fight it, with town hall meetings and listening tours and stops by the old neighborhood. But your schedule dictates that you move in a different orbit from most of the people you represent. And perhaps as the next race approaches, a voice within tells you that you don't want to have to go through all the misery of raising all that money in small increments all over again . . . The path of least resistance—of fund-raisers organized by the special interests, the corporate PACs, and the top lobbying shops—starts to look awfully tempting, and if the opinions of these insiders don't quite jibe with those

you once held, you learn to rationalize the changes as a matter of realism, of compromise, of learning the ropes.

Popular culture has been perhaps even more likely to question the honesty and ethics of our leaders. In his book, *Roughing It*, Mark Twain wrote: "The government of my country snubs honest simplicity, but fondles artistic villainy, and I think I might have developed into a very capable pickpocket if I had remained in the public service a year or two." His most famous quote, however, was that America "has the best government that money can buy." Will Rogers, the celebrated humorist and (somewhat reluctant) Democrat, summed up what a lot of people think when he said "The Democrats and the Republicans are equally corrupt where money is concerned. It's only in the amount where the Republicans excel."

But invoking a skeptical tradition and offering pithy quotes are merely suggestive. What do the data say with respect to perceptions of corruption in the United States? The American National Election Study (ANES) has included several relevant items in its time series, including measures of corruption and trust. Since 1958, ANES has asked its respondents "how many people in the federal government are crooked?" In Figure 3.1, we see that the percentage of people who think "quite a few" are crooked has ranged from

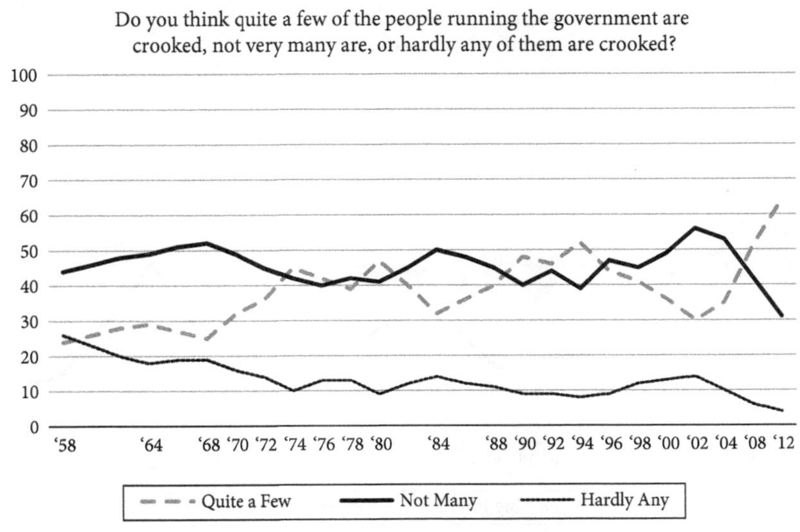

Figure 3.1 How Many People in Government Are Crooked?
Source: American National Election Studies Cumulative Survey File, 1952–2012.

a low of around 25 percent (1958) to a high of around 65 percent (2012). Interestingly, there has been an uptick in the number of people saying, "quite a few" since 2002, which is the year that the Bipartisan Campaign Reform Act (BCRA, often referred to as McCain-Feingold), the last significant revision of federal campaign finance laws since the 1970s, was signed into law. Historically, the percentage of people choosing "quite a few" over "not many" or "hardly any" increased from the 1950s through Watergate (1974), after which it leveled out until the mid-1990s. The "quite a few" percentage then declined from 1996 through 2002, before shooting upwards.

Of course, this item is not the only measure of perceived corruption. Other questions, however, mostly tell the same story. For example, in Figure 3.2 we see the results for an ANES item in which people were asked whether they think the government is "mostly run by a few big interests looking out for themselves" or is it "mostly run for the interests of all Americans." The percentage saying the government is "run by a few big interests looking out for themselves" increased from 31 percent in 1964 (the first year the question was asked) to 73 percent in 1974. After 1974, the "few big interests" number fluctuated between 70 and 80 percent with two notable exceptions: it dropped to 59 percent in 1984 and again to 49 percent

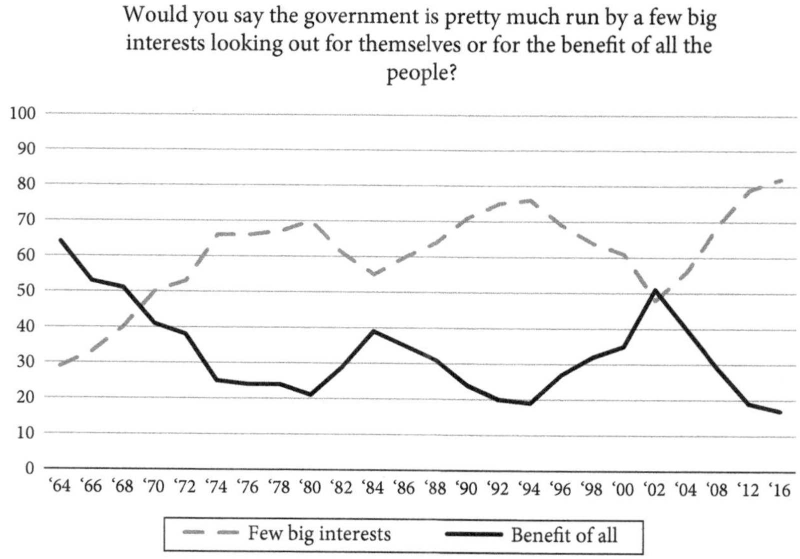

Figure 3.2 Is Government Run for the Benefit of All or for a Few Big Interests?
Source: American National Election Studies Cumulative Survey File, 1952–2016.

in 2002. Since 2002 the "few big interests" percentage has risen again, to an all-time high of 82 percent in 2016. The zero-order correlation between the "crooked" measure and the "run by a few big interests" measure is a statistically significant 0.43.

Why would perceptions of corruption increase after 2002? The obvious answer is that general measures of government and politicians improved considerably in the wake of the economic boom of the 1990s and (especially) the 9/11 attacks on New York and Washington, DC in 2001. Subsequently, disaffection with the wars in Afghanistan and Iraq and then the economic collapse of 2008–2009 caused negativity toward the political system to increase, with perceptions of corruption following suit. However, the argument that perceived corruption would rise in response to policy failures is, at best, contentious. Then there is the fact that the increase in perceptions of corruption also coincided with the passage of a major campaign finance reform law—the Bipartisan Campaign Reform Act of 2002.[5]

We are not the only ones to notice this recent trend. This increase in perceived corruption since 2002 has drawn the attention of public opinion scholars and survey research experts. In 2012 and 2016, the ANES introduced an additional item that sought to distinguish between the existence of corruption in government and its pervasiveness. The item specifically asks respondents "how many people in government are corrupt?" In 2012, 30 percent said "all" or "most" people in government are corrupt; by 2016 the number climbed to 36 percent. Similarly, the percentage saying "none" or "a few" dropped from 37 percent to 29 percent. So, it is not just that Americans think the federal government is corrupt in some general sense; more than one-in-three Americans believe that "all" or "most" of their government officials are corrupt.

The notion that one-third of voters today believe that most governing officials are corrupt is further backed by data from our own national surveys of public opinion. In 2009 and again in 2016, we conducted nationally representative samples to ascertain opinions about money in politics.[6] Among other items, we asked respondents to rate the "honesty and ethics" of (a) the average representative in Congress, (b) their own representative, and (c) their own senator. We are especially interested in the comparison between general ratings of the institution and specific ratings of members. It seems to us rather easy to say that Congress, as an institution, is corrupt—but do Americans think that the average rank-and-file member is lacking in honesty and ethics? And, given that incumbent members who run for re-election win about 90 percent of the time, do voters rate their own members low on this dimension?

As might be expected, the average representative does not fare well. In 2009, 65 percent rated the level of honesty and ethics for an average legislator as "not so good" or "poor." Contrary to our other findings, negative attitudes on this measure decreased slightly between 2009 and 2016. During the 2016 election campaign, "only" 59 percent said the level of honesty and ethics for an average legislator was "not so good" or "poor." Ratings of one's own legislators are, as expected, better overall: by about 20 percentage points. In 2009, 38 percent said their representative had "not so good" or "poor" honesty and ethics, while 44 percent rated their honesty and ethics as "excellent" or "fair." For their senators, 36 percent of respondents gave them "not so good" or "poor" ratings, compared to 45 percent scoring them as "excellent" or "fair." Still, even when it comes to their own legislators, the American public offers only mixed ratings on core measures of integrity.

The more general ratings of the Congress from our own polls are at least as negative as ratings of the federal government offered by the ANES. For example, in 2016 84 percent said corruption is a "very" or "somewhat" serious problem in the U.S. Congress. Only 14 percent said corruption is either "not a very serious problem" or "not a problem at all." These numbers are comparable to those in 2009, when 82 percent said corruption in the U.S. Congress was a "very" or "somewhat" serious problem. Roughly speaking, more than four out of five Americans think corruption is a problem for the country's main democratic institution.

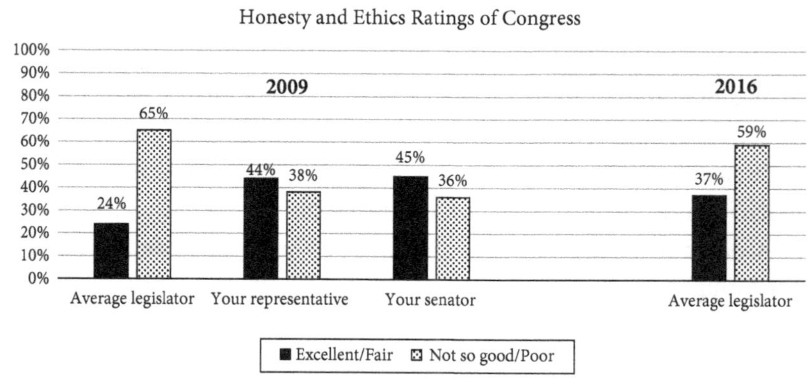

Figure 3.3 Integrity of Congressional Representatives, 2009–2016

In short, the data tell a consistent story. Americans today are more likely than ever to see their political system as corrupt. It remains to be ascertained whether concerns with the state of campaign finance—the magnitude, sources, and concentration of money in politics—in the United States play any part in this level of perceived corruption. Only then is there a comfortable foundation upon which the Court could advance a compelling interest sufficient to overcome the speech limitations inherent in laws restricting money in politics.

Who Sees Corruption? Why?

Given these data, it is plausible for journalists, pundits, and commentators to assume that many (most?) Americans think that the government is corrupt. But the plausibility of this assumption should not preclude us from searching for interesting and important variation in who, exactly, is most likely to embrace the notion that the political system is corrupt. Nor is it self-evident that everyone sees the specific sources of corruption in quite the same way. We are interested in assessing who is most skeptical about the honesty and ethics of governing officials, as well as who (or what) voters believe to be the primary source of corruption in the American political system. Both inquiries help us consider the Court's reasoning in justifying limits on political speech.

To assess general perceptions of corruption, we combine two items from our own 2016 U.S. national survey: (1) How honest and ethical is the average member of Congress? (2) How serious a problem is corruption? Both items are scored 1–5, with 1 representing less corruption and 5 representing more corruption. The zero-order correlation is a statistically significant 0.53, and factor analysis suggests that the items each tap into a common first dimension. We therefore combine the items into an additive, nine-category (2–10, which we re-score to range from 0–8) measure of perceived corruption.[7]

Our measure is of a piece—if somewhat distinct—from previous empirical research in the area. Recall that Persily and Lammie (2004) examined three different questions from the ANES to gauge the correlates of corruption: "crookedness" of the government, the extent to which government is run for the benefit of "special interests," and level of "distrust" of the government. The authors report the correlations between and amongst these variables (which are quite high) but never take advantage of the fact that they almost certainly tap into the same dimension. They also fail to specify and estimate a single model for any of their corruption attitudes. Rosenson (2009) offers a more compelling model of corruption attitudes but relies on journalists' (elite) assessments of statewide corruption using government ideology, membership in Common Cause, and population as instruments in a two-stage least squares (TSLS) model. Given all this, we think our approach will yield more reliable estimates of the key relationships.

We proceed by estimating a least squares equation in which our measures of campaign finance regulation and per capita campaign spending—along with campaign finance knowledge (see Chapter 2), statewide population, and several demographic and attitudinal variables—are used to predict perceived corruption.[8] The demographic and attitudinal variables we included are standard for models of political opinion: sex (being male), race (being Black), ethnicity (being Hispanic), age (being either under thirty years of age or sixty-five years of age and older), education (having a college degree or more or having a high school education or less), religion (being Catholic or being Jewish), religiosity (attending church at least once a week), union status (living in a union household), party identification (being Republican or being Democratic), political interest (low to high), and news media usage (yes or no for television, newspapers, or social media). These variables are useful for both substantive and methodological reasons. Substantively, they have all been shown to correlate with distinct political opinions and attitudes (Delli Carpini and Keeter, 1996; Bardes and Oldendick, 2015) and we think it at least plausible that they might drive corruption perceptions.[9] Methodologically, excluding them might bias our estimates of the independent effects of our other substantive variables, especially those gauging campaign finance regulations.

The estimation technique also merits additional comment. Note that the population, campaign regulation, and spending data are from the state level. In light of this, we performed an additional analysis in which we added fixed effects for the states and then calculated robust clustered standard errors for the predictor variables. The results of this analysis are substantively similar to those obtained for the least squares equation.[10] For ease of presentation and interpretation, we rely on the least squares estimates in Table 3.1.

So, what is the most powerful predictor of lower perceived corruption? Whether the respondent identifies as a partisan. Democratic identification reduces perceived corruption by about 0.86 points on the summary scale.[11] Republican identification reduces it by about 0.49 points. This point

Table 3.1 Predicting Perceived Corruption, 2016

	DV: Summary measure of perceived corruption		
	Est. Coeff.	S.E.	Prob = 0
Constant	6.059	0.0257	0.000
Summary of knowledge of campaign spending	0.108	0.023	0.000
Summary of knowledge of restrictions on special interests in campaigns	−0.371	0.056	0.000
Summary measure of limits on individuals, parties, PACs, corporations, unions	0.067	0.022	0.002
Average total candidate and committee expenditures per capita, 2006–2016	−0.005	0.010	0.606
Statewide population, 2016 (in millions)	−0.007	0.004	0.079
Political interest	0.058	0.037	0.116
TV usage	−0.141	0.096	0.143
Newspaper usage	−0.105	0.088	0.234
Social media usage	−0.004	0.093	0.965
Male	−0.037	0.087	0.670
African American	−0.331	0.141	0.019
Latino	0.036	0.146	0.808
Under 30 years of age	−0.268	0.141	0.056
65 years of age and over	0.426	0.148	0.004
College degree or more	−0.102	0.111	0.357
High school degree or less	−0.181	0.100	0.071
Democrat	−0.856	0.123	0.000
Republican	−0.490	0.124	0.000
Union household	0.091	0.141	0.519
Church attendance	0.004	0.101	0.969
Catholic	−0.250	0.108	0.021
Jewish	−0.347	0.267	0.195
Total cases (*N*)	1,995		
Standard error	1.84		
Adjusted R-Squared	0.072		

Note: Estimates derived from least squares estimator.

Source: University of Texas Modules for the 2016 Cooperative Congressional Election Study.

is key: partisan identification, of any sort, reduces the likelihood that an individual perceives the system as corrupt in 2016. Because divided government existed before the 2016 election (Democrats controlling the presidency and Republicans controlling the Congress), we hasten to add that it does not necessarily undercut the argument that attitudes concerning corruption are driven by a partisan reaction to one side (or the other) being in power. More on this shortly.

Beyond party identification, several other demographic and attitudinal variables affect perceived corruption. Corruption attitudes are decreased by being Black (by about −0.33 points on the summary scale), Catholic (−0.27), being under 30 (−0.27), and having a high school degree or less (−0.18). On the other side of the ledger, corruption attitudes are increased by being a senior (+0.43). None of these findings strikes us as surprising. For example, if we assume that the longer and more closely one is exposed to the system, the more likely one is to see its flaws and experience frustration, we would expect perceived corruption to be higher amongst the more attentive and the more experienced. Similarly, those who do not "buy into" the system enough to identify with one of the two major parties should also be more likely to see politics as corrupt.

The contrast between Blacks and Latinos is instructive here. Blacks are less likely to see the system as corrupt, most likely because they are a critical constituency within one of the dominant political parties and have managed to secure—through decades of social, political, and legal struggle—a seat at the table of power. In contrast, Latinos are much less well integrated into the existing political party system and often believe that they do not have a seat at the table of power (Bardes and Oldendick, 2016; Bowler and Segura, 2011). In addition, many first-generation—and even some second-generation—Latinos come from countries with long traditions of political corruption, and they carry these attitudes with them in appraising the U.S. political system. Consequently, it is not surprising that they are slightly more likely to see the political system as corrupt.

On its face, the impact of religious denomination on corruption attitudes is perhaps surprising. Compared to others, Catholics and Jews are less likely to see the political system in the United States as corrupt. The most obvious explanation is that adherents of these religions are more likely to be comfortable with centralized authority and to see corruption with a certain amount of context. Admittedly, however, this is speculative (for an interesting overview, see Mensah, 2014).

What about the possibility that campaign finance knowledge might be correlated with perceived corruption? In its disclosure arguments, the Court suggested that more information about campaign contributions leads to more knowledge, which may well lead to *less* corruption. That is, the light of disclosure reduces the incentives that politicians have to engage in quid pro quo behavior. More pragmatically, however, work by Ansolabehere, Snowberg, and Synder (2005) indicates that the more news people consume, the *less* accurate their knowledge of campaign finance is. Our data suggests that campaign finance information does influence corruption attitudes, although this influence is mixed.

The regression model estimates suggest that knowledge of campaign spending positively correlates with perceived corruption; correctly answering one of these items is associated with a 0.11-point increase in perceived corruption. Conversely, knowledge of restrictions on special interests in campaigns is negatively correlated with perceived corruption; correctly answering one of these items is associated with a 0.37-point decrease in perceived corruption. In sum, people who know more about money and politics are not necessarily less likely to see the government as corrupt. They are if they know about the prohibition on corporate contributions to candidates or about "dark money" or about 501(c)(4)s not having to disclose contributors. But they are more likely to see the government as corrupt if their knowledge is about campaign spending.

Then there are the twin questions of whether either campaign spending or campaign finance regulation affects perceived corruption. With respect to the former, the answer is "no." The average amount of per capita dollars spent in federal elections from 2006 to 2016 is insignificantly correlated with perceptions of corruption. In fact, the direction of the effect is negative; that is, more spending tends to decrease beliefs that the system is corrupt, although the tendency is extremely weak. With respect to the latter, which is much closer to the Court's reasoning in *Buckley*, the summary measure of campaign finance reform and regulation is correlated with higher levels of perceived corruption. The suggestion is that more regulation is associated with an increased belief that politics and politicians are corrupt. Of course, we cannot speak to the issue of causality. It may be, for instance, that states in which perceptions of corruption are the highest are states prone to responding with campaign finance regulations. But our findings are consistent with those of Rosenson (2009), who explicitly attempts to correct for exactly this sort of endogeneity in her model of perceived corruption.

Did these associations exist before the critical judicial decisions of the late 2000s were rendered? Mostly, although some important differences are evident. Before examining the results from the 2009 survey, however, two measurement issues merit attention. First, it is worth pointing out that the political corruption measure for the 2009 equations is slightly different in our post–*Citizens United* poll: here, we use an additive scale of four items, creating a 0–12 scale that we transform to 0–10 for purposes of presentational clarity. The other measurement issue is that our campaign finance knowledge variable for 2009 is a single, simple variable. Otherwise, the 2009 equation is similar to the 2016 version: it includes variables for political interest, news media usage, sex, race, ethnicity, age, education, partisanship, population, campaign finance regulations, and per capita campaign spending.[12]

Table 3.2 presents the results of the 2009 equation. Several results stand out.

- Political interest was significantly correlated with increased perceptions of corruption, but so was news media usage. This is distinct from 2016, where news media use had no impact on perceptions of corruption.
- Unlike 2016, partisanship has an asymmetric effect on perceived corruption in 2009, as Democratic identifiers are less likely to think the system is corrupt whereas Republicans are (marginally) more likely to believe this. This is unsurprising given that the Democrats controlled both the White House and the Congress in 2009 and strongly suggests that perceived corruption is (at least somewhat) driven by a partisan reaction to who is holding the keys of power at a given point in time. It is worth reiterating, however, that general perceptions that the system is corrupt were quite prominent in 2009.
- African-Americans, people under thirty years of age, and those with a college degree are much less likely to see the political system as corrupt.
- Knowledge of the campaign finance system, the state campaign finance regulatory environment, and per capita campaign spending are uncorrelated with perceptions of corruption.

* * *

The empirical models thus tell a coherent story. In general, those who are younger and less experienced and those who are committed to one of the major political parties are much less likely to see the political system as corrupt. Those who are older and more experienced, those who are attentive to

Table 3.2 Predicting Perceived Corruption, 2009

	DV: Summary measure of perceived corruption		
	Est. Coeff.	S.E.	Prob = 0
Constant	6.216	0.221	0.000
Summary of campaign finance knowledge	−0.012	0.051	0.813
Summary measure of limits on individuals, parties, PACs, corporations, unions	0.008	0.023	0.741
Statewide population, 2008 (in millions)	0.003	0.004	0.400
Total statewide candidate and committee expenditures per capita, 2008	−0.001	0.008	0.905
Political interest	0.269	0.038	0.000
Media usage	0.040	0.018	0.003
Male	−0.045	0.081	0.578
African American	−0.582	0.137	0.000
Latino	−0.138	0.127	0.277
Under 30 years of age	−0.715	0.100	0.000
65 years of age and over	0.255	0.127	0.045
College degree or more	−0.351	0.110	0.001
High school degree or less	−0.062	0.098	0.527
Democrat	−0.575	0.105	0.000
Republican	0.141	0.109	0.196
Total cases (*N*)	1,913		
Standard error	1.73		
Adjusted R-Squared	0.136		

Note: Estimates derived from least squares estimator.

Source: University of Texas Money in Politics Survey (Shaw and Roberts, 2009).

the news, and those who are more politically independent are much more likely to see the political system as corrupt. A small handful of other studies have been done in this vein, and they are mostly consistent with what we show here. Most notably, Persily and Lammie (2004) show that race and social status, along with attitudes toward government, are correlated with perceived corruption. While we are not exactly tilling virgin soil, rarely have the effects of demographic variables on perceived corruption been specified with appropriate controls as they are in this analysis. Furthermore, in our view, the specific relationship between identification with the political parties and diminished perceptions of corruption in 2016 is new and something that the Court has not considered at all in its campaign finance reform rulings. Put simply, divided government may drive—through partisanship—diminished perceptions of corruption.

Then there are the relationships between perceived corruption and campaign knowledge, spending, and regulation. The 2016 data clearly demonstrate that knowing some things (such as the nature of legal limits on contributions) tends to decrease perceptions of corruption, while knowing other things (such as how much money is spent in federal election campaigns) tends to increase perceptions of corruption. We know of no other research on this relationship, and these findings obviously present a more complex reality than the one assumed by the Court in *Buckley*.

To some degree, our other results are also counterintuitive. For instance, the data show that the amount of campaign spending does not have much influence on perceived corruption. One might argue that campaign spending is only an imperfect measure of the total amount of money in politics—and therefore ought not correlate with the public's perception of money corrupting politics. But this seems a strained argument, at best. The data also show that residing in a state with more substantial campaign finance regulations and reforms coincides with *increased* perceived corruption. Despite the consistency of this finding with previous work (Rosenson, 2009), we offer these results with all appropriate caution because we do not explicitly control for potential bias due to endogenous relationships.

* * *

While there has been substantial research documenting perceived levels of corruption, much less has been done on *why* voters think this corruption occurs. Our 2009 and 2016 surveys employ different conceptualizations of corruption. We are interested in whether voters think corruption mainly occurs (a) because people with an agenda offer money to candidates so that the candidates will help advance their policies when in office or (b) because candidates solicit funds from people who might be affected by their policy decisions should they win. The former is the "classic" conceptualization of corruption and is often characterized as an anticipated quid pro quo. The latter conceptualization gets less attention in the news media but is well-known among wealthy contributors and interest groups as the "shake down."[13]

So, which is it? Voters think both occur quite often but are a little more likely to say interest groups and wealthy contributors are leading this corruption dance. In 2016, when asked how often members vote based on contributors' demands, 62 percent choose "all the time" or "often," while 29 percent choose "sometimes" or "never" (see Figure 3.4). By comparison, when asked how often corruption flows from members' demands for contributions, 53 percent choose "all the time" or "often," while 34 percent choose "sometimes" or "never." Although still quite high, the percentage of Americans saying that either form of corruption occurs "all the time" or "often" decreases slightly—by about 5–6 percentage points—from 2009 to 2016.

What if we pose these two different "corruption" scenarios directly against each other to see which voters think is the primary culprit? In 2016, a majority (53 percent) say that both occur with equal frequency, with 15 percent choosing "politicians demanding money from contributors" and 10 percent choosing "politicians changing votes in response to contributors." In 2009, a comparable majority (52 percent) said both occur with equal frequency, with 10 percent choosing "politicians demanding money from contributors" and 9 percent choosing "politicians changing votes in response to contributors." It seems that most Americans think that politicians, special interests, and contributors are all in bed with one another and that all sides contribute to this corruption.

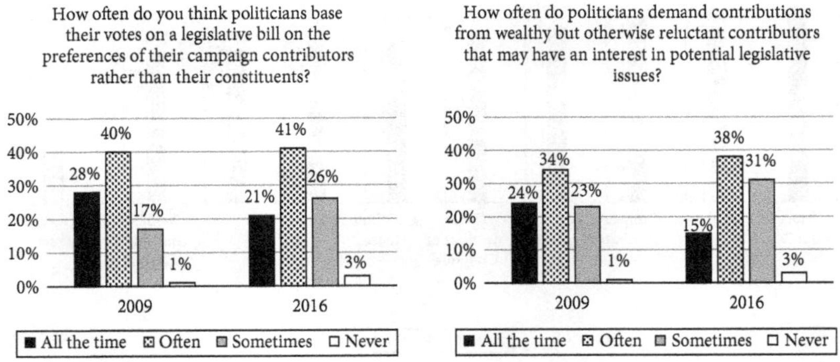

Figure 3.4 Sources of Corruption

Source: University of Texas Money in Politics Surveys (Shaw and Roberts, 2009). University of Texas Modules for the 2016 Cooperative Congressional Election Study.

Do voters view some interests and contributors as more influential than others? In both 2009 and 2016, we asked respondents to rate the influence of several factors (and groups) on congressional member voting. To make things simple, we had people use a 0–10 scale, with 0 representing almost no influence and 10 representing too much influence. Figure 3.5 shows that in 2016, three groups score almost a full percentage point higher than anything else: Super PACs (8.48), lobbyists (8.40), and campaign contributors (8.03). All are major sources of campaign money.[14] In 2009, prior to the *Citizens United* decision, we did not ask about Super PACs, but lobbyists (7.63) and campaign contributors (7.66) were deadlocked for the top spot, along with political party.

The perception that influence is directly linked to campaign contributions—trumping party, ideology, and a politician's sincere beliefs—is quite stunning in its naked cynicism. Note the difference between the perceived influence of lobbyists (8.4 in 2016 and 7.6 in 2009) and the preferences of the member's constituents (6.5 in 2016 and 5.8 in 2009); respondents think that both are important (each score well over the midpoint of 5), but lobbyists are judged to be two points *more* influential (on a 0–10 scale) than those who vote in the election. That translates to almost 20 percent more important.[15]

Of course, these ratings items do not ask voters to pit one source of corruption against another or to pick the most important source of corruption. In both the 2009 and 2016 surveys we therefore followed the ratings battery

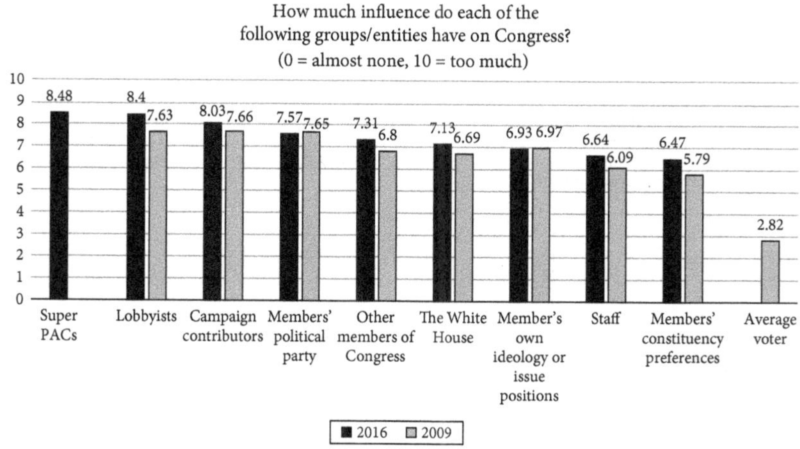

Figure 3.5 Influence on Congressional Member Voting

Source: University of Texas Money in Politics Surveys (Shaw and Roberts, 2009). University of Texas Modules for the 2016 Cooperative Congressional Election Study.

by asking about the "primary source of corruption in U.S. politics." In 2009, respondents chose political parties first (27 percent), followed by interest groups (26 percent), corporations (20 percent), and candidates (9 percent). This was slightly different in 2016, when respondents selected interest groups (26 percent) over political parties (21 percent), followed by wealthy individuals (19 percent), corporations (16 percent), candidates (15 percent), and unions (4 percent). Part of this difference may be because "wealthy individuals" was not offered as a choice in 2009. Still, the data clearly indicate that many Americans see political parties as a major source of political corruption, on par with interest groups, wealthy individuals, and corporations. The partisan differences in responses to this question were, predictably, striking. Independents were much more likely to see political parties as the main source of corruption, whereas partisans were much more likely to point to other groups. Democrats were more likely than Republicans to say wealthy contributors and corporations are the main sources of corruption, although these differences are not as great as one might assume. The finding that there are two very different strands of perceived corruption—one that sees it as flowing through the political parties and another that sees it as flowing through interest groups—is a critical one that we do not think has been recognized in the Court's previous rulings on campaign finance.

Given the overwhelming data suggesting that voters see a link between contributing to a politician's campaign and influencing that politician (classic quid pro quo corruption), we are intrigued by how people think this works. In particular, we wish to consider the question of amount. To the mind of the average voter, how much money must someone (or some group) contribute to unduly influence a senator in a $10 million election campaign? We asked precisely this question in our 2016 survey. The average across all responses is $3.4 million, with a median response of $2.7 million and a modal response of $5.3 million. In other words, voters think the average "price" for influence is quite high.[16]

However, it is possible that the scope of our inquiries about influence and the behavior of members of Congress is too narrow. One might reasonably argue that voters may think Congress is corrupt or even that special interest groups have disproportionate influence over American government but still see other sources of power as equally or more important. We therefore asked a more general question in 2016 about the level of power exercised or held by a variety of distinct groups (see Figure 3.6). Using a 0–10 scale from least to most power, respondents gave political lobbyists the top average

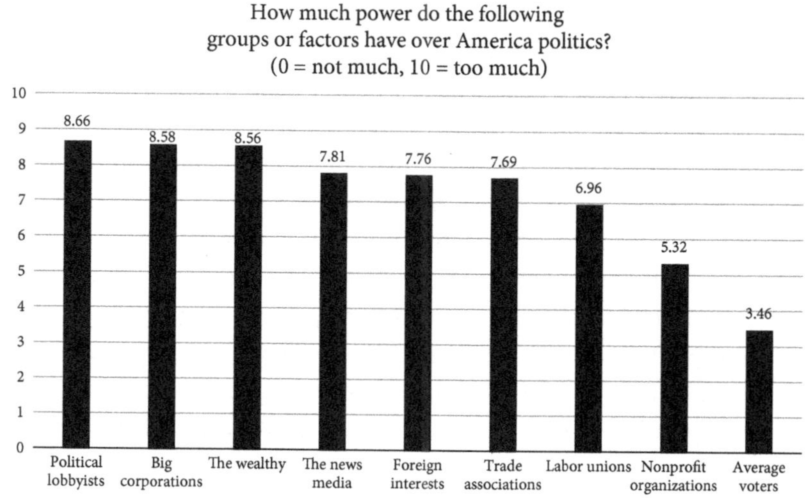

Figure 3.6 Power over American Politics
Source: University of Texas Modules for the 2016 Cooperative Congressional Election Study.

score of 8.7, followed by big corporations (8.6) and the wealthy (8.6). Behind these, we see a secondary clustering made up of the news media (7.8), foreign interests (7.8), trade associations (7.6), and labor unions (7.0). Bringing up the rear—not exactly powerless, but nowhere near the top—are nonprofit organizations (5.3) and average voters (3.5). The upshot is that a more expansive consideration of power players simply reinforces the argument that many Americans believe that the political system is influenced by moneyed interests, above and beyond mass media and foreign actors and well beyond average Americans. The perceived corruption that so troubles the Court is, in fact, pervasive.

Do Voters Support Campaign Finance Reforms?

If we accept that many Americans are convinced that their government is corrupt, it seems appropriate to ask about laws or regulations or policies that might reduce this cynicism. The Court, of course, asserts a link between legislation and regulation curtailing political speech and diminished perceptions of corruption. We wish to explore this linkage in detail. Let us first examine the extent to which Americans support specific campaign finance reforms and then turn to the question of whether these reforms affect behavior. Here we focus on our survey data from 2016, which demonstrates considerable support for many different sorts of campaign finance reforms. In Figure 3.7, which plots the mean support for various reforms on a 0 (strongly opposed) to 10 (strongly support) scale, we see support for a range of restrictions, including modest support for public funding. The responses to enhanced disclosure offer subtler insights. Requiring fuller disclosure of contributors to outside interest groups garners the highest support, but the reluctance to treat more disclosure as an acceptable tradeoff to freeing candidates to accept unlimited individual contributions speaks to the limits disclosure has as a corruption deterrent.[17]

According to the 2012 and 2016 ANES surveys, voters are willing to not only limit corporations or unions giving to political candidates but to also ban this sort of political spending. Sixty percent favor limiting corporate and union PAC contributions to federal election campaigns (14 percent oppose this) and 42 percent favor banning contributions from these sources altogether (22 percent oppose). Moreover, 69 percent favor more general limits on campaign spending, whereas only 8 percent oppose them.

Does this mean that the public does not think interest groups have the same constitutional right to free speech that individuals have? Somewhat surprisingly, there is substantial support for the theoretical notion that these groups have free speech rights. Notably, when asked about the essence of the *Citizens United* decision, which holds that corporations and unions have the same free speech protections as individuals, the public is split. Forty-three percent say these groups ought to have the same free speech rights as individuals, while 25 percent say they should have fewer rights and 17 percent

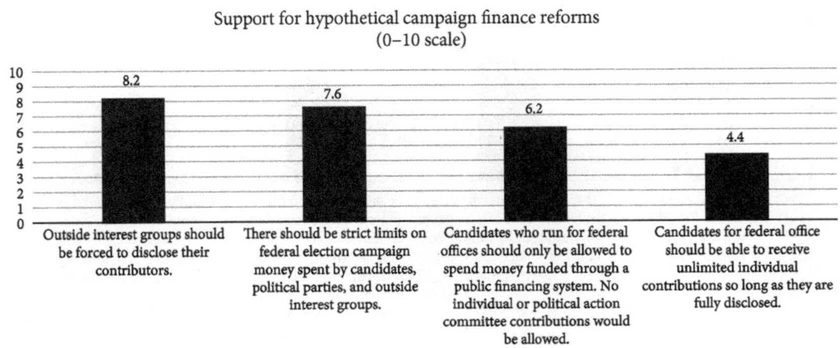

Figure 3.7 Estimating Support for Campaign Finance Reforms and Regulations
Source: University of Texas Modules for the 2016 Cooperative Congressional Election Study.

say they should have no free speech rights. But this viewpoint seems disconnected from political reality. In fact, when asked about the *Citizens United* decision directly, only 14 percent say the decision was correct and that corporations have free speech rights. Conversely, 31 percent say the decision was correct but that we should amend the Constitution to limit these free speech rights for corporations, while 26 percent say the decision was incorrect and that corporations have no free speech rights (29 percent were unfamiliar with the decision).

However we measure it, the appetite for reform is undeniable. A sizable percentage of Americans—somewhere around 40 percent—are supportive of almost any attempt to limit money in politics or to increase transparency. In theory, people acknowledge free speech rights for groups, but in practice they are willing to limit those rights, and many would even be willing to amend the Constitution to do so.

Do Voters Think Reforms Will Reduce Corruption?

Given the high support for campaign finance reforms and regulations, one would assume that people think these reforms will reduce political corruption and improve the overall quality of democracy in the United States. A cursory glance at responses to our 2016 questions asking about the effectiveness of prospective reforms supports this assumption. In Figure 3.8 we see that

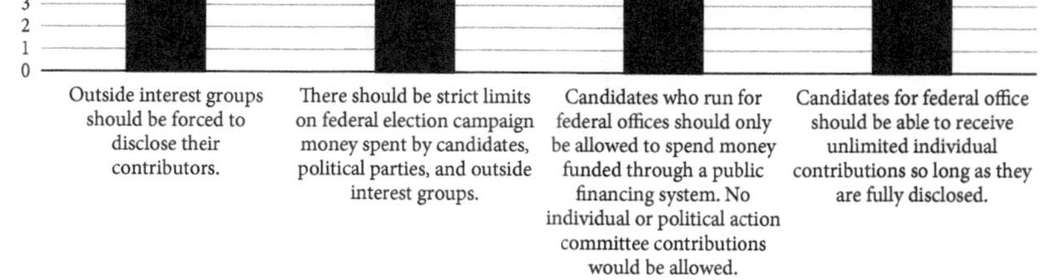

Figure 3.8 The Effectiveness of Reforms
Source: University of Texas Modules for the 2016 Cooperative Congressional Election Study.

each of the four reforms that we tested is predicted to be either extremely effective (7.1 on a 0–10 "effectiveness" scale for disclosure requirements for outside groups, and 6.8 for strict limits on campaign contributions) or at least moderately effective (5.9 for public financing and 4.6 for unlimited spending with full disclosure).

Interestingly, this rather rosy assessment occurs even though Americans do not believe that past reforms and regulations were effective. When asked in 2016 how effective campaign finance reforms have been at reducing the amount of corruption in politics, only 22 percent say they have been effective (2 percent say "extremely" effective, while 20 percent say "somewhat" effective). Conversely, 78 percent say either "not very" effective (40 percent) or "not at all" effective (39 percent).

It could be that this reflects a native optimism about "new" policies and efforts to address persistent problems. Or it could be that voters do not understand that many of the proposed reforms have been tried in one form or another—public financing for presidential elections, for example—and haven't had the desired effect.[18] Whichever of these is closer to the truth, Americans support reform and regulatory efforts to curtail the influence of money in politics.

How Has Campaign Finance Reform Affected Money and Attitudes?

We have spent much of our time in this chapter examining attitudes about the political system and government, what people know about the campaign finance system, and how receptive they are to attempts to "fix" the system. The upshot of these analyses is that many Americans are convinced that the political system is deeply corrupt, they see money from nefarious sources everywhere, and they say that they are willing to try most anything to fix their politics.

But all of this is complicated by two things. The first complication has been pointed out by scholars and campaign practitioners: few Americans rate campaign finance reform as one of the most important problems facing the United States. In May 2016, an NBC News/Wall Street Journal survey asked about the most important issue for the federal government to address: at the head of the list were jobs and economic growth (26 percent) and national security and terrorism (21 percent), followed by the deficit and government spending (16 percent) and healthcare (15 percent). *Not a single respondent offered campaign finance reform as the most important issue.* Furthermore, this finding is hardly an outlier; less than 1 percent of respondents cited campaign finance reform as the most important issue facing the country in the 2016 ANES pre-election survey. This may partially explain why neither Democrat Hillary Clinton nor Republican Donald Trump mentioned campaign finance reform in their convention speeches or in the three presidential debates in 2016.[19] As former U.S. House of Representative Bill Frenzel (R-MN) once said, "no one ever lost a congressional election by opposing campaign finance reform."[20]

A second complication is that it is unclear what the "real-world" effects of campaign finance reform and regulation are. We have had three major changes to campaign finance laws since 1970: the Federal Election Campaign Act (1971, 1974) and the Bipartisan Campaign Reform Act (2002). None interrupted steady increases in spending on federal election campaigns. Looking at the ANES data from Figures 3.1 and 3.2, none appears to have improved citizen perceptions about corruption in federal government.

But let us more systematically unpack the different elements at play here. When looking at the "real world" effects of campaign finance reform, the first and most obvious thing worth considering is whether campaign finance laws reduce the amount of money in the system, an overriding goal of the campaign finance reform community, if not the Court. If we regress our summary measure of state campaign finance reforms and regulations—using the 0–7 scale, where 7 represents maximum regulation—on per capita campaign spending in each of the states in 2016, we find that relatively greater regulation has almost no effect on spending. We repeat this exercise for every election year from 2006 to 2014 and find the same thing: states with more regulation do not experience less per capita spending (see Table 3.3). Although the relationship is never statistically significant, it tends to be positive—more regulation is associated with slightly more per capita spending—and is slightly more substantial in midterm elections. Irrespective of how one looks at it, though, there is no evidence that more regulation of campaign finance decreases the amount of money that campaigns spend per voter.[21]

One might reasonably argue (as discussed earlier) that the causal-temporal direction of this relationship is hazy. It may be that states with high levels of campaign spending pass campaign finance reform laws and regulations to redress this relationship: spending impacts reform, not the other way around. This is entirely plausible. Considering the minimal correlation

Table 3.3 The Effects of Campaign Finance Reforms on per Capita Election Spending

	Per capita campaign spending			
	Coeff.	**S.E.**	**Prob = 0**	**Adjusted R Squared**
Summary measure of campaign finance reforms and regulations				
2016	−0.192	0.642	0.766	−0.019
2014	0.774	0.659	0.246	0.008
2012	0.075	0.595	0.900	−0.021
2010	0.241	0.318	0.453	−0.009
2008	0.225	0.453	0.622	−0.016
2006	0.459	0.504	0.366	−0.004

Notes: Data based on least squares regressions estimating the effects of campaign finance regulations on statewide per capita campaign spending for each election from 2006 to 2016. $N = 50$ for each year.

shown in Table 3.3, however, one wonders at what point such reform reduces spending.

Another possibility worth considering with respect to "real-world" effects is whether campaign finance laws and regulations decrease voters' perceptions that the system is corrupt. From Table 3.1, we know that states with broad limits on contributions—individuals, parties, PACs, corporations, and unions—tend to have higher levels of perceived corruption. This relationship is entirely at odds with the Court's understanding of how regulations and reforms might affect how citizens view the political system. Once again, there is the question of causality: perhaps states with higher levels of perceived corruption are more likely to pass reform laws.[22] But while this is not an interpretation that we can discount, Rosenson does account for this possibility and still finds no relationship. It is also true that the number of states that have passed new campaign finance laws over the past several years is exceedingly small. This suggests current attitudes about corruption are unlikely to be "in flux" as new campaign finance reforms change how voters regard the political system.

Finally, it is worth restating the finding that increased average spending in federal elections has virtually no impact on perceived corruption (see Table 3.1). This contradicts the implied notion (which some campaign finance reform supporters have read into the Court's reasoning in the *Buckley* case) that lower per capita spending will result in voters feeling more efficacious about the American political system. Furthermore, here the causal relationship is less theoretically ambiguous. It seems unlikely that the attitudes of people who think the system is corrupt are driving campaigns to spend more money. Rather, the lack of a relationship in the data casts doubt on the notion that spending directly causes negative attitudes toward the government (Coleman and Manna, 2000).

Conclusion

Empirical analyses of some of the main linkages posited by the Supreme Court to bolster their decision to allow restrictions on money in politics produce mixed findings. In bringing data to bear on the Court's assertions regarding perceived corruption, we see the precariousness of the Court's logic. The difficulty, of course, is that they were right about many things but still produced a bad judgment. So, while the Court's basic assumptions with respect to high levels of perceived corruption and an appetite for reform are borne out by our survey data, the efficacy of its decision in *Buckley* and other cases is questionable because of its incorrect assumptions about how campaign finance reforms affect attitudes about political corruption. Still, there are other attitudes besides perceived corruption, as well as aspects of political behavior that are important above and beyond the attitudes that might influence them. In the next chapter, we take up an attitude that may be more broadly relevant for our and the Court's understanding how citizens think of their political system: political trust.

4

Perceived Corruption and Trust in Government

In this chapter we take aim at a second attitudinal linkage suggested by the Court: perceptions of corruption lead to decreased trust in government. Despite the fact that our empirical tests in Chapter 3 offered little support for the idea that increased regulation reduces perceived corruption, we also test the Court's assumption that states with more substantial campaign finance regulations will evince greater trust in government. Finally, we examine the related notion—implicitly suggested by the Court's teleology—that lower levels of campaign spending are likely to be associated with greater trust in government.[1]

Thinking about Trust

While old in theory, the idea that government is based on a social compact agreed upon by the people is relatively new in practice. In the American case, the preeminence of the individual, replete with "unalienable" rights, is broadly accepted as gospel and serves as the cornerstone of the Constitution. Americans also embrace the related idea—manifest in the Declaration of Independence as well as the Constitution—that the people have the power to dissolve the government if it fails to protect the rights of the people. Critically, for our purposes, this perspective suggests that public trust in government is essential to its legitimacy and survival.

But while scholars have long noted the importance of trust in government as an indicator of systemic health, conceptualizing and measuring this notion has produced some interesting conflicts. For example, some researchers use "confidence in government" as their main measure of public attitudes toward the American government.[2] Others have focused on the concept of political efficacy, which encompasses both internal and external elements. "Internal efficacy" is the extent to which someone thinks that they are smart

The Appearance of Corruption. Daron R. Shaw, Brian E. Roberts, and Mijeong Baek, Oxford University Press (2021).
 DOI: 10.1093/oso/9780197548417.003.0004

enough and capable enough to make sense of politics; it is weakly correlated with broader feelings about the U.S. government. In contrast, "external efficacy" refers to the extent to which someone thinks that the political system is responsive to the input of people like themselves; it is strongly correlated with the perceived functioning of government.[3] In fact, some academics have examined shifts in external efficacy when gauging the impact of either perceived corruption or campaign finance reform and regulation on more general attitudes (Persily and Lammie, 2004).

We think that measuring both confidence in government and external efficacy is worthwhile on their own, as well as serving as a legitimate means of assessing the Court's claim that perceptions of corruption damage the bond between the American people and their government. Furthermore, by these metrics there is some prima facie plausibility to the Court's intuition. Figures 4.1a–b, for instance, demonstrate that confidence and external efficacy have decreased monotonically over the past six decades, dropping precipitously after events like the Vietnam War, Watergate, Iran-Contra, and the (unpopular) impeachment of Bill Clinton, rising in the wake of the 9/11 attacks, and then dropping again with setbacks in the Iraq and Afghan Wars and with the collapse of the U.S. economy in 2008–2009.

Studies of governmental trust in the United States have also traditionally aimed to expose the source(s) of political disaffection, with several classic analyses contending that political trust is a function of popular reactions to political issues and public policy (Citrin, 1974; Miller, 1974). Prior to the mid-1960s, however, many scholars tended to focus on individuals' background and personality characteristics as a way to understand political cynicism and alienation. The prevalence of work on governmental "confidence" and "efficacy" during this early era reflects this perspective. The Vietnam War and Watergate, though, produced a change in the way political scientists thought about political trust. Individual personalities and attributes surely condition attitudes toward government, but politics and governmental performance are the proximate explanations of how people feel about their government. Since the 1990s, studies of trust in government have chronicled the decline of trust in government, connecting these trends to the foreign policy and social upheaval of the 1960s and 1970s (e.g., Abramson and Finifter, 1981; Hetherington, 2006). Some have gone even further, arguing that the decline in governmental trust in the United States has undermined liberal public policy positions and proposals and caused tension in the party

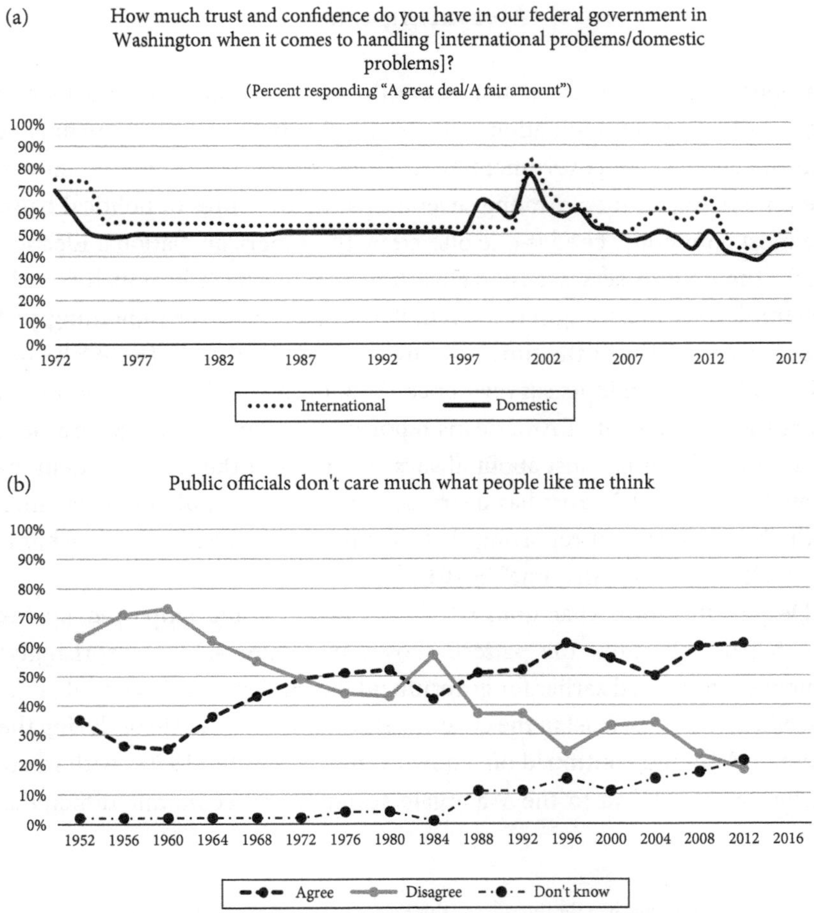

Figures 4.1a–b Trust/Confidence in Government & Political Efficacy, 1972–2016

Source: Gallup Poll (the question was not asked from 1977–1996).

Source: American National Election Studies Cumulative Survey File, 1952–2016.

coalitions (Hetherington, 2006). For present purposes, we think confidence and external efficacy are still one degree of separation removed from the most appropriate variable for a study assessing the behavioral model posited by the Court in *Buckley*. We therefore concentrate our analysis on the measure of the attitude most clearly related to the Court's explicit model of behavior: trust in government.

Measuring Trust

Apropos of the earlier discussion about the need for conceptual clarity and rigor, we begin our examination of the connection between campaign finance and citizens' trust in government by seeking a strong, consistent measure of the underlying attitude. Among several existing measures of political trust, the most commonly cited is one offered by the American National Election Study: the ANES assesses trust in government by asking "How much time do you think you can trust government in Washington to do the right thing: just about always, most of the time, or only some of the time?" The ANES has asked this question in its surveys since 1958; in that midterm election year, more than 75 percent of Americans reported that they trusted government to do the right thing "just about always" or "most of the time." As demonstrated in Figure 4.2, trust has decreased among the population over time, with about 25 percent reporting that they trust the government to what is right "all" or "most of the time" in 2012.[4]

Despite the somewhat unusual "how often?" frame employed by the ANES trust question, the pattern shown in Figure 4.2 (unsurprisingly) matches those noted earlier for governmental confidence and external political efficacy. That is, trust in the government declined in the 1960s during the Vietnam War and continued on a downward trend in the 1970s, with many attributing this trend to the Watergate scandals and economic difficulties

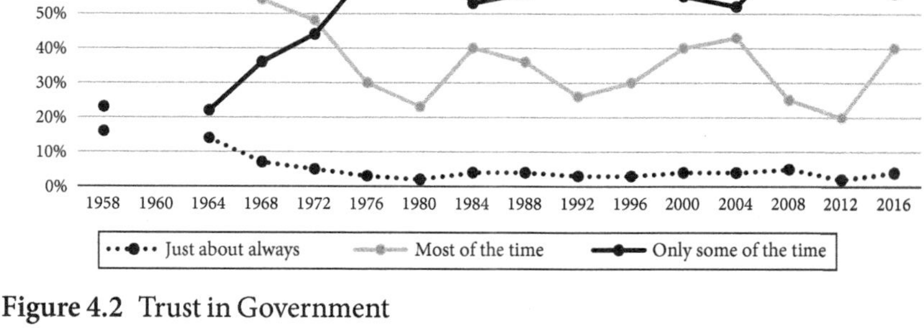

Figure 4.2 Trust in Government

Source: American National Election Studies Cumulative Survey File, 1958–2016.

of the era (Abramson and Finifter, 1981; Hetherington, 2006). The level of trust increased in the mid-1980s but fell again in the mid-1990s; recovered in the late 1990s; increased significantly after the 9/11 terrorist attacks; and then dropped in the mid- to late 2000s. Curiously, in 2016 we see an increase such that approximately 44 percent of Americans trust government "always" or "most of the time." This uptick may be related to the economic recovery and (ironically) the populist movement spearheaded by Donald Trump and Vermont Senator Bernie Sanders. Both Trump and Sanders vilified the political establishment while simultaneously proposing substantial additional spending and activity on the part of the federal government. Or it may simply be a reversion to a level closer to the mean level of trust that we saw from 1984 to 2004.

The Relationship between Perceived Corruption and Trust

If existing measures of government trust seem somewhat odd, measures of perceived corruption are, as we observed earlier, limited and inconsistent over the course of the ANES time series. This compromises our ability to use these data to test the relationship between the appearance of corruption and trust in government. As noted in Chapter 3, since the 1950s the ANES has asked a question about whether "politicians are crooked." In 1964, they added two more questions that can be considered indirect measures of corruption: "Do you think that people in the government waste [a lot/some/not much] of the money we pay in taxes?" and "Would you say the government is pretty much run by a few big interests looking out for themselves or for the benefit of all the people?" Many previous studies of political trust use these four items—trust in government, politicians are crooked, waste tax dollars, and big interests—not to estimate perceived corruption's effect on trust distinctly,[5] but rather to create a more omnibus measure of political trust (e.g., Hetherington, 1998; Lipset and Schneider, 1983). In fact, a "true" corruption item (beyond the "crooked" question) does not appear on the ANES questionnaire until 2012. In 2012 and 2016, the survey asked participants: "How many of the people running the government are corrupt?" with response options "all," "most," "about half," "a few," or "none."

The fuzziness of the trust and corruption concepts leads us to rely on our own measures, which were included in our 2016 U.S. national survey.[6] For political trust, we asked respondents how *much* they trusted the federal government on a 0–10 scale, where 0 means "do not trust the federal government at all" and 10 means "completely and totally trust the federal government." Note that our scale assesses the *depth* of trust rather than the relative *frequency* or *incidence* of trust (as with the ANES measure). Furthermore, the question yields an easily interpretable scale, with a true midpoint (5) and equidistant intervals.[7] The results (displayed in Figure 4.3) show that 66 percent of voters rated their level of trust in the federal government lower than 5.0 while 34 percent rated it higher than 5.0. A small number of people (roughly 3 percent) reported complete and total trust in the federal government. The overall mean is 4.2.

For perceived corruption, we combine the two corruption items from our 2016 survey: (1) "How honest and ethical is the average congressperson?" (2) "How serious a problem is corruption?" As we explained in Chapter 3, this combined/additive measure accounts for perceptions of corruption among public officials and the salience of this problem.

In an effort to uncover the causal path from perceived corruption to decreased political trust, we predict governmental trust as a function of perceived corruption along with several demographic, population, and attitudinal variables. In previous studies of political trust, these control variables have been shown to correlate with trust in government (Hetherington, 1998), and so we include them here. Perhaps even more importantly, we also allow knowledge of campaign finance laws (see Chapter 2) and state-level campaign spending to predict trust.[8] As discussed later in the chapter, our

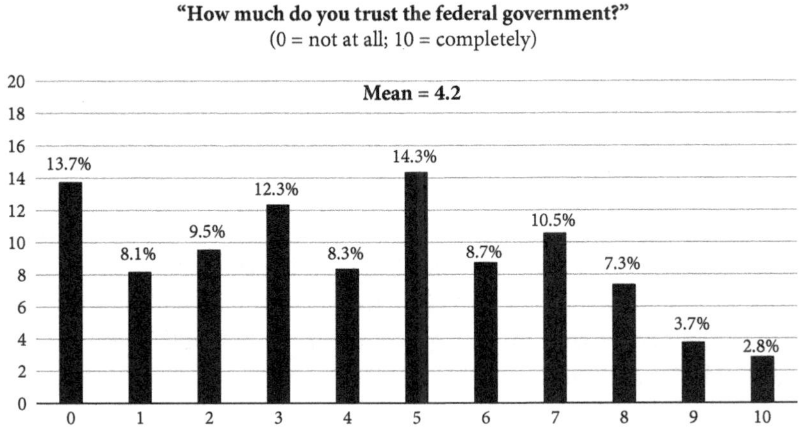

Figure 4.3 Trust in the Federal Government
Source: University of Texas Modules for the 2016 Cooperative Congressional Election Study.

composite measure of the actual restrictiveness of state-level campaign finance regulations is used as an instrumental variable in our two-stage least squares (2SLS) model explaining trust in government.

As we will see, we estimate multivariate models of trust in government as a function of perceived corruption and state-level campaign finance variables,[9] as well as other attitudinal and demographic variables. Table 4.1 reports the results for ordinary least squares (OLS) and two-stage least squares (2SLS) models side by side. The OLS models provide the best possible estimates as long as they satisfy the OLS assumptions. In our model of political trust, however, the main predictor, perceived corruption, is suspected to be endogenous. In other words, our predictor variables might be functions of other variables present in the system and may therefore be correlated with the disturbance term of the general equation, violating the Gauss-Markhov assumptions and biasing our OLS estimates. Preliminary diagnostic tests for endogeneity suggest that our concerns are valid.[10] In light of this, we adopted a 2SLS approach to produce better estimates of the key relationships. In the following, we will offer a brief discussion of the OLS estimates and then will move on to the 2SLS models for detailed discussions about the results.

The OLS results unequivocally back the Court's specific claim that there is a positive connection between lower levels of perceived corruption and higher levels of trust in government. Table 4.1 shows that this relationship is statistically and substantively significant; if voters see politicians as more corrupt (less honest and ethical), they are less likely to trust the federal government. In fact, OLS coefficients from the model suggest that perceived corruption is one of the most powerful factors affecting political trust. This result, however, is methodologically suspect, as we cannot exclude the possibility of reverse causality; to wit, those who mistrust government are more likely to perceive corruption in government. The 2SLS models accounts for this endogeneity problem.

The first stage 2SLS regression models perceived corruption, with the composite state-level campaign finance variable employed as our instrument. We turn again to the Court's behavioral model in this choice of instrument. The exclusion restriction that the instrument only affects the dependent variable of interest—trust—indirectly, through perceptions of corruption, follows directly from the Court's corruption teleology: campaign finance restrictions lower perceptions of corruption which in turn increase trust. Moreover, a common approach to estimating an instrumental variable when the endogenous variable is perceptual is to use some measure of the "reality" to

Table 4.1 Explaining Trust in Government, 2016

	OLS		2SLS			
	DV: Trust		First stage DV: Corruption		Second stage DV: Trust	
	Coeff.	S.E.	Coeff.	S.E.	Coeff.	S.E.
Constant	2.542***	0.40	8.037	0.27	−2.017	4.13
Perceived corruption	−0.369***	0.03	—		0.181	0.50
State-level regulation	—		0.058***	0.02	—	
Expenditures per capita	−0.032***	0.01	−0.010	0.01	−0.003**	0.01
State population	0.013***	0.01	−0.005	0.00	0.015***	0.01
Knowledge of regulations	0.189***	0.07	−0.358***	0.05	0.386**	0.09
Knowledge of campaign spending	0.021	0.03	0.080***	0.02	−0.023	0.05
TV use	0.033	0.12	−0.113	0.09	0.010	0.14
Newspaper use	0.087	0.11	0.017	0.08	0.085	0.12
Social media use	−0.209*	0.11	0.046	0.09	−0.226*	0.12
Presidential approval	0.418***	0.05	−0.087**	0.04	0.466***	0.07
Congressional approval	0.324***	0.05	−0.391***	0.04	0.539***	0.20
Evaluation of the economy	0.499***	0.06	−0.208***	0.05	0.612***	0.12
College degree or more	−0.132	0.13	−0.084	0.11	−0.084	0.15
High school degree or less	−0.123	0.12	−0.262***	0.10	0.0230	0.19
Under 30 years of age	0.117	0.17	−0.232*	0.13	0.251	0.22
Over 65 years and older	−0.230	0.18	0.408***	0.14	−0.462*	0.29
African American	−.645***	0.17	−0.281**	0.13	−0.498**	0.23
Male	0.130	0.10	−0.017	0.08	0.135	0.11
Democrat	0.442***	0.17	−0.215*	0.13	0.566***	0.21
Republican	0.321**	0.16	−0.611***	0.12	0.662*	0.35
Total cases	1,979				1,979	
Adjusted R-Squared	0.38				0.27	
Standard error	2.23				2.42	

Note: *** $p < 0.01$, ** $p < 0.05$, * $p < 0.1$.

Source: University of Texas Modules for the 2016 Cooperative Congressional Election Study.

predict the "perception." Thus, the composite measure of state-level regulatory restrictions is used as the instrument. Based on the first stage regression estimates, we use "estimated" perceived corruption and run the second stage regression for trust in government.

The 2SLS model is based on the assumption that the changes in the instrumental variable—state-level campaign finance laws—are associated with changes in perceived corruption but do not explain changes in trust in government other than indirectly through perceived corruption. In *Buckley*, the Court's sole rationale for upholding campaign finance laws is to limit actual or perceived corruption, not for ameliorating trust directly. Thus, our theoretical assumption is that restrictive campaign finance laws lower perceptions of corruption, but they affect trust in government only indirectly, if ever, through perceptions of corruption.[11]

The first stage regression shows that the restrictiveness of state-level campaign finance regulation has a significant effect on perceived corruption. The substantive relationship, as we found in Chapter 3, is not consistent with the Court's expectations: more restrictive campaign finance regulations are associated with *higher* levels of perceived corruption.

The second stage regression outcome is distinct from the OLS reported in Table 4.1. Perceived corruption is no longer a significant predictor of trust in government. Inconsistent with the second attitudinal linkage suggested by the Court, perceptions of corruption do not lead to decreased trust in government. The disappearance of the causal relationship after accounting for endogeneity suggests that, although people who are less trustful of government perceive more corruption, such perceptions do not affect trust, a key behavioral claim of the Court.

Beyond that key difference, the effects of the 2SLS framework produces mostly consistent results. It is notable, however, that, after taking into account endogeneity, the coefficient size of many exogenous variables gets larger. Especially, the estimated coefficients for knowledge on restrictions on special interest contributions, congressional approval, and partisan identification (particularly Republican identification) significantly increase in the 2SLS model. In addition, people sixty-five and over gain a statistically significant level ($p < 0.1$), as they are found to be less trustful of government than younger respondents.

A few of these relationships merit additional comment. Take, for example, our finding that the summary measure of knowledge of limits on special interests in campaigns is positively correlated with trust in government.

People who have better knowledge about regulations concerning special interests and their influence on campaigns tend to express higher trust in government. In Chapters 2 and 3, respectively, we found that respondents tend to exaggerate both the absolute and relative amount of money coming from special interest groups and refer to them as a major source of political corruption. The positive relationship between public's knowledge of special interests and political trust may suggest that political distrust is to some extent driven by the public's misperception of special interests' influence in campaigns.

Similarly, it should also come as no surprise that identifying as a partisan also increases trust in government: Republican and Democratic identifiers are more trustful of government than independents. It is understandable that party identifiers show significantly higher levels of trust in the federal government than independents. The latter group is less directly connected to the people responsible for the federal government, who are (of course) Democrats and Republicans.

Other relationships are, perhaps, less obvious. When people report receiving campaign information from different media types, levels of trust in government vary. People who rely on the traditional mass media outlets, television and newspapers, are more likely to trust government, but the estimates are not statistically significant. By contrast, social media use has a negative (but weak) effect on trust in government ($p = 0.07$). This finding is consistent with the widespread suspicion that social media outlets are more likely than traditional news to focus on or amplify stories of corruption and malfeasance. Our results also corroborate studies showing that social media consumption facilitates motivated reasoning and confirmation bias in political deliberations (e.g., Lee, et al., 2014).

It may also be somewhat surprising that our models show that a voter's evaluation of the national economy is the most powerful predictor explaining political trust, followed by congressional and presidential job approval. While the magnitude of the relationship is striking, the logic is straightforward. Collectively, these relationships demonstrate that how people evaluate government performance greatly influences public trust.

What about the possibility that greater campaign spending leads to decreased trust? The estimates from Table 4.1 indicate that more money in politics lowers political trust. More specifically, our variable capturing average statewide campaign spending per capita (for candidates and campaign committees) between 2006 and 2016 shows a regression coefficient that is negative and statistically significant. In other words, higher spending does appear to coincide with lower trust in government. This finding is particularly interesting given the absence of a positive relationship between spending and perceived corruption in Chapter 3.

Lastly, and consistent with previous research, we find that African Americans remain significantly less trusting of government than other racial or ethnic groups. This is particularly interesting given the first stage results in Table 4.1 and our analysis in Chapter 3, which suggest that Black respondents are also less likely to see corruption. In other words, perceived corruption does not appear to be a critical factor explaining higher levels of government mistrust among African Americans. Instead, governmental mistrust is undoubtedly powerfully connected with vestigial skepticism about the motives of White elected officials, a skepticism grounded in the history of Blacks in the United States.

Discussion

In the *Buckley* decision, the Supreme Court offered a plethora of testable research hypotheses about the political attitudes and behavior of American voters. In this chapter, we focus on key relationships that occur in the middle of the posited behavioral chain. Most obviously, we ask whether attitudes concerning political corruption correlate with trust in government. The Court asserts that higher levels of perceived corruption are correlated with lower levels of political trust. The data are not consistently supportive of this line of reasoning. While the OLS models show that perceived corruption is closely associated with trust in government, the 2SLS model that accounts for endogeneity shows that perceived corruption does not have a significant impact on trust in government. Rather, the analyses reaffirm the importance of government performance—as embodied by public evaluations of the president, Congress, and the national economy—for assessments of trust (Citrin, 1974; Miller, 1974).

To some extent, the absence of a consistent, direct, and independent effect of perceived corruption on political trust casts doubt on the Court's broader behavioral model. This seems especially the case given the absence of a relationship between perceived corruption and either campaign finance regulation or campaign spending, as shown in Chapter 3. Still, the (somewhat) negative influence of campaign spending and the indirect effect of campaign finance regulation on governmental trust is worth noting. The obvious next step is assessing whether perceived corruption and trust in government influence the participatory behavior of American voters. Chapter 5 assesses this connection.

5

Perceived Corruption and Political Participation

Until this point, we have focused on either how attitudes and opinions affect other attitudes and opinions or how certain policy environments affect attitudes and opinions. This is reasonable given that many of the linkages posited by the Supreme Court in *Buckley* are, in fact, between perceived corruption and other political attitudes or between regulatory environments and perceived corruption. Our focus in this chapter, though, is on another linkage asserted by the Court: between perceived corruption and political participation. In allowing regulatory limits on campaign contributions—and thus limits on political speech—the Court has taken the position that perceived corruption dissuades people from getting involved in politics or voting. The implicit logic is that people who think the U.S. government is corrupt are too discouraged to vote, too disgusted to vote, or both. High levels of perceived corruption therefore require remedy because they discourage political participation, and this, in turn, corrodes the legitimacy of a democratic republic (Verba and Nie, 1972; Piven and Cloward, 2000). The Court has consequently allowed limits on political speech because these regulations presumably reduce perceived corruption, thereby encouraging greater participation and enhancing systemic legitimacy.

In Chapters 3 and 4, we presented evidence that casts doubt on the assertion that increasing campaign finance regulations reduces perceived corruption. However, we did not examine the linkage between the key attitude—perceived corruption—and the key behavior—voting in elections. Nor did we explore the extent to which campaign finance regulation is associated with participation more broadly conceived. As we have seen throughout this study, unpacking causal pathways is difficult, but measuring associations is both possible and instructive.

The Appearance of Corruption. Daron R. Shaw, Brian E. Roberts, and Mijeong Baek, Oxford University Press (2021).
 DOI: 10.1093/oso/9780197548417.003.0005

In this chapter, we examine the general nature of political participation in the United States and the influence that political attitudes and campaign money have on turnout. More specifically, we begin by examining a broad range of participatory activities in the United States, offering evidence on turnout but also establishing the extent to which Americans engage in high-end participatory acts (such as attending political meetings) and low-end participatory acts (such as discussing politics with friends). In so doing, we are not exactly breaking new ground; rather, we are updating previous studies (e.g., Leighley and Nagler, 2013; Verba and Nie, 1972; Verba, Schlozman, and Brady, 1995) and expanding the range and scope of our baseline knowledge of political participation from 2008 through 2016. In addition, we also position ourselves to comment more convincingly on how broader political attitudes shape participation.

Following this, we connect the findings from Chapter 4 to political participation: most obviously, we explore the relationship between trust in government and political participation. Are people more likely to vote when they trust the government to do what is right? Alternatively, are they more likely to vote when they distrust the government? The Court assumes the former, but it seems to us that low trust in government might prompt people to go to the polls to "reclaim" the political system from entrenched, corrupt interests.

Our next area of interest is the extent to which campaign finance laws and regulations influence participation and turnout at the state level. Are people in states with greater regulatory limits and prohibitions on campaign spending more or less likely to cast ballots in elections? Even though the data analyses from Chapters 3 and 4 suggest that regulating campaign finance does not necessarily reduce perceived corruption, we do not know whether it affects political participation.

We are also intrigued by the relationship between campaign money and political participation. What happens to turnout and other forms of participation when campaign spending is relatively high? The Court seems to imply that money increases a sense of corruption and erodes trust, causing people to stay away from the polls. But our analysis in Chapter 3 demonstrates that the relationship between increased per capita spending and perceived corruption is somewhat different; in fact, lower spending is associated with higher levels of perceived corruption. Similarly, we think money might facilitate increased turnout by increasing political engagement and information.

Our final area of inquiry in this chapter is a direct examination of the relationship between perceived corruption and turnout. We now know that perceptions of the U.S. government and political system as corrupt are commonplace among Americans, but the antecedents of these attitudes are not as simple as the Court has assumed, and it is possible that their behavioral implications are equally surprising. Indeed, the idea that corruption attitudes are positively linked with political participation squares with the fact that presidential election turnout has increased since 1996 (see Figure 5.1) as perceived corruption has likewise ticked upward.

With these foci in mind, the remainder of this chapter relies on analyses of our national surveys from 2009 and 2016 to consider the linkages between attitudes, regulatory environment, and political behavior. While the virtues of nationally representative polls are well-known, it is worth pointing out that survey-based analyses rely on self-reported activities. Because of this, the relationships we are estimating can be affected by the tendency of people to misreport whether they voted or went to a meeting or signed a petition. Previous research indicates that the effects of these tendencies are substantively minor. Most relevant for our purposes, studies that use self-reported behavior slightly exaggerate the magnitude of known correlates of the vote (e.g., Silver, Anderson, and Abramson, 1986). In other words, it's not that education does not affect turnout (it does), but by relying on self-reported behavior we produce estimates that overstate that relationship compared to what we find when we use validated data on turnout.[1]

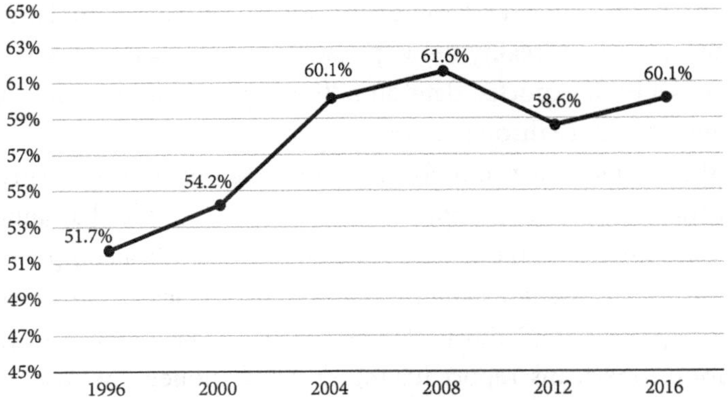

Figure 5.1 Voter Turnout in U.S. Presidential Elections, 1996–2016

Notes: Turnout is among the voter-eligible population.

Source: McDonald, 2020.

What Do We Know about Political Participation?

If you happen to journey to Washington, DC and make a trip to Ford's Theatre, we recommend that you walk across the street and visit the Abraham Lincoln museum next to the house where the sixteenth president passed away. Within the museum is a three-story "sculpture" made of books about Lincoln. The point of the sculpture is that there are as many books about Lincoln as there are about any other figure in American (and perhaps world) history. The public's appetite for all things Lincoln is remarkable. With all due respect to President Lincoln, however, the literature on political participation is equally impressive. Political scientists have covered this topic from almost every conceivable angle, with studies of almost every country imaginable. Indeed, a "literature review" of scholarship on political participation is guaranteed to offend—by omission—some appreciable portion of the dozens of authors still living who have contributed to our knowledge of this most basic of democratic acts. Still, the fact that studies of turnout and participation continue to be published tells us either we do not know everything or what we know is constantly subject to change as new democracies, new voters, and new elections occur.

In the United States, a country with a credible claim to having the oldest and longest-running mass democratic system, election data and public opinion surveys have yielded treasure troves of data on political participation. In the broadest terms, the facts are simple and consistent: most Americans talk about politics occasionally with family and friends and vote in some elections, but relatively few Americans engage in more demanding forms of political participation. Even in an era of significant partisan polarization—one featuring the first "reality show" president—these facts persist. In Figure 5.2, we present self-reported data on political participation from the four-year period from 2012 through 2016.

Note that Americans routinely engage in less demanding forms of political participation. For example, from Figure 5.2 we see that almost two out of three Americans report discussing politics, while a comparable percentage say they voted in a primary election. Nevertheless, the drop-off for activities requiring more effort, knowledge, and engagement is steep. Only one in four Americans report having donated money, for instance, and fewer than one in seven say they attended a political rally. Then there is another drop-off for the high-end participatory acts: only one in twenty say they worked for a campaign or contacted a newspaper. Furthermore, one in

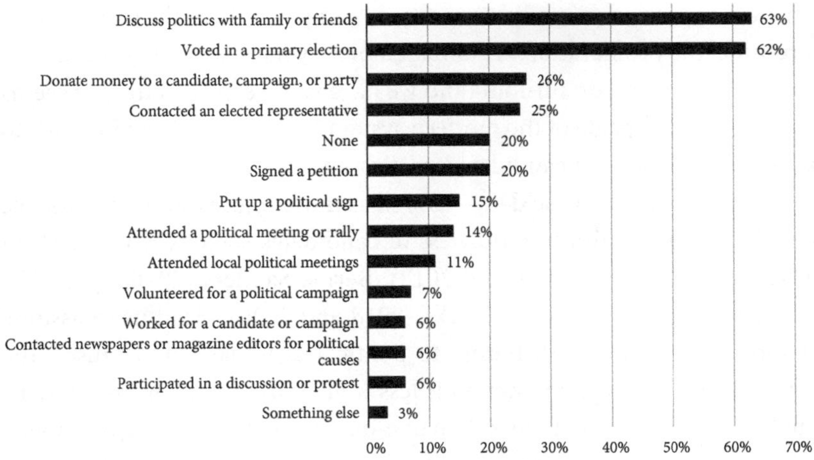

Figure 5.2 Political Participation in the U.S., 2012–2016

Note: Four items were asked referent to "the last year" rather than "over the past four years": Have you attended a local meeting; put up a political sign; worked for a candidate or campaign; donated money to a candidate?

Source: University of Texas Module for the 2016 Cooperative Congressional Election Study.

five Americans say they did not participate in politics at all over this four-year period.

But while the estimated levels of participation for high-end political acts do not match some of the effusive descriptions of the American citizenry of the early nineteenth century (e.g., Tocqueville 1838), we think the data paint a rather balanced picture overall, with little evidence that political participation is trending downward. Roughly 80 percent of Americans report engaging in some kind of political activity over a single presidential cycle, with somewhere between one-quarter and one-third stating that they engaged in some kind of relatively demanding activity. Moreover, election turnout information indicates that participation has increased since the mid-1990s (see Figure 5.1), and other data suggest that some other activities—most notably, contributing money—have also become more common.

Campaign Contributions as Political Participation

Although we are currently looking at political participation generally, we are struck by the proportion of Americans (26 percent) reporting that they have contributed money to a candidate, party, or campaign. If, as the Court seems to presume, the proliferation of campaign money has had deleterious effects on political trust and on turnout (and we have yet to establish this), it seems that one possible upside of the modern system is more people giving cash to express their support for candidates, parties, and causes.

Nevertheless, while these data—as well as more impressionistic evidence about the online fundraising prowess of candidates such as Howard Dean (2004), Barack Obama (2008 and 2012), Bernie Sanders (2016 and 2020), Ted Cruz (2016), and Beto O'Rourke (2018 and 2020)—lead us to assume that more people are contributing to political candidates and causes, the precise nature of this phenomenon is less well established. For instance, although our data show that more than one-quarter of Americans gave money to candidates, parties, or some political cause over the 2015–2016 cycle, data from the American National Election Study (ANES) surveys show the percentage contributing to a political campaign at less than half this figure. In Figure 5.3, which covers the period from 1968 (the last election before passage of the Federal Election Campaign Act, or FECA) through 2016, we see that about 12 percent of ANES respondents self-report giving money to a campaign in either 2012 or 2016. In part, the nature of the survey question explains this. Our 2016 survey asks about contributions to candidates, campaigns, or political parties, while the ANES question confines itself to contributing to a political campaign. There are also methodological differences that could explain the discrepancy: ANES conducts both

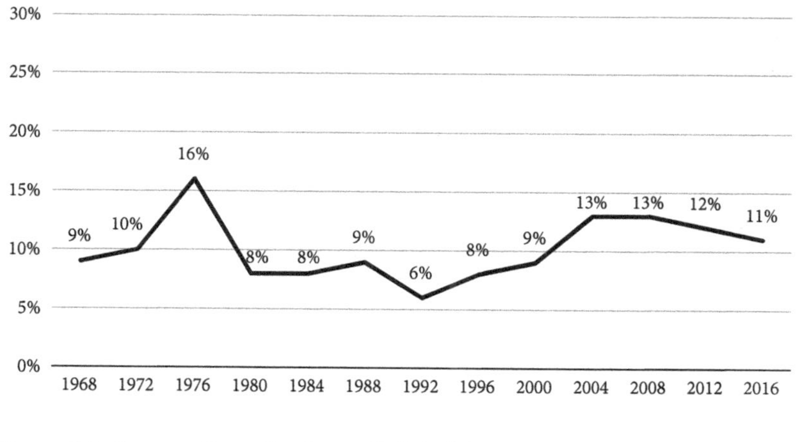

Figure 5.3 Percent Contributing to Political Campaigns
Source: American National Election Studies Cumulative Survey File, 1968–2016.

face-to-face and online interviews, which increases response rates and representation among the less affluent (who are presumably less likely to contribute money). Still, these differences notwithstanding, the broad contours of the story remain comparable across these different surveys—the percentage of Americans contributing to politics has increased since 1992.

This makes sense. In the "old days," someone wishing to contribute to a candidate or campaign would have to stuff cash or a check into an envelope, look up the appropriate address, and mail in the contribution. Today, one can contribute via credit card or Venmo or ApplePay online within seconds. While the cost of the contribution itself has remained the same, the transactional costs associated with contributing to a political candidate or cause have been slashed since the early 1990s. The following figures lend empirical support to this storyline. In Figure 5.4a, we provide data from our 2016 survey on *how* people contributed; via phone, mail, online, and so forth. In Figure 5.4b, we provide data on *where* people sent their money; to candidates, political parties, PACs, and so on. Both figures offer evidence supporting the stylized contention that Americans have taken advantage of a more convenient and diverse contributor environment.

In Figure 5.4a, we see that 16 percent of all respondents say that they contributed online between 2012 and 2016. For context, this represents 81 percent of people who self-report contributing to politics. By contrast, 6 percent contributed by mail (30 percent of all contributors), 4 percent at a donor event (20 percent of all contributors), and 2 percent via phone (10 percent of all contributors). The takeaway is that online has become the dominant means by which Americans contribute to politics.

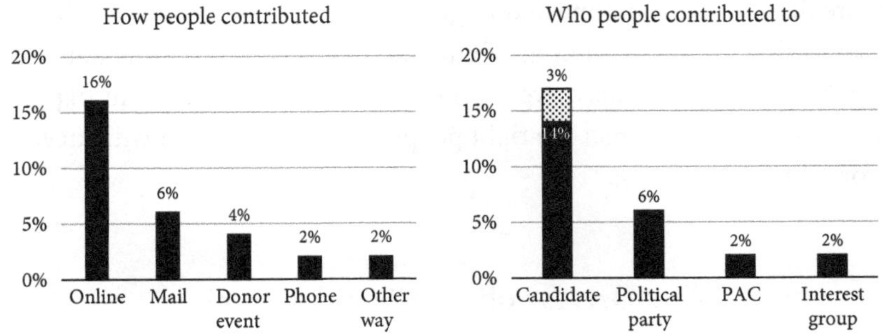

Figures 5.4a–b Political Contributions in the 2016 Election
Source: University of Texas Module for the 2016 Cooperative Congressional Election Study.

In Figure 5.4b, we see that 17 percent of all respondents contributed to a political candidate between 2012 and 2016. In other words, of those contributing money to politics during the last presidential election cycle, 85 percent contributed to a candidate. By comparison, 6 percent of Americans gave to a political party (32 percent of contributors), 2 percent gave to PACs (8 percent of all contributors), and 2 percent gave to interest groups (12 percent of all contributors). These numbers do not speak directly to the argument made by advocates of campaign finance reform that Super PACs and special interest groups will become dominant forces in politics in the wake of the *Citizens United* decision, but they do tell us that individuals continue to concentrate their contributions on candidates and, to a lesser extent, parties rather than outside entities.

Within the broad category of "candidate," it is worth noting that contributions to presidential candidates dominate. One-in-seven, approximately 14 percent of all people, gave to a presidential candidate between 2012 and 2016; that translates to 82 percent of those contributing. By comparison, 3 percent gave to a U.S. Senate candidate in their state (19 percent of contributors), 2 percent gave to a U.S. Senate candidate in another state (14 percent of contributors), 2 percent gave to a U.S. House candidate in their state (14 percent of contributors), 2 percent gave to a U.S. House candidate in another state (9 percent of contributors), and 2 percent gave to a candidate for state office (11 percent of contributors). Within the category of "political party," 4 percent gave money to a PAC (22 percent of contributors).[2] Within the category of "PAC," roughly 1 percent gave to a PAC at work (6 percent of contributors) and another 1 percent gave to a PAC outside of work (again, 6 percent of contributors).

In short, data from the 2016 election cycle suggest that while Americans are not very likely to contribute money to politics, when they contribute, they are likely to do so online and to give to presidential candidates. This is not surprising given the amount of attention lavished on presidential election politics by news media, as well as the relatively substantial ability of presidential campaigns to target the right people and provide them with an easy platform for contributing.

What Drives Political Participation?

In the remainder of this chapter, we rely on models of political participation (in general) and election turnout (in particular) in 2016 and 2008 to test some of the specific linkages asserted by the Supreme Court in *Buckley* with respect to money and political behavior. In other words, we will attempt to ascertain whether certain attitudes and policies affect voting and participation. Our first step in this endeavor is to develop an appropriate "summary" measure of political participation to go along with the more obvious measure of turnout ("did you vote in the election?"). Using our national surveys from 2016, our first instinct was to use a simple additive measure including all possible "examples" of political participation.[3] This yielded a 0–14 scale, encompassing a range of participatory acts, some easy and some demanding. However, a detailed examination of this scale reveals that there is almost no meaningful variation after one reaches five participatory acts. In fact, 82 percent of respondents score in the 0–4 range. Because of this, we opted for a 0–5 scale and placed those who claim five or more participatory acts in the top category.[4] Correlational analyses suggest that single acts of participation are highly correlated with one another, validating the use of such an additive scale.

We then examined turnout on its own, comparing the results to those for participation writ large.[5] We think that turnout and participation are (potentially) distinct enough to merit separate analyses. The key measure here is the self-reported turnout question, asked in our post-election surveys. By this measure, 65 percent of respondents voted in the 2016 general election. This is 6 points higher than the actual turnout rate of 59 percent.

Trust in Government and Political Participation

Initially, we focus on the correlation between political trust and political participation because of the Court's key posited linkage between the two. Recall from Chapter 4 that we have a scaled measure of political trust, in which respondents rated their level of trust in the federal government, with 0 representing not trust at all and 10 representing complete and total trust. The zero-order correlation between this measure of political trust and our measure of political participation is 0.028, which is positive but statistically and substantively insignificant. The zero-order correlation between political trust and turnout in 2016 is −0.018, which is (again) statistically and substantively insignificant. This obviously calls into question the assumption that improving trust in government will increase the probability that an individual will participate politically.

To get a better sense of what drives participation, we employ a range of predictor variables in equations for both political participation and turnout. Many of these are familiar by now—we include demographic and attitudinal variables that are known to correlate with participation such as political interest, gender, race, ethnicity, age, education, partisanship, religion, and union status, as well as our measures of perceived corruption, campaign finance knowledge, campaign finance regulations, campaign spending, and political trust.

Table 5.1 shows the results of our multivariate least squares model of political participation. The results for political trust are enlightening—the relevant coefficient is −0.015, which is statistically insignificant at conventional levels. At least for 2016, there appears to be no appreciable relationship between trust in government and political participation. This result holds even when we use more complex estimations strategies (such as 2SLS and fixed-effect models) to account for potential endogeneity and collinearity issues or for the mixing of state and individual-level data.

Other Factors and Political Participation

Although governmental trust seems to have little impact on political participation, the data suggest that political interest and campaign finance knowledge have major effects. Table 5.1 shows that those expressing an interest in politics are significantly more likely to have been active politically in 2016, while both knowledge of campaign finance regulations and (especially) knowledge of campaign spending have a positive and statistically significant effect on participation. For example, moving from the minimum (0) to maximum (9) on the campaign spending knowledge scale increases the average participation score by approximately 3 points on the 0–5 scale.

A few other results stand out for 2016:

- Perceptions of corruption do not appear to influence participation.
- Greater campaign finance regulation does not seem to affect political activity.
- Increased campaign spending is very weakly correlated with greater participation. This effect disappears in our more sophisticated models, however, leaving us to conclude that the impact of statewide expenditures is minimal.

Table 5.1 Explaining Political Participation, 2016

	Regression Coefficients		
	Coeff.	S.E.	Prob = 0
Constant	−0.920	0.307	0.003
Trust in the federal government	−0.015	0.014	0.286
Perceived corruption	0.000	0.019	0.984
Summary measure of contribution limits	0.014	0.017	0.389
Average total campaign expenditures per capita, 2006–16	0.009	0.008	0.249
Statewide population, 2016 (in millions)	0.001	0.003	0.661
Presidential approval	−0.061	0.045	0.180
Congressional approval	0.213	0.042	0.000
Evaluations of the national economy	−0.075	0.040	0.064
Political interest	0.351	0.028	0.000
Newspaper usage	0.214	0.066	0.001
Social media usage	0.118	0.070	0.093
Summary of knowledge of campaign spending	0.302	0.017	0.000
Summary of knowledge of restrictions on special interests in campaigns	0.106	0.043	0.000
Male	−0.148	0.066	0.025
African American	−0.535	0.108	0.000
Latino	−0.311	0.112	0.005
Under 30 years of age	−0.075	0.106	0.476
65 years of age and over	0.492	0.112	0.000
College degree or more	0.132	0.084	0.114
High school degree or less	−0.737	0.076	0.000
Democrat	0.059	0.107	0.583
Republican	0.006	0.098	0.949
Union status	0.547	0.107	0.000
Church attendance	0.241	0.077	0.002
Catholic	−0.105	0.082	0.202
Jewish	0.423	0.201	0.036
Total cases (*N*)	1,979		
Adjusted R-Squared	0.464		
Standard error	1.382		

Note: Appendix 2.4 offers descriptive statistics for all variables.

Source: University of Texas Modules for the 2016 Cooperative Congressional Election Study.

- Exposure to television, newspapers, and social media produces relatively higher levels of political activity.

With respect to demography, the data indicate that several factors have a strong impact on participation, as union household members, college graduates, Jewish people, church attenders, and older Americans are all relatively more likely to engage in political activity of some sort. By contrast, those without a high school degree, Blacks, Latinos, and men are relatively less likely to participate.

What about Turnout?

The same variables animate our equation for 2016 turnout, although here we must use a logistic regression estimator to account for the binary nature of the dependent variable. From Table 5.2 we see that trust in government did not have a statistically significant influence on turnout in the 2016 presidential election. Perceptions of corruption are also an insignificant factor, as is the statewide level of campaign finance regulation.

Conversely, average per capita campaign spending is positively and (somewhat) significantly correlated with turnout, as are campaign finance knowledge and political interest. Exposure to television and social media have, if anything, a mildly suppressive effect on turnout, while reading a newspaper increases the likelihood of casting a ballot. Finally, demographic variables, such as education, age, and gender influence turnout: those with a college education, seniors, and females were relatively more likely to cast a ballot in 2016. Partisanship also matters, as Republican and Democratic identifiers were much more likely to have voted than independents.

Logistic regression coefficients are notoriously difficult to interpret, so we present the substantive impact of our key predictor variables on turnout in Figure 5.5. From this, we see that if one were to move a single unit on the 0–10 trust scale, the estimated change in predicted turnout probability is −0.001 points. The effect of perceived corruption is similarly miniscule. On the other side of the ledger, increasing the knowledge and interest measures by a unit increases turnout probability by between 0.03 and 0.04 points. In general, the influences of key political and demographic variables dwarf those associated with campaign spending and the statewide level of campaign finance regulation.

Table 5.2 Explaining Turnout, 2016

	Logistic Regression Coefficients		
	Coeff.	S.E.	Prob = 0
Constant	–4.568	0.638	0.010
Trust in the federal government	–0.002	0.029	0.945
Perceived corruption	–0.005	0.040	0.904
Summary measure of limits on individuals, parties, PACs, corporations, unions	0.024	0.036	0.505
Average total candidate and committee expenditures per capita, 2006–2016	0.027	0.016	0.090
Statewide population, 2016 (in millions)	–0.014	0.007	0.029
Summary of knowledge of campaign spending	0.518	0.039	0.000
Summary of knowledge of restrictions on special interests in campaigns	0.915	0.095	0.000
Political interest	0.291	0.053	0.000
TV usage	–0.027	0.152	0.856
Newspaper usage	0.429	0.140	0.002
Social media usage	–0.383	0.147	0.009
Presidential approval	0.008	0.091	0.927
Congressional approval	0.488	0.090	0.000
Evaluations of national economy	0.062	0.083	0.455
Male	–0.298	0.138	0.031
African American	–0.273	0.216	0.206
Latino	0.086	0.226	0.703
Under 30 years of age	–0.506	0.216	0.019
65 years of age and over	1.058	0.271	0.000
College degree or more	0.543	0.192	0.005
High school degree or less	–0.804	0.153	0.000
Democrat	0.821	0.213	0.000
Republican	1.056	0.196	0.000
Union status	–0.105	0.228	0.644
Church attendance	0.184	0.162	0.256
Catholic	–0.011	0.171	0.947
Jewish	–0.091	0.493	0.854
Total cases (*N*)	1,977		
Cox & Snell R-Squared	0.563		
–2 Log Likelihood	1,518		

Source: University of Texas Modules for the 2016 Cooperative Congressional Election Study.

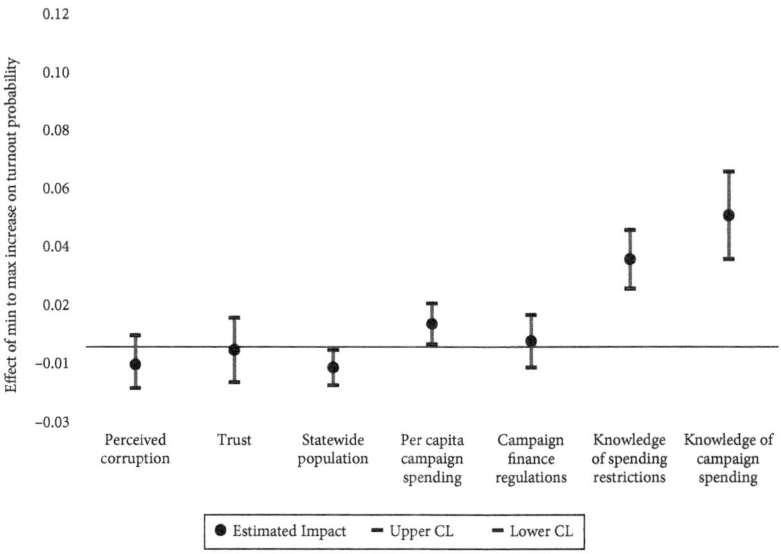

Figure 5.5 Explaining Turnout in the 2016 Election

Notes: The circles represent the estimated change in the probability of voting in 2016 based on a minimum to maximum shift in the predictor variable. Lines extend to represent the upper and lower confidence bounds (95% level) associated with these estimates.

Source: University of Texas Module for the 2016 Cooperative Congressional Election Study.

Has the Participation Story Changed Since *Citizens United*?

Given the lack of a relationship between trust and participation in 2016, we are interested in exploring whether this has "always" been the case—that is, whether trust and participation were more closely linked before the *Citizens United* decision—by leveraging our survey data from 2009. We attempted to replicate our models of political participation (again operationalized as a summary measure) and self-reported turnout for the 2008 election cycle, which occurred after the passage of the BCRA (2002) but before the *Citizens United* decision (2009). As shown in Table 5.3, our key explanatory variables include campaign finance environment, statewide per capita campaign spending, perceived corruption, political interest, and knowledge about campaign finance, as well as a set of demographic and political variables including gender, race, ethnicity, age, education, income, partisanship, and statewide population.[6] Unfortunately, the 2009 survey does *not* include a measure of trust in government—so while we strived to specify equations

Table 5.3 Explaining Political Participation and Turnout, 2008

	Regression Coefficients					
	Participation			Turnout		
	Coeff.	S.E.	Prob = 0	Coeff.	S.E.	Prob = 0
Constant	−1.459	0.294	0.000	−1.847	0.427	0.158
Perceived corruption	0.071	0.023	0.002	0.147	0.037	0.000
Summary measure of limits on individuals, parties, PACs, corporations, unions	0.014	0.022	0.520	−0.052	0.037	0.167
Total candidate and committee expenditures per capita, 2008	0.029	0.008	0.000	−0.023	0.014	0.099
Summary measure of campaign finance knowledge	−0.018	0.054	0.732	0.116	0.088	0.190
Statewide population, 2008 (in millions)	0.005	0.004	0.218	0.001	0.006	0.932
Political interest	0.615	0.041	0.000	0.366	0.055	0.000
News media consumption	0.047	0.019	0.016	0.093	0.028	0.001
Political knowledge	0.002	0.033	0.941	−0.043	0.054	0.427
Male	0.212	0.080	0.008	−0.018	0.130	0.888
African American	−0.410	0.135	0.003	0.159	0.226	0.481
Latino	−0.321	0.132	0.015	−0.418	0.187	0.026
Republican	0.380	0.112	0.001	1.836	0.168	0.000
Democratic	0.228	0.114	0.045	1.630	0.151	0.000
Under 30 years of age	0.023	0.105	0.827	−0.365	0.150	0.015
Over 65 years of age	0.174	0.115	0.132	0.694	0.264	0.009
High school or less	−0.483	0.098	0.000	−0.635	0.154	0.000
College or more	0.319	0.102	0.002	0.449	0.204	0.028
Total cases (*N*)	1,456			1,912		
Adjusted R-Squared/ Nagelkerke Adjusted R-Squared	0.306			0.373		
Standard Error/ −2 Log Likelihood	1.49			1,585		

Notes: The equation for political participation in 2008 is based on a least squares estimator. The equation for turnout in 2008 is based on a logistic regression estimator.

Source: University of Texas Money in Politics Survey (Shaw and Roberts, 2009).

close in spirit to the 2016 equations, we cannot directly assess whether trust "mattered" prior to *Citizens United*.[7]

Unlike 2016, perceptions of corruption are *positively and significantly correlated with participation and turnout*. Thus, pre–*Citizens United* data show that people who thought the system was corrupt were *more* likely to vote and participate in politics.[8] This comports with the notion of political anger or backlash—citizens who think the system is dominated by insider deals and special interests are relatively more likely to show up at the polls to vent their frustrations. It is intriguing that this relationship was actually stronger in the pre–*Citizens United* era.

Our measure of the statewide campaign regulatory environment had little influence on participatory variables in 2008. This is the same finding we have for 2016 and constitutes yet another blow to the Court's presumption that campaign finance regulations will improve democratic participation. On the other side of the ledger, increased per capita campaign spending in 2008 is associated with increased political participation but not increased turnout. In 2016, one will recall, campaign spending is positively (though weakly) correlated with both participation and turnout, so the 2008 data indicate that things have changed.

Predictably, in 2008 political interest and news consumption also drove statistically significant increases in participation and turnout. Our measure of campaign finance knowledge did not have the same positive and significant effect that it had in 2016, however. Nor did our more general measure of political knowledge. We believe this is mostly because these measures are less reliable and precise than the multi-item scales we used in our more recent survey. Finally, the results indicate that partisanship and education were powerful predictors of participation and turnout in 2008. The only noteworthy over-time change in this regard is the diminished tendency for partisan identification to drive political participation; in 2016, independents were just about as likely as Republicans or Democrats to engage in participatory acts, although partisanship still drove turnout.

* * *

While we cannot comment on the historical tendency of trust to be uncorrelated with political participation, we can say that perceived corruption has not reduced participation in either the pre– or post–*Citizens United* world; in fact, there is considerable evidence that those who feel the system is corrupt are disproportionately more likely to vote. More generally, the attitudinal underpinnings of political participation do not seem to be what the Supreme Court had in mind in *Buckley* or any of its other relevant decisions.

A Closer Look at What Affects Participation and Turnout

Campaign Regulations and Campaign Spending

Throughout this study we have focused on the conundrum of public support for campaign finance regulation and reform existing alongside skepticism that these efforts will effectively curb the influence of money on politics. We now wish to narrow our focus to the specific proposition that campaign finance regulation and reform will encourage relatively higher levels of political participation and electoral turnout. Our 2009 and 2016 surveys offer stand-alone questions that help us gain additional leverage on how much these attitudes matter for political behavior.

In our 2016 surveys, we asked voters directly about the extent to which campaign contributions are relevant to them when they decide whether to vote. Figure 5.6 presents these results. On a 0–10 scale, where 0 means the item was not important at all to them and 10 means the item was extremely important to them, respondents rated "how much money the candidates have raised in the race" at 3.6. We also asked them to rate the importance

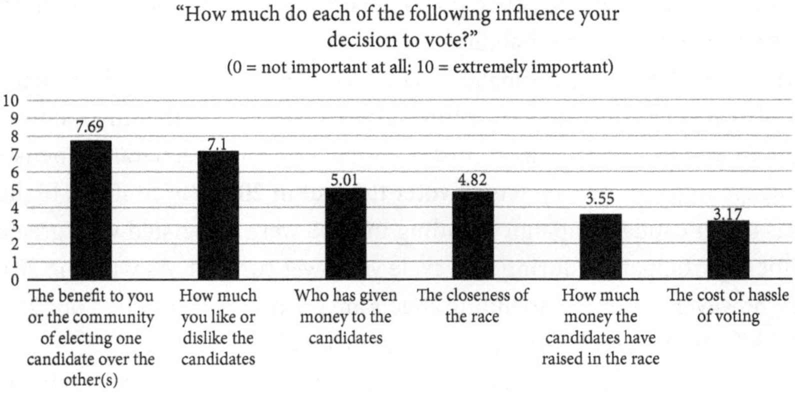

Figure 5.6 Factors Affecting Turnout in the 2016 Election
Source: University of Texas Module for the 2016 Cooperative Congressional Election Study (N = 1,000 adults).

of "who has given money to the candidates," and the average rating was 5.0. These campaign finance factors score slightly higher in importance than "the cost or hassle of voting" (3.2) and about the same as "the closeness of the race" (4.8) but well behind "the benefit to you or the community of electing one candidate over the other" (7.7) or "how much you like or dislike the candidates" (7.1). They are not irrelevant, but neither are they at the top of the list when it comes to the drivers of turnout. Of course, these are measures where voters rate themselves; such ratings are always subject to "desirability" biases. Few people will admit, for example, that the "hassle" of voting might dissuade them from participating. Furthermore, these measures do not establish whether more spending or contributions from certain sources will make you less (or more) likely to cast a ballot.

These results from these "subjective" assessments reinforce the mixed (at best) results we see in the equations, which rely on objective assessments and control for other effects. Table 5.1 shows that campaign finance restrictions and regulations are positively (but very weakly) correlated with overall participation in 2016. In fact, the relationship is statistically indistinguishable from zero. Increased per capita spending has a marginally positive relationship with participation but disappears in the fixed-effects model. Similarly, Table 5.2 shows that respondents from states with stricter campaign contribution limits were essentially no more likely to vote in 2016 than those from states with no limits. A 1-unit increase in the campaign regulation variable produces a miniscule 0.002-point increase in 2016 turnout probability (Figure 5.5). A $1 million increase in per capita campaign spending increases voting . . . but just barely; such a change corresponds to a 0.001-point increase in 2016 turnout probability.

The limited effect of campaign finance regulation on political participation also appears consistent over time. Our equations find that the statewide regulatory environment has almost no impact on either general propensity to engage in participatory acts or voter turnout in 2008. By contrast, higher levels of per capita campaign spending in 2008 were associated with greater political participation during that cycle yet lower turnout. As with the 2016 data, however, campaign spending effects are greatly diminished in our 2008 fixed-effects models of participation and turnout.[9]

In sum, our analyses indicate that stronger limits on campaign contributions have only a trace effect on political participation, while increased per capita campaign spending seems to have a small but intriguing positive effect.

Perceived Corruption

Beyond the correlation between political participation and campaign finance regulations and spending, we remain perhaps even more fundamentally interested in whether perceived corruption itself influences participation. To this point, we have introduced empirical evidence suggesting that an increase in the appearance of corruption does not correlate with reduced participation. This is, however, a relationship worthy of more careful consideration.

Toward this end, our surveys include questions asking voters how they would react to the occurrence of corruption in specific election contests. More specifically, in our 2016 national surveys we asked voters two distinct questions about whether corruption would dissuade them from voting. The first asked about an election in which overall corruption is high, and the second asked about a race in which a candidate for a specific office is corrupt (see Figure 5.7). The self-reported effects of increased perceived corruption on voting are mixed but are mildly positive. On the item asking about an election with generally high levels of corruption, a plurality (42 percent) say they would be unaffected, 37 percent say they would be more likely to vote, and 21 percent say they would be less likely to vote. On the item asking about the corruption of a specific candidate, 35 percent say it would not affect their

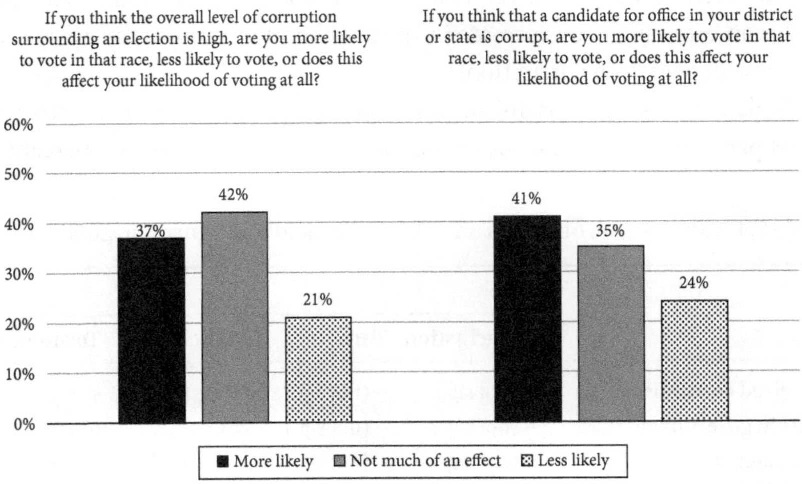

Figure 5.7 Perceived Corruption and Turnout, 2016

Source: University of Texas Module for the 2016 Cooperative Congressional Election Study (N = 1,000 adults).

turnout decision while 41 percent would be more likely to vote, and 24 percent would be less likely.

Interestingly, the mobilizing effect of corruption seems to be greatest among partisans. Those identifying as either Democrats or Republicans were among the most likely to say that their response to a corrupt election or a corrupt candidate would be to make sure that they cast a ballot in the next election. Older voters were also more likely to participate despite corrupt activities. In contrast, younger and independent respondents were more likely to say that news of corruption would either dissuade them from voting or have no impact on their turnout.

While we are intrigued in how people say they would respond to corruption, we are of course more interested in how they actually behave. Our equations estimating the impact of a full range of contextual and control variables, including perceived corruption, on political participation in 2016 show a positive effect—that is, greater perceived corruption is correlated with higher scores on the 0–5 political participation scale—but the relationship is statistically weak (see Table 5.1). The influence of perceived corruption is very slightly negative for turnout in 2016 (see Figure 5.5), although once again it is quite possible (likely?) that the effect is statistical noise. Things are less ambiguous for 2008, as the equation (see Table 5.3) shows that for every unit increase on the perceived corruption response scale, there is a 0.07-unit increase on the political participation scale. The turnout equation is trickier, but converting the logistic regression coefficient to a predicted probability yields an estimated 0.02 increase in the likelihood of turnout for every unit increase in perceived corruption.

Table 5.4 presents a useful summary of the findings from the 2016 and 2008 participation and turnout equations, and the upshot is that perceived

Table 5.4 Comparison of Effects on Political Participation/Turnout, 2008–2016

	2016		2008	
	Participation	Turnout	Participation	Turnout
Perceived corruption	+ (not sig.)	– (not sig.)	+ (sig.)	+ (sig.)
Trust in government	– (not sig.)	– (not sig.)	NA	NA
Campaign finance regulation	+ (not sig.)	+ (not sig.)	+ (not sig.)	+ (not sig.)
Per capita campaign spending	+ (not sig.)	+ (sig.)	+ (sig.)	– (not sig.)

corruption attitudes operated differently in our pre- and post-*Citizens United* elections, with corruption attitudes driving greater participation and turnout in 2008 but not in 2016.

Demography and Political Attitudes

In positing its behavioral model in the *Buckley* case, the Supreme Court did not directly comment on the need to properly control for other (potentially confounding) factors. For social scientists, it is too much to hope for the Court to use the phrase "omitted variable bias" in a landmark case (or in any other case, for that matter). Still, these other factors—such as gender, age, race, education, and a host of attitudes—almost certainly influence political participation and turnout and thus worth considering more thoroughly when characterizing the nature of political participation in U.S. elections.

Our analyses confirm much of the conventional wisdom about political participation and turnout (see, e.g., Verba and Nie, 1972; Leighley and Nagler, 2013). Since the main relationships hold for both participation and turnout, let us focus on political participation where the data reveal few surprises. In both 2008 and 2016 older Americans were much more likely to participate than those under thirty years of age. In fact, seniors were roughly 50 percent more likely to engage in a participatory act or to vote in a presidential election than those belonging to the youngest age cohort. There is a comparable difference between those who have attended college and those who have a high school degree or less. The education gap, however, is primarily a function of extremely low-participation rates among the least well educated. Then there is the fact that partisanship is highly correlated with political participation in 2008 but not 2016; the idea of highly engaged and active independent voters is largely a myth until the Trump-Clinton contest. Prior to 2016, partisans—Democrats and Republicans—participated in politics, while independents mostly sat on the sidelines.

The 2016 models also tell us about the role of religion and union membership in facilitating political participation.[10] As seen in Tables 5.1 and 5.2, Catholics are slightly less likely to participate politically, while Jewish people are slightly more likely. These tendencies, though, are statistically weak. These findings do, however, fit with past studies, as well as with anecdotal evidence about the extent to which religious leaders from specific denominations encourage participation in secular politics.

As might be expected, even stronger effects are associated with church attendance and union membership. Those who report attending church at least once a week are almost 2 percent more likely to engage in a participatory act than their less observant brethren are. Those belonging to a union are more than 5 percent more likely to engage in a participatory act. Both findings are consistent with the idea that participation in one sort of civic activity has "carry-over" effects for other activities.

Conclusion

The statistical models analyzing political and electoral participation demonstrate the relevance of general political interest, partisanship, age, and education for political participation and voting. Conversely, when it comes to political trust or perceived corruption, the correlations with participation are minimal. Equally important, campaign finance regulations and campaign spending have a minimal influence on political participation. In fact, increased spending appears to coincide with slightly more participation.

We do not wish to overstate our findings here. The associations between greater perceived corruption and political participation—and between greater campaign spending and political participation—are consistent enough directionally to be intriguing, but they are not large enough (statistically speaking) for us to be confident that they are real. Still, the lack of evidence supporting some of the central assertions of the Supreme Court with regard to participation in American politics and elections is disconcerting.

Furthermore, while our pre- and post-*Citizens United* equations do not replicate one another exactly, they are similar; similar enough to suggest that the explanatory power of our critical variables for political participation has not changed much since 2008. This, again, casts some doubt on the efficacy of the Court's implicit assumptions concerning campaign finance and the regulation of contributions.

6

Campaign Contributions and Partisan Vote Choice

In previous chapters, we tested the Court's stated assumptions regarding the effect of campaign finance information on citizens' attitudes (such as perceptions of corruption and political trust) and behaviors (such as turnout and participation). In this last empirical chapter, we switch gears and investigate the effects of campaign finance information on partisan (candidate) vote choice. Although the link between campaign finance information and the preferences of voters is not explicitly stated in the *Buckley* rulings, we think it is implied strongly in the Court's behavioral reasoning with respect to disclosure rules. Our claim, with all its intriguing ramifications, requires some elaboration.

At the heart of the Supreme Court's argument in favor of campaign finance disclosure, articulated most fully in its *Buckley v. Valeo* (1976) decision, is the conviction that the informational value to voters of disclosed campaign finance information trumps valid concerns over chilled speech. The Court ruled that disclosure rules enacted by the Federal Election Campaign Act (FECA) Amendments of 1974 were entirely constitutional, in part because they provide for the dissemination of valuable information to voters about the ideology of candidates—their place on the "political spectrum"—and thus facilitate more informed voting decisions. The Court—in a curious nod to the spatial theory of voting (Downs, 1957)—asserted that such information, "allows voters to place each candidate in the political spectrum more precisely than is often possible solely on the basis of party labels and campaign speeches." In other words, campaign finance information is alleged to provide voters with critical information about candidates *beyond* knowing their party affiliations and policy positions. To the extent voters act on this information the Court has, again, posited a behavioral model. It is only recently that scholars have begun to test aspects of this strong empirical claim by the Court (Sances, 2013; Dowling and Miller, 2014).[1]

The Appearance of Corruption. Daron R. Shaw, Brian E. Roberts, and Mijeong Baek, Oxford University Press (2021).
 DOI: 10.1093/oso/9780197548417.003.0006

In this chapter we examine the tenets of the Court's voter information argument, analyzing whether the candidate preferences of survey respondents are influenced by specific information about campaign contributions—the sort of information routinely disclosed by candidates and disseminated by the Federal Election Commission—to a hypothetical candidate. Throughout the chapter, we draw on information theories to develop and test expectations concerning the sensitivity of the American public to campaign contribution information. We begin with some intuitive theoretical assumptions about uncertainty, information, and political behavior. For illustrative purposes, and because we ultimately wish to focus our study on voters' preferences, we frame this discussion in terms of candidates and voting rather than issues and policy positions. As election campaigns unfold, we assume that voters "update" their attitude toward a candidate based on low cost, easily available information such as a candidate's party and whether the candidate is the incumbent officeholder (Lodge, et al., 1995), as well as other heuristics (Tversky and Kahneman, 1974; Popkin, 1991; Lupia, 1994).We further assume that bits of information about a candidate's friends, supporters, and contributors are best understood as heuristics; they provide voters with a low-cost basis for developing impressions about the candidate and what she will do if elected.[2]

This perspective leads to the Supreme Court's contention that campaign finance information (i.e., information about how much and from whom a candidate has raised money) could affect voters' candidate preferences and, presumably, act upon them. The underlying logic and attendant assumptions proffered by the Court ought to be directly observable in how people react to information about a candidate's campaign funding. Information about the amount and source of a candidate's campaign contributions should influence support for the candidate. There is a twist, however: the direction of this influence is not obvious. With respect to contribution amounts, a candidate receiving tens of millions of dollars in contributions may be viewed more favorably to the extent this demonstrates broad support. Conversely, she may be viewed less favorably because she may be allied with moneyed interests. With respect to contribution sources, money flowing from a group could increase support by signaling a connection with a preferred cause. Or, it could decrease support by signaling a connection with a despised interest.

In setting our sights on voters and candidates, we draw on (and seek to bolster) the voluminous literature on partisan vote choice in the United

States. We know, for example, that voters rely on party identification to infer things about candidates; specifically, their issue positions (Campbell et al., 1960; Lewis-Beck et al., 2008) and competencies (Petrocik, 1996), their personal traits (Hayes, 2006), and their standing with certain demographic and political groups (Berelson et al., 1954; Lewis-Beck et al., 2008). But we do not know whether information about campaign funding—at a level and from a specific source—adds anything to the vote choice equation. It is possible, for example, that voters may assume that candidates from one party are more likely to raise substantial amounts of money or to collect contributions from certain groups or organizations. In this way, actual information about contributions may not influence their likelihood of voting for a candidate. Given what we know about motivated reasoning (Taber and Lodge, 2006; Redlawsk et al., 2010), it is also possible that voters might discount or rationalize information that their party's candidate accepted major contributions from a disreputable source. Indeed, despite our theory suggesting how campaign finance information might be used by voters to inform their candidate preference, there is little direct evidence of the impact of campaign finance information. Furthermore, if there is a conventional wisdom in the voting literature on this matter, it is probably that information about campaign contributions is unlikely to be noticed by voters (Delli Carpini and Keeter, 1996) and, contrary to the Court's assumptions, unlikely to move voters even if they encounter it.

What Affects Partisan Vote Choice?

The most obvious way to ascertain what influences voters' candidate preferences is to ask them. The University of Texas module of the 2016 Cooperative Congressional Election Study (CCES) did just this, querying respondents on what factors affected who they voted for. More specifically, they were asked to rate the degree to which various factors (including campaign finance information) matter for their 2016 congressional vote choice. As shown in Table 6.1, on a 0–10 scale voters rated issues (average score of 8.6), representative of "people like me" (8.1), candidate traits (7.5), and party affiliation (6.4) as important factors in their candidate preference. The campaign finance information, "who has given money to the candidate," scored a 5.2 on the vote choice importance scale, while how much money the candidates earned an average rating of only 3.9.

Table 6.1 Factors Affecting Who You Vote For, 2016

	Avg. (0–10)	Very important (6–10)	Medium important (5)	Not important (0–4)
Candidates' issue positions	8.61	87%	9%	4%
Whether the candidate represents people like you	8.06	81%	13%	6%
Personal traits of the candidates	7.46	76%	15%	9%
Political party	6.35	58%	22%	20%
Who has given money to the candidates	5.20	41%	23%	36%
How much money the candidates have raised and spent in the race	3.94	25%	26%	49%

Source: University of Texas Modules for the 2016 Cooperative Congressional Election Study. $N = 1{,}000$.

The data are thus even more nuanced than we expected. They suggest that voters take information on contribution sources seriously but are less interested in information about how much the candidates have raised. If this finding holds up, it would be a distinct and important twist on the behavioral model implicit in the Court's decisions.

However, while this result potentially sheds light on the role of campaign finance information for candidate preferences, it is based on self-assessments of how much different kinds of information matter; such data do not necessarily reflect what is *actually* going on in the minds of voters or how they *actually* behave (see, for example, Silver, Anderson, and Abramson, 1986; Snyder, 1974; Epley and Dunning, 2000). Moreover, we still don't know *how* information about campaign contributions affects their vote choice or *how* other factors (such as the party affiliation of the candidates and/or voters) interact with this information. In the next section, we address some of these issues by exploring the results of survey-based experiments that test the impact of campaign finance information on the candidate preference of survey respondents.

The Survey Experiment

To estimate the impact of various types of campaign contribution information on voting behavior, we follow the lead of a small clutch of innovative studies on this topic that draw on survey experiments (most notably, Sances, 2013 and Dowling and Miller, 2014). More specifically, in our 2009 and 2013 surveys we embedded randomized experiments designed to gauge respondents' likelihood of voting for a hypothetical U.S. Senate candidate (the generic "Chris Jones").[3] Respondents were first asked to read a (slightly doctored) news story in which the electoral prospects of a hypothetical U.S. Senate candidate—Chris Jones—are discussed. Here is an abbreviated version of the story used for the 2009 experiment (items in brackets were randomly assigned to respondents):[4]

> WASHINGTON, D.C.—When it comes to next year's primaries for U.S. senators, a few challengers may get lucky as their opponent incumbents are feeling a lot like Rodney Dangerfield: They can't get any respect. . . . As a(n) [Independent / Republican / Democrat], Chris Jones hopes to take advantage of the current political climate to win a Senate seat in November 2010. If his fundraising is any indication, his chances seem pretty good so far. Since last December, Jones has raised [$20 million / $50,000], with the majority of this money coming from [the tobacco industry / trial lawyers / friends and acquaintances]. Jones may get lucky, if the transcending trend of his popularity and fundraising keeps up. Over the next year, Jones will rely more and more on his staff and growing army of volunteers to launch his campaign with an eye toward an eventual victory in November 2010.

For 2013, the article was slightly updated and streamlined, with oil companies and green energy replacing the tobacco industry and trial lawyers. Here is an abbreviated version of the story used for the 2013 experiment (items in brackets were randomly assigned to respondents):

> "WASHINGTON, D.C.—Heading into next year's midterm elections, politicians and candidates sense that voters are skeptical that the political system can handle the challenges of the 21st century. [Independent / Republican / Democrat], Chris Jones hopes to take advantage of the current political climate to win a Senate seat in November 2014. If his fundraising is any indication, his chances seem pretty good so far. Since last

> December, Jones has raised [$20 million / $50,000], with the majority of this money coming from [oil companies / green energy companies / friends and acquaintances]. Jones may get lucky, if his popularity and fundraising continue to grow.

The fact that we have survey experiments for both pre– and post–*Citizens United* is a critical improvement on previous studies that have sought to assess the vote choice-campaign finance information relationship. We are uniquely positioned to comment on how the *Citizens United* decision has (or has not) changed voting behavioral dynamics.

A few technical features of the design also merit attention. First, note that we have a 3 x 2 x 3 design; respondents were randomly assigned into one of eighteen treatments. For a relatively small-*N* survey, this design might be somewhat problematic, as the number of respondents in the different treatment cells could be too small to assume a random distribution of important covariates or to generate statistically significant differences. But our surveys of 2,100 in 2009 and 2,000 in 2013 produced 1,606 and 1,950 valid responses (respectively), with an average of 89 and 108 responses per cell, obviating (if not eliminating) these statistical concerns.[5]

Also, note that we did not have a traditional control group, as it would be counterproductive to ask about the likelihood of voting for Chris Jones without offering any information about the candidate. Rather, we follow common experimental practice (Gadarian and Albertson, 2014) and use the most innocuous of treatments—independent candidate, $50,000 raised, contributions primarily from friends and acquaintances—as our baseline.

Following the news story, respondents were asked to rate the likelihood of voting for Chris Jones on a 0–10 (11-point) scale. Their numbers serve as the key dependent variable in our analysis. Focusing on this dependent variable is not as obvious a choice as one might think. Although we are ultimately interested in whether (and to what extent) information about campaign contributions affects vote choice, we might also have focused on whether such information affects voters' perceptions of corruption or systemic efficacy, or whether it affects voters' ability to place the candidates on an ideological scale. These are, after all, assertions implicit in the Court's previous holdings.[6] Ultimately, however, our emphasis on vote choice is a matter of theoretical and practical necessity. Theoretically, we want to know about the behavioral impact of contribution information; opinions, especially those aimed at the election system, are much less interesting if they do not result in action. Practically, voters already express substantial cynicism toward the financing of elections in the United States. It is unclear whether a treatment that moves self-rated cynicism from, say, 80 percent to 90 percent will register as either statistically or substantively significant. Still, we acknowledge that our choice here means we are left to assume, rather than test, some interesting causal mechanisms.

How Contribution Amount Affects Vote Preferences

Although federal campaign finance laws limit the amount of contributions to individual candidates from individuals and political committees,[7] they do not limit the amount of money that a congressional candidate can raise or spend. To test the effect of the size of aggregate contributions raised by a candidate on the political behavior of voters, we randomly assign survey respondents to one of two treatments. In the first treatment, respondents are informed that a candidate for office has raised, in total, $50 *thousand* ($50K); in the second, they are informed that he has raised $20 *million* ($20M). The idea is to expose respondents to extremes—the "high-end" and "low-end" contribution amounts a Senate candidate is likely to raise—and to see how they react.[8] These specific numbers were derived from responses in our pilot surveys to questions about how much money voters *thought* was coming from major contributors—we wanted our treatments to be significantly above and below the average and median response.

Based on the Court's logic, respondents should recoil from a candidate raising $20M from a clearly identified source or interest; they might support the other candidate, or they might stay home, but they should be less likely to support the well-heeled candidate. Our expectations are not so singular. From our perspective—again, based on generalizations from information theory and public opinion research—voter reactions could go in different directions. Given what we know about Americans' cynicism toward our politicians (Delli Carpini and Keeter, 1996), there could very well be no reaction whatsoever. If there is a reaction, though, our expectation is that it could either increase or decrease support for the relevant candidate. On the one hand, the amount raised from any one class of contributors could evoke concerns about political indebtedness—the quid pro quo that so concerns the Court—and cause voters to take their support elsewhere. On the other hand, the ability to raise a substantial amount of money may signal candidate strength and appeal to voters seeking affiliation with a resourceful winner or fellow ideological traveler.

How Contribution Source Affects Vote Preferences

As with contribution amount, our goal with the experiments was to offer respondents relatively extreme treatments. That is, the information conveyed in the treatment had to be strong enough to provoke (potentially, at least) a reaction without straining credulity. In the case of possible sources of campaign contributions, there was no shortage of provocative characters from which to draw. After much debate, for 2009 we settled on three primary sources of contributions to our fictitious Mr. Jones—friends and acquaintances, tobacco companies, or trial lawyers.[9]

The first of these—a network of friends—arguably represents the least provocative source of support (so long as they're not identifiable as a bunch of Wall Street bankers . . .). Conversely, tobacco companies represent a group embroiled in considerable controversy, particularly in the judgment of liberals and Democrats. Trial lawyers have a similarly poor reputation (though perhaps not quite so bad) and are held in particular disdain by conservatives and Republicans. Thus, two of our treatment groups are designed to provoke negative reactions, with the potential for a differential partisan effect as our theoretical perspective suggests that Republicans and Democrats selectively search for heuristics to aid their vote choice (Bonica, 2013; Lupia, 1994; Popkin, 1991). If voters are prepared to forgive "friendly" third-party contributions, then we might expect, for instance, a Democratic candidate to be punished relatively less for receiving lawyer rather than tobacco money.

Again, information theory and the more generalized research on political opinion suggest that this information could very well have little to no effect on voters' behavior. But we think it is equally plausible that we will see something consistent with campaign finance reform rhetoric, which places information about corporate money in a class of its own, as the most likely to elicit the greatest negative voter response. This would be followed, using the Court's implied logic, by a slightly less vehement reaction to trial lawyers' contributions (though reactions could vary depending on both the party of the candidate and the partisanship of the respondent). Finally, the least amount of backlash—and perhaps even a slightly positive reaction—would be expected toward a candidate acquiring campaign funds from friends and acquaintances.

In designing the 2013 study, we opted to update and expand the range of contribution sources, while leaving the aggregate contribution treatment from the 2009 experiment. Why change the contribution source treatment? First, based on our own observations and conversations with political consultants in 2012, we decided that tobacco companies and trial lawyers were less relevant in 2013 than they may have been in 2009. Second, while these entities served our initial purpose of measuring how potentially controversial contribution sources influence the attitudes of respondents, some might consider them too unusual to allow us to generalize. Tobacco companies, for example, have been prominent contributors in states such as Kentucky and Virginia, but are much less relevant in states such as Arizona or Minnesota. Similarly, trial lawyers frequently contribute to candidates in New York and California but are relatively absent in Montana and Alabama. So, for 2013 we used oil companies and green energy companies, along with friends and acquaintances, as treatments.

Our discussions with political consultants and other experts led us to several additional, more specific expectations. Initially, we expected that Democratic voters would be relatively unfavorable toward oil companies, while Republican voters would be relatively unfavorable toward green energy companies. Next, assuming there is a negative reaction to Mr. Jones, we expected it to be greatest in response to oil company contributions given the combination of big business and an eco-unfriendly reputation. We expected green energy companies, on the other hand, to produce a mixed reaction—Republicans may recoil at stories of cronyism and other government-subsidized boondoggles,[10] but Democrats and independents may temper their concerns about corporate money given the positive social message of such enterprise. At any rate, the 2013 experiment ought to expand the depth and range of our understanding of contribution effects, particularly in comparison to the 2009 experiment.

How Partisanship Affects the Role of Campaign Finance Information

Beyond understanding more about how voters generally react to information about the nature and amount of campaign money going to a candidate, we are also interested in how potential effects are influenced by (a) the partisanship of the candidate, (b) the partisanship of voters, and (c) the interaction of *a* and *b*. The survey experiments directly reflect (and facilitate) this interest.

As discussed earlier, given the historical reputations of the parties and their ties with demographic and interest groups, we thought it likely that contribution source (and perhaps even contribution) amount effects would vary depending on whether the candidate is a Democrat or a Republican. Accounting for candidate partisanship is simple: the experiments randomly varied the party of Jones, allowing us to gauge how voters react to candidate partisanship and how candidate partisanship influences the impact of specific information on campaign contributions on the voting decision. Jones was alternatively presented as a Republican, a Democrat, or an independent, with the last of these treatments offered to provide a contrast with the experiments' partisan conditions.

In addition to the impact of candidate party affiliation, we are interested in the effect of voter party identification. Specifically, how do partisans react to campaign contribution information about their "own" candidate versus the "other" candidate? And how do independent voters react to campaign contribution information about partisan candidates? So, while we are theoretically interested in how partisans react to contribution information about out-party candidates, we expect support to be low across the board and are more interested in whether such information affects how they view in-party candidates. Similarly, as a practical matter we are relatively less interested in reactions by voters to the (rare) independent candidate; we want to know how independents react to contribution information about the major party candidates. More generally, we think this focus—and the attendant estimated effects—will yield important and practical insight with respect to mobilization and persuasion.[11]

Finally, we want to know how candidate partisanship and voter partisanship interact when Americans are presented with information about campaign contributions. Our expectations were largely informed by our reading of the voting literature and our own intuition. Perhaps most notably, we expect that the extreme treatment—$20M from tobacco companies/trial lawyers—could be less impactful (i.e., damaging) for certain partisan candidates. Partisan candidates may be assumed to be "in bed" with their respective moneyed interests, such that information conveyed by the treatment may not be "new" and may, in fact, already have been factored into the vote choice. Republican candidates may be relatively immune to disclosure given their ties to business and moneyed interests compared to Democratic candidates (Herrnson, 2009).

Findings

Does Campaign Contribution Information Affect Vote Preference?

As we can see in Table 6.2, contribution source mattered both pre- (2009) and post-*Citizens United* (2013). Chris Jones received his highest support

Table 6.2 Voting Likelihood for Jones by Contribution Source, Amount, and Candidate Party

	2009			2013		
	N	Likelihood of voting for Jones (0–10)	Std. Dev.	*N*	Likelihood of voting for Jones (0–10)	Std. Dev.
Contribution source						
Friends and acquaintances	500	4.58	2.69	672	4.26	2.77
Trial lawyers/Oil companies	547	3.69	2.68	654	3.90	2.83
Tobacco/Green energy companies	559	3.64	2.78	637	4.18	2.80
Contribution amount						
$50,000	766	3.95	2.68	1,005	4.20	2.74
$20,000,000	840	3.95	2.81	958	4.03	2.85
Candidate party						
Republican	563	4.27	3.00	658	4.09	2.90
Democrat	537	3.58	2.60	669	3.96	2.90
Independent	506	3.99	2.56	636	4.29	2.57
Total	**1,606**	**3.95**	2.75	**1,963**	**4.11**	**2.80**

Source: University of Texas Money in Politics Surveys (Shaw and Roberts, 2009; Shaw and Roberts, 2013).

when raising most of his money from friends and acquaintances. His support drops significantly if he received contributions from the tobacco industry, trial lawyers, or the oil industry ($p < 0.05$). The consequences of raising money from green energy sources, however, are statistically indistinguishable from those of friends and acquaintances. Conversely, contribution amount did *not* matter. In both 2009 and 2013, support for candidate Jones was unaffected by the amount of money he received ($p > 0.5$). Again, we are left with the intriguing possibility that voters care about *who* gives to a candidate but not about *how much* they give.

Similarly intriguing is the estimated impact of partisanship. Our expectations on this front were only partially confirmed. In the 2009 experiment, Jones does worse if he is identified as a Democrat regardless of contribution source and amount (his average support as a Democrat is 3.58, compared to 4.27 as a Republican and 3.99 as an independent). This difference is statistically significant ($p < 0.01$) and almost certainly reflects the mood of the nation at the time of the survey; in the fall of 2009 Republicans and independents were energized (and angry) while Democrats were divided and defensive over issues such as Wall Street bailouts and healthcare reform. Still, the pro-GOP edge is striking and perhaps prescient considering the Republican electoral victories of 2009 and 2010. This Republican advantage mostly disappears in the 2013 experiment, however, as the mean rating between Republican Jones (4.09) and Democratic Jones (3.96) is statistically insignificant. This almost certainly reflects the public's frustration with the two major parties due to partisan stalemates over the federal budget and debt ceiling. This impact of partisanship goes well beyond this cursory review, though, as we detail in the next section.

Does Information about Campaign Contributions Vary by the Candidate's Party?

Figure 6.1 displays the mean support for candidate Chris Jones in 2009 and then again in 2013 by contribution source, amount, and his party. Let us focus first on the pre–*Citizens United* experiment (see the top two graphs in Figure 6.1). The 2009 data demonstrate that contribution source had a clear and consistent effect on the likelihood of supporting Jones. When Jones received most of his financial support from friends and acquaintances, he always scored higher than when he garnered contributions from either trial

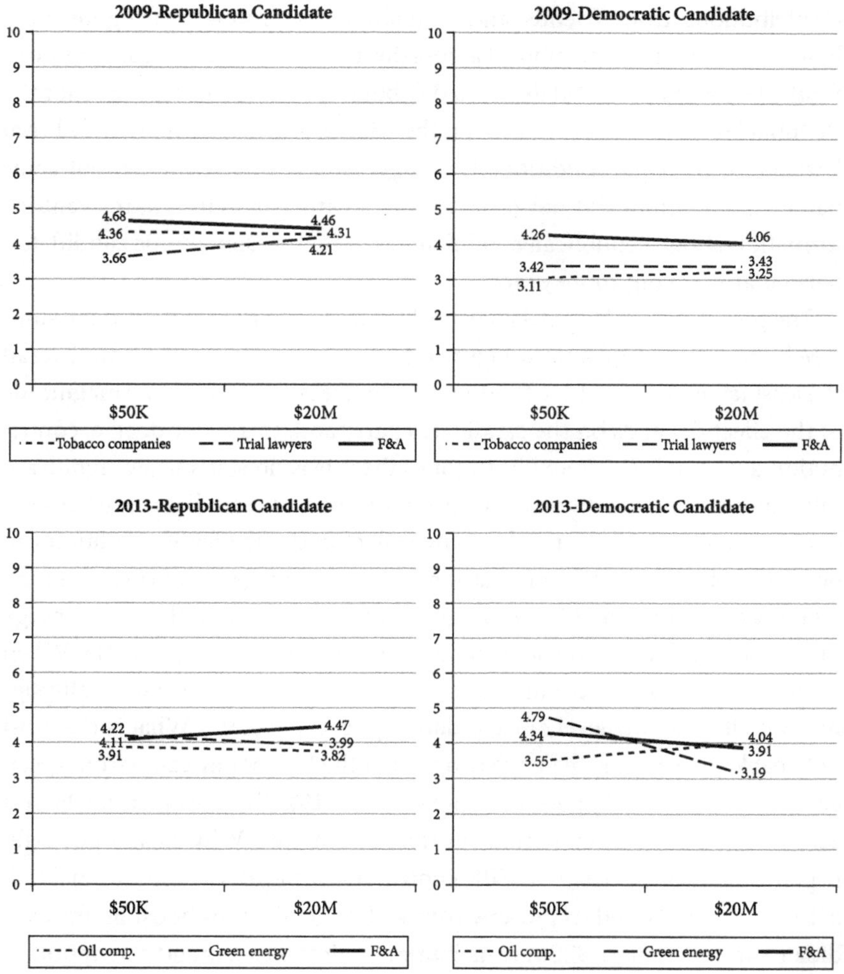

Figure 6.1 Voting Likelihood for Jones by Contribution Source, Amount, and Candidate Party (All Voters)

lawyers or tobacco companies, regardless of his party affiliation. When candidate party affiliation is factored in; however, we find differential effects. A Republican Jones, for instance, obtained higher support when he received donations from sources tied to the tobacco industry than to trial lawyers; the opposite is true for a Democratic Jones, for whom tobacco money did the most damage.

It is also worth noting that in 2009 contribution information seems to have had a greater impact on a Democratic (as opposed to a Republican) Jones.

Contributions from friends and acquaintances produced a significantly higher level of candidate support across the different amount of contributions for the Democratic candidate ($p < 0.05$), but such a difference is found for the Republican candidate only between the friends and acquaintances and trial lawyers in the $50K condition. This suggests that information about campaign contributions did not provide voters with as much new, relevant information about Republican candidates as it did for Democratic candidates, particularly in a big-money race.

The post–*Citizens United* data from 2013 add a layer of subtlety to the story (see bottom two graphs from Figure 6.1). While the oil industry was overall the least favored of the three funding sources (recall Table 6.2), the magnitude of the effect depends on the candidate's party and, to a lesser degree, contribution amount. For a Republican Jones there was no statistically significant difference among the different contribution sources regardless of the contribution amount. By contrast, the source effect under the $50K condition can be clearly observed for Democrat Jones, whose average support score in the oil industry condition (3.55) was significantly lower than in the green energy (4.79) and the friends and acquaintances (4.34) conditions ($p < 0.01$). When we move to the $20M condition, the source did not have a statistically significant effect on the level of candidate support ($p = 0.35$). What is the most noticeable, however, is the large drop when the big money came from green energy companies—33 percent (from 4.79 to 3.19). This decline is the largest across all experiment conditions in the 2013 survey. Why such a powerful negative reaction? Perhaps a $50K contribution suggests a conventional link between the party and its pro-environmental agenda, thus boosting the candidate support, while a $20M contribution indicates excess and corruption.[12]

In sum, campaign contribution source mattered to voters, especially when the candidate was a Democrat. On the other side of the ledger, campaign contribution amount did not matter to voters, except when large contributions provided substantively important signals. The most notable example was when a Democratic candidate received big money from green energy (his support decreased).[13]

Are There Differences by Voters' Partisanship?

One possibility discussed earlier that we have not yet explored is that the party identifications of voters shape their responses to information about contribution source and amount. We know partisans are likely to reject the out-party candidate, so a critical question is whether campaign contribution information affects the enthusiasm of partisans for their own candidate. The other important question is whether (and how) independent voters are influenced by contribution information about Democratic and Republican candidates. Considering this, we re-sort the results of the experiment, separating respondents by their party identification.

Collectively, our data analysis shows the continued and powerful effects of party on voter decision-making. In Figures 6.2 and 6.3, we segment the experimental treatments by respondent party identification. In both 2009 and 2013, we find a strong and consistent tendency for voters to reject a candidate from the other side of the partisan aisle; they are relatively less affected by information about campaign contribution source or amount. Voters *do* respond to campaign finance information about their own party's candidate, however, as both Democrats and Republicans are more likely to support in-party candidates when those candidates receive campaign contributions from friends and acquaintances.[14]

The detailed results are worth delineating more carefully. As shown in Figure 6.2, the 2009 experiment results tell us that Republican respondents were much more likely to support Republican Jones than Democrat Jones. They also preferred friends and acquaintances to the other two contribution sources, while favoring trial lawyers the least. Yet, the size of the source effects depends on the candidate's party and contribution amount. In the case of a 2009 Republican candidate, when the contribution amount was \$50K, their preference for friends and acquaintances over trial lawyers was statistically significant ($p < 0.01$), while their preference for friends and acquaintances over the tobacco industry was not. When evaluating a 2009 Democratic candidate, typically neither source nor amount had a statistically significant effect on the support level. The major (and curious) exception to this finding is that Republican antipathy toward a Democrat receiving money from the trial lawyers did not kick in unless the amount was \$20M.

Democratic voters' most preferred funding source was friends and acquaintances and the least preferred was the tobacco industry. The higher levels of Democratic support for Democrat Jones when he received contributions from friends and acquaintances were statistically significant, especially when those contributions were at the \$50,000 level ($p < 0.05$). But while Democrats factored in campaign finance information about their own candidate in the pre–*Citizens United* survey experiment, they did not seem

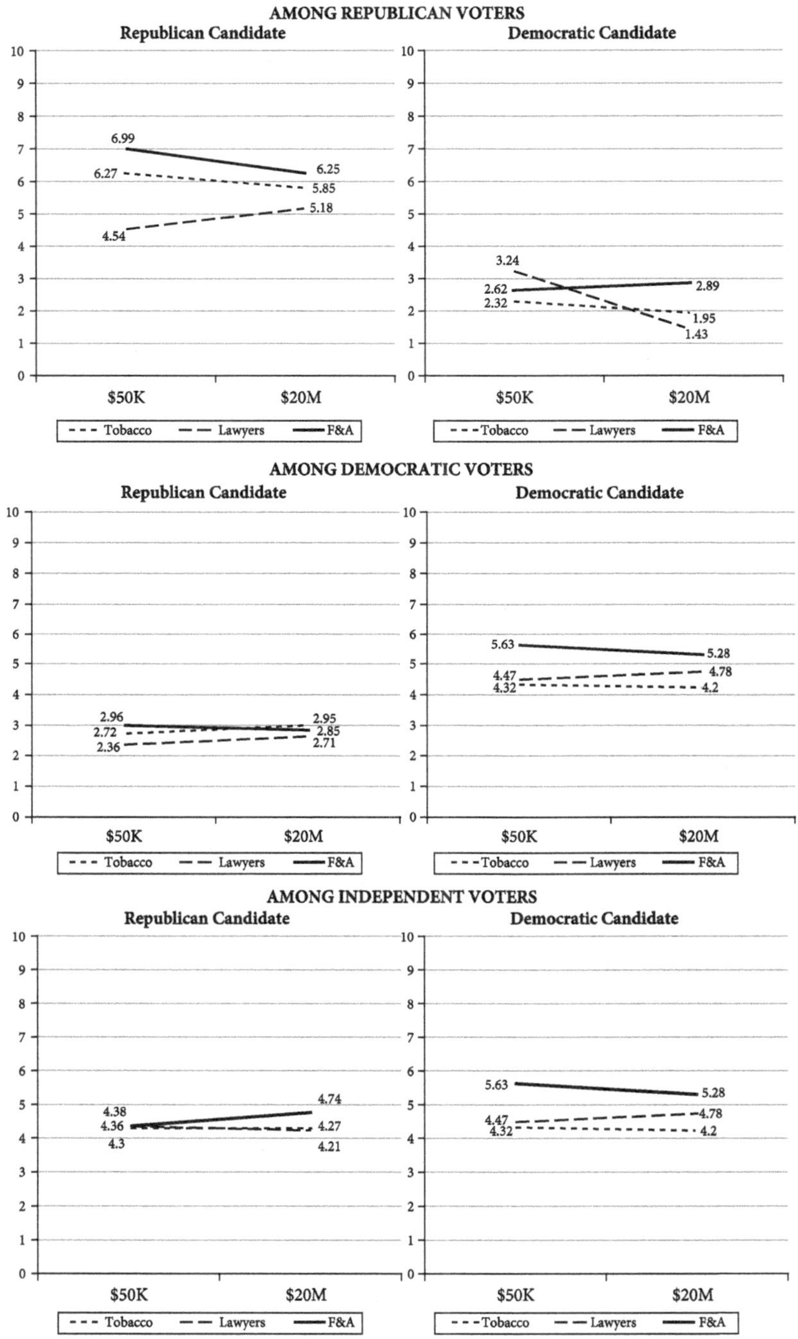

Figure 6.2 Voting Likelihood for Jones by Contribution Source, Amount, and Candidate Party in 2009 (by Party ID)

to factor in campaign finance information about the other side's candidate. Democratic support for a Republican candidate did not vary by source nor by amount.

It is intriguing to observe that a candidate's party appears to have conditioned how independent voters viewed information about campaign contributions in 2009 (as we suggested earlier). Independents were much less likely to support a Democratic Jones receiving money from either trial lawyers or tobacco companies ($p < 0.05$). By contrast, independent voters were almost completely unaffected by contribution source when considering a Republican Jones. Furthermore, as with partisans, contribution amount did not have any substantial influence on independents.

Looking at the post-*Citizens United* survey experiment from 2013 (Figure 6.3), we again witness partisan differences in evaluating campaign finance information. Let us start with the Republicans. Initially, we notice that Republican respondents were much more supportive of a Republican candidate irrespective of information about campaign contributions. Beyond this, we see that Republican voters were most supportive of a GOP candidate who received contributions from friends and acquaintances, followed by a candidate who received contributions from oil companies, followed by a candidate who received contributions from the green energy industry.[15]

The results were different when Republicans were presented with a Democratic Jones in 2013. Republican voters gave him low marks across all treatment categories—neither contribution source nor amount moved these Republicans. The only caveat to this "non-effect" result is that there was a sharp decline in Republican support for Democrat Jones when he received $20M (as opposed to $50K) from green energy companies. This parallels the 2009 study's finding that Republicans were much less supportive of Democrat Jones only when he received big money from the trial lawyers. For Republican voters considering a Democratic candidate, negative source effects appear to kick in when the contribution amounts are substantial.

What about Democratic voters in 2013? In the broadest terms, Democrats were also much more supportive of Jones when he was "their" candidate, irrespective of campaign finance information. Like Republicans, Democrats liked Democrat Jones when he received $50K from green energy sources but soured noticeably when he received $20M from the same source. Beyond these, some interesting differences catch the eye. For example, Democratic voters preferred green energy companies in 2013 over other funding sources, irrespective of Jones's party. The only instance in which they favored another

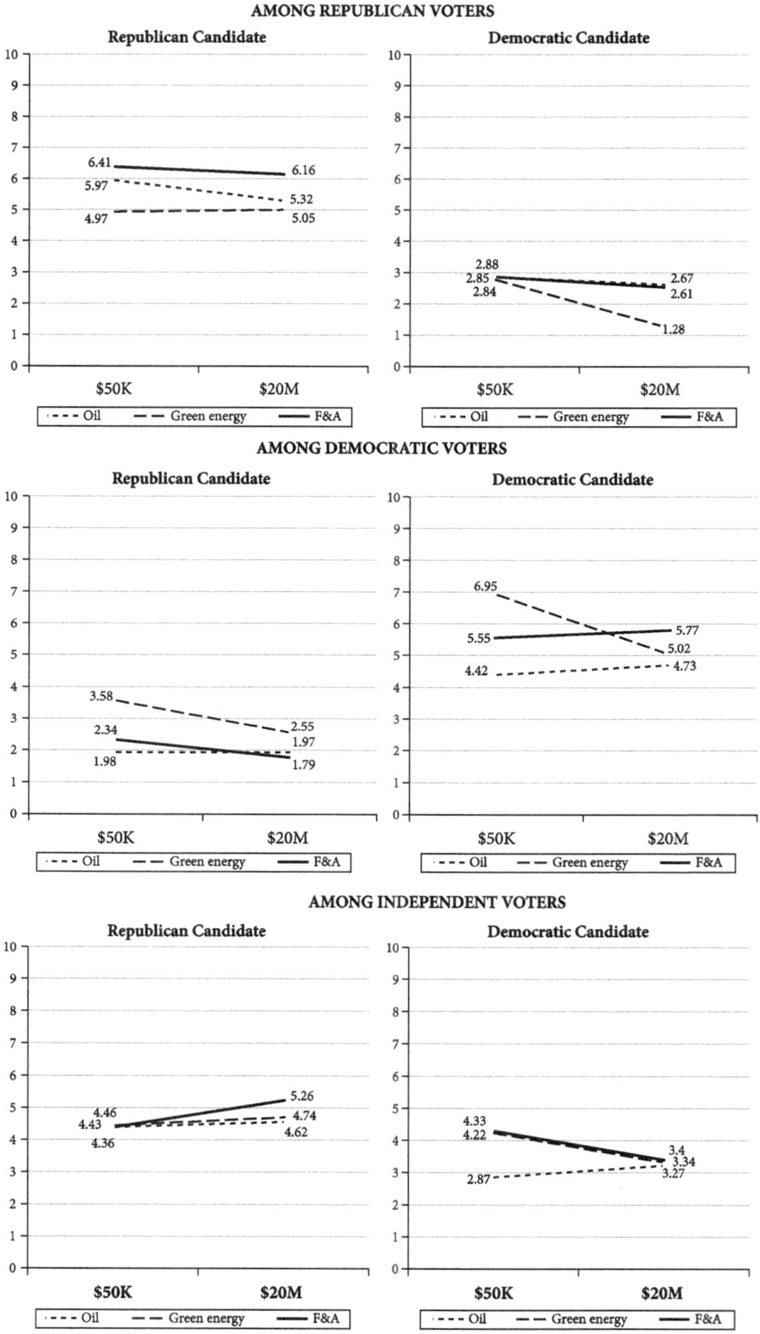

Figure 6.3 Voting Likelihood for Jones by Contribution Source, Amount, and Candidate Party in 2013 (by Party ID)

funding source (friends and acquaintances) is for Democrat Jones at the \$20M mark. By contrast, their preference for friends and acquaintances over the oil industry was only significant for Democrat Jones; this tendency is decidedly insignificant for Republican Jones.

Similarly, independent voters were less likely to support candidates who drew money from oil companies, whereas they were equally supportive of candidates who gathered money from green energy companies or friends and acquaintances. The partisanship of the candidate, however, was consequential. When considering a Republican candidate, the funding source did not matter. It *did* matter for Democrat Jones ($p < 0.07$), although this effect was driven by the disdain of independent voters for lower level contributions from the oil companies. While the contribution amount in general did not consistently make a difference in independents' evaluation of Jones, some effects are discernible. For example, independent voters joined their Republican and Democratic counterparts in also disliking Democratic candidates who received \$20M from green energy companies. The difference in means between the \$20M and \$50K conditions for the green energy contribution to the Democratic candidate was statistically significant ($p < 0.01$). Independents also gave slightly higher scores to Republican candidates getting \$20M in contributions; they gave Democrats getting \$20M from big oil companies slightly higher scores as well, but were less supportive of Democrats getting big money from friends and acquaintances or (as noted earlier) green energy.

The findings in Figures 6.2 and 6.3 are generally consistent with our expectations. Voters are more likely to support someone who shares their partisan inclinations, and this tendency reduces the value of campaign finance information. This conditioning effect is especially powerful when voters are considering someone from the other party; under these circumstances the only impact we observed was a further *reduction* in support when high-level contributions were received from noxious sources. On the other hand, campaign finance information concerning an in-party candidate occasionally had a meaningful effect on support among co-partisans. There was also a slight tendency for voters—especially independent voters—to consider such information more seriously when they evaluated a Democratic candidate. And while we did not attempt to formally compare the pre– and post–*Citizens United* results, there do not seem to be important differences across the two studies. In other words, we do not see obvious evidence that voters are influenced by campaign contribution information in the post–*Citizens*

United era. Finally, one specific finding merits mentioning again: big money contributions from green energy companies to a Democratic candidate decreased his support across the partisan spectrum.

Multivariate Model Results

Although simple means comparison tests are highly instructive, we need to ensure that the effects discussed are not influenced by systematic differences in assignment to treatment groups. As Imai (2005) notes, random assignment does not necessarily eliminate the possibility that estimated effects are driven by demographic or attitudinal variance between and amongst cell populations. To control for this possibility and to specify conditional effects, we offer multivariate models of support for candidate Jones.

Given our continuous measure and the plausibility of "independence of irrelevant alternatives" (IIA) assumptions, we use an ordinary least squares estimator to analyze the effects of our identified factors on support probability. The dependent variable is the 0–10 scale of support for Jones, our hypothetical U.S. Senate candidate. Our key independent variables include the source and amount of contributions to Jones, along with Jones's party. In addition, we control for a range of political and demographic variables that—were they not randomly distributed—might account for variation in vote intention.[16] Importantly, we estimate separate models for Republican, Democratic, and independent respondents. Finally, we also add a composite index of the respondents' perception of corruption in politics, with which we can test the Court's assumption that such a perception might influence voting behavior.

Table 6.3 focuses on 2009 and offers the regression estimates of the base and full models with all respondents, Republicans, Democrats, and independents, respectively. Notice that the full models include multiplicative interaction terms for contribution source and the candidate's party.[17] Other potential interactive relationships were estimated (including those between the candidate's party and contribution amount, and between contribution source and amount), but none proved significant. We also included the three-way interaction term for contribution from trial lawyers, contribution amount, and a Democratic candidate to account for the preliminary finding that the mean difference between $50K and $20M contributions from trial lawyers to a Democratic candidate is significant among Republican respondents (this finding is confirmed by the multivariate model).[18]

Table 6.3 Support for Candidate Jones by Treatment, 2009

	All (simple)	All (interactions)	Reps	Dems	Inds
Constant	6.07***	6.57***	6.45***	6.71***	6.43***
	(0.40)	(0.43)	(0.84)	(0.64)	(0.77)
Tobacco	−0.93***	−1.80***	−1.45**	−1.84***	−1.83***
	(0.17)	(0.31)	(0.61)	(0.44)	(0.59)
Trial lawyers	−0.89***	−1.33***	−1.86***	−1.12**	−1.06*
	(0.17)	(0.31)	(0.62)	(0.45)	(0.58)
$20 million	−0.02	−0.05	−0.16	0.00	−0.11
	(0.14)	(0.15)	(0.28)	(0.23)	(0.27)
Republican candidate	0.49***	−0.39	1.36**	−1.95***	−0.48
	(0.17)	(0.31)	(0.61)	(0.47)	(0.59)
Democratic candidate	−0.02	−0.69**	−2.25***	0.72	−0.66
	(0.14)	(0.31)	(0.60)	(0.45)	(0.63)
Tobacco X Republican	—	1.73***	0.75	2.11***	1.83**
	—	(0.42)	(0.81)	(0.64)	(0.79)
Tobacco X Democrat	—	0.80*	0.72	0.80	0.67
	—	(0.42)	(0.82)	(0.63)	(0.82)
Trial lawyer X Republican	—	0.79*	0.21	0.71	1.13
	—	(0.42)	(0.83)	(0.66)	(0.77)
Trial lawyer X Democrat	—	0.46	2.07**	−0.01	−0.51
	—	(0.48)	(0.92)	(0.74)	(0.89)
Trial lawyer X Democrat X $20 M	—	0.08	−1.64*	0.34	0.70
	—	(0.44)	(0.91)	(0.70)	(0.75)
Republican respondent	0.25	0.23	—	—	—
	(0.18)	(0.18)	—	—	—
Democratic respondent	−0.40**	−0.43***	—	—	—
	(0.17)	(0.17)	—	—	—
Age	−0.02	−0.01	−0.01	−0.02	0.11
	(0.06)	(0.06)	(0.11)	(0.09)	(0.11)
College	−0.06	−0.06	−0.32	−0.11	0.09
	(0.15)	(0.15)	(0.29)	(0.24)	(0.27)
Union	0.33*	0.35*	−0.28	0.55**	0.36
	(0.19)	(0.19)	(0.41)	(0.27)	(0.36)
Female	−0.24*	−0.26*	−0.00	−0.29	−0.24
	(0.14)	(0.14)	(0.28)	(0.22)	(0.26)
Income	−0.01	−0.00	0.22	−0.18	−0.12
	(0.09)	(0.09)	(0.16)	(0.14)	(0.17)

(Continued)

Table 6.3 Continued

	All (simple)	All (interactions)	Reps	Dems	Inds
Knowledge	−0.20	−0.16	0.15	−0.53	−0.84*
	(0.26)	(0.26)	(0.50)	(0.43)	(0.45)
Corruption	−0.17***	−0.18***	−0.20***	−0.18***	-0.11
	(0.04)	(0.04)	(0.07)	(0.06)	(0.07)
Total cases (N)	1,442	1,442	369	498	417
Adjusted R-Squared	0.057	0.069	0.276	0.174	0.092

Notes: Standard errors in parentheses; *** $p < 0.01$, ** $p < 0.05$, * $p < 0.1$.
Source: University of Texas Money in Politics Surveys (Shaw and Roberts, 2009).

In examining the models for 2009 in Table 6.3, we see that these more sophisticated statistical analyses largely confirm the patterns and relationships described earlier. Perhaps most notably, the data indicate that candidate support is *not* influenced by contribution amounts. However, the source of campaign contributions exerts a significant impact: compared to contributions made by friends and acquaintances, those from the tobacco industry or trial lawyers clearly decreased the likelihood of supporting Jones. For example, campaign donations to Jones from tobacco companies decreased the likelihood of voting for him by almost 1 point on the 0–10 scale, holding all other factors constant. A similar but slightly lesser effect is found in the case of trial lawyers.

As for the candidate's partisanship, we again find that when Jones was presented as a Republican candidate, the 2009 vote probability score was significantly greater than when he was an independent or a Democrat, *even controlling for the respondent's party identification*. The data here clearly foretells subsequent GOP triumphs in Virginia, New Jersey, and Massachusetts, where Democratic candidates were swamped by an energized GOP base and disgruntled independent voters in November 2009 and January 2010 (respectively).

What of the interactive relationship between the candidate's party and contributions? Results from the full model show that the candidate's partisanship did indeed change the relative importance of funding sources in the vote decision. More specifically, the interaction effect is statistically significant when Jones was identified as a GOP candidate and contributions came from the tobacco industry. Furthermore, in this instance (when Jones was identified as a Republican), the overall effect associated with contribution source disappears. All of this means that when the candidate was Republican, the negative effects associated with campaign contributions from the tobacco industry and trial lawyers (to a lesser degree) declined. When the candidate was Democratic, the negative effect of tobacco contributions is reduced in comparison with an independent candidate, but they still decreased his support.

These findings suggest that when Jones was labeled independent, the contribution source effect is largest. Indeed, these regression results show that Republican candidates were relatively immune to negative blowback from financial connections with corporations or special interest groups. The public's expectations seem to have been that independent and (to a lesser extent) Democratic candidates were less tied to corporate interests so that information establishing such a connection had a more dramatic influence on voters' appraisals. Conversely, voters were generally more tolerant of the Republican Party regarding the potential influence of corporate or special interest groups, perhaps because (as we postulated earlier) the GOP was already assumed to be sympathetic to corporate interests.

Finally, when looking at the baseline models (simple and with interactions), we note that only two of the control factors—being a Democrat and being female—had any influence on the probability of supporting Jones. This persists even when controlling for different treatments. Perceptions of corruption (another attitude) also exerted a statistically significant negative influence on support even after controlling for different treatments. For our purposes, this finding is quite important. Put plainly, those who think the system is corrupt were *less* likely to support Jones.

The last three columns of Table 6.3 report the regression estimates by respondents' party identification. These models offer a more rigorous examination of the relationships and associations explored in our earlier graphs (see Figure 6.2). More specifically, they further demonstrate that voters' partisanship affected how (and how much) campaign finance information mattered for candidate evaluations in 2009. Several findings from these regressions merit mention.

- Voters across all partisan groupings were less supportive of Jones when he received money from either tobacco companies or trial lawyers. Partisans (and nonpartisans) were, however, differentially negative toward these funding sources. Even though everyone preferred friends and acquaintances as a contribution source, Republicans preferred tobacco companies to trial lawyers while both Democrats and independents preferred trial lawyers to tobacco companies.

- Among Democrats and independents, Republican Jones did relatively better when he received money from tobacco companies. This is not as strange as it might sound. Democrats and independents were less supportive of a Republican candidate and were less supportive of a candidate who received tobacco money—the combination of these two factors helped mitigate what was otherwise an overwhelmingly negative reaction.
- In somewhat the same way, Republican voters were significantly more positive toward a Democratic candidate if he received $50K in contributions from trial lawyers compared to other contribution sources and amounts. Put in more precise statistical terms, the coefficient for the interaction term between trial lawyers and a Democratic candidate (2.07) outweighs the negative coefficient of trial lawyer (−1.86). This interactive effect, combining source and amount alongside party, did not exist among Democrats or independents. Indeed, this finding was quite unique: contribution amount mattered only for a specific source (trial lawyers) and only among a specific partisan group (i.e., Republicans). It also contradicts the more general result that Republicans were unaffected by contribution information about Democratic candidates.

The regression analyses for 2013 are presented in Table 6.4. We tried to make the models as comparable as possible to 2009 and deviated only when important substantive improvements could be made.[19] Taken as a whole, the estimated results reaffirm what we found in the 2009 analyses, while displaying some unique dynamics given the different funding source treatments and the timing of the survey.

As with the 2009 analysis, the base model for 2013 shows that the source of campaign contributions, not the amount, provided more impactful information for candidate evaluations. Oil industry contributions significantly reduced the level of likelihood of supporting Jones compared to contributions from friends and acquaintances (coefficient = −0.554, $p < 0.01$). Green energy contributions had a smaller, marginally significant negative effect (coefficient = −0.335, $p < 0.10$).

Table 6.4 Support for Candidate Jones by Treatment, 2013

	All (simple)	All (interactions)	Reps.	Dems.	Inds.
Constant	5.72***	5.63***	6.22***	4.29***	6.54***
	(0.33)	(0.34)	(0.74)	(0.51)	(0.49)
Oil	−0.55***	−0.69**	−0.48	0.24	−1.46***
	(0.17)	(0.30)	(0.55)	(0.48)	(0.45)
Green energy	−0.34*	−0.17	−1.92***	1.80***	−0.55
	(0.17)	(0.30)	(0.58)	(0.50)	(0.42)
$20 million	−0.12	0.08	0.07	−0.08	0.21
	(0.14)	(0.15)	(0.29)	(0.23)	(0.22)
Republican	−0.40**	−0.35	1.09**	−1.09**	−0.59
	(0.17)	(0.29)	(0.53)	(0.49)	(0.43)
Democrat	−0.28	−0.27	−1.53***	2.02***	−1.24***
	(0.17)	(0.29)	(0.58)	(0.48)	(0.42)
Oil X Republican	—	0.01	−0.70	−0.35	1.19*
	—	(0.42)	(0.76)	(0.68)	(0.65)
Oil X Democrat	—	0.35	0.23	−1.07	0.97
	—	(0.423)	(0.84)	(0.66)	(0.64)
Green X Republican	—	−0.13	0.73	−1.07	0.41
	—	(0.42)	(0.81)	(0.68)	(0.63)
Green X Democrat	—	0.55	1.16	−0.49	0.79
	—	(0.48)	(0.92)	(0.78)	(0.68)
Green X $20M X Democrat	—	−1.75***	−1.83**	−1.65**	−1.30**
	—	(0.45)	(0.82)	(0.76)	(0.65)
Republican respondents	0.01	0.02	-	-	-
	(0.19)	(0.19)	—	—	—
Democratic respondents	−0.37**	−0.39**	—	—	—
	(0.16)	(0.16)	—	—	—
Age	−0.01***	−0.01***	−0.02**	−0.01	−0.02***
	(0.00)	(0.00)	(0.01)	(0.01)	(0.01)
College	0.03	0.03	−0.11	−0.13	−0.02
	(0.18)	(0.18)	(0.33)	(0.29)	(0.26)
Income	0.05**	0.05*	0.04	0.05	0.04
	(0.03)	(0.03)	(0.05)	(0.04)	(0.04)
Female	0.15	0.14	0.35	0.40*	−0.33
	(0.15)	(0.15)	(0.28)	(0.23)	(0.23)
Knowledge	−0.10	−0.11	−0.20	−0.22*	−0.07
	(0.07)	(0.07)	(0.14)	(0.12)	(0.11)
Corruption	−0.51***	−0.49***	−0.29*	−0.44***	−0.51***
	(0.09)	(0.09)	(0.16)	(0.14)	(0.13)
Total cases (*N*)	1,520	1,520	318	617	585
Adjusted R-Squared	0.055	0.066	0.291	0.234	0.098

Notes: Standard errors in parentheses; *** $p < 0.01$, ** $p < 0.05$, * $p < 0.1$.
Source: University of Texas Money in Politics Surveys (Shaw and Roberts, 2013).

Another consistent result was that the candidate's party was an important factor affecting support. However, unlike in 2009, being a Republican in 2013 did not necessarily help Candidate Jones. As we discussed earlier, this is hardly surprising. The political climate in 2013 was not as favorable to the Republicans as it had been in 2009, as the Republican-led Congress battled with the newly re-elected Democratic president. As a result, both Republican Jones and Democrat Jones received lower support than independent Jones.

We also see some consistencies in the effects of the respondent's partisanship, demographic characteristics, and attitudes—our so-called control variables—across the pre- and post-*Citizens United* survey experiments. Most notably, those who scored high on the summary measure of perceived corruption were less likely to support the candidate. Voters who thought the system corrupt were also more skeptical about a new candidate. In addition, Democratic voters were once again less likely to support Jones. Unlike the 2009 experiments, though, age was a significant factor (older voters were less likely to support Jones) as was income (more affluent voters were more likely to support Jones).

As in 2009, in 2013 the three partisan groups had different evaluations of the proffered funding sources. Republicans clearly ranked green energy industry contributions the lowest, while the Democrats ranked them highest. Independents, on the other hand, ranked oil industry contributions the lowest and were ambivalent with respect to contributions from the green energy industry versus friends and acquaintances. Indeed, the largest partisan difference was found in the specific reaction to green energy industry contributions.

Although we did not find many significant interaction effects between the funding source and the candidate's party in 2013, several findings stood out. Initially, we note that independent respondents were turned off when Democrat Jones received contributions from the oil industry whereas they were unaffected by this when Jones was Republican. Perhaps more significantly, the interaction models showed a strong negative effect in the case of a Democratic candidate who received \$20M in green energy contributions. This finding was ubiquitous across the three partisan groups, although the effect was largest among Republicans. While we do not have direct evidence for this, we suspect that voters may have ambivalent attitudes toward eco-energy companies, liking them when they are modest in size and reach (i.e., when they look like "David") but disliking them when they grow in size and scope (i.e., when they look like "Goliath"). More to the point, voters may suspect that a candidate receiving \$20M in green energy contributions is somehow at odds with the non-materialistic ethos of the environmental movement. In general, voters do not like hypocrites. This finding is consistent with the interaction effect from the 2009 analysis where Republicans expressed significantly lower support for Democrat Jones when he received big money from trial lawyers.

In sum, both pre- and post-*Citizens United* regression estimates confirm our expectation that *some* campaign contribution information modestly affected voters' candidate preferences in experiments in 2009 and 2013. More specifically, when it comes to information about a candidate's campaign contributions, the experimental regression models demonstrate that voters care about where the money comes but care far less about how much the candidate raises. The multivariate and interaction term analyses from the models also show that the effects associated with information about campaign contributions are conditioned by the candidate's partisanship and the voters' partisanship. Thus, while information about campaign contributions had statistically significant effects in certain circumstances, even these were only a point or two on a 0–10 support scale.

It is also important to point out that while there were subtle differences between the 2009 and 2013 models, these probably owe more to design than to any substantive change in the post-*Citizens United* political environment. In fact, we see little reason to conclude that changes in the aftermath of the *Citizens United* decision have influenced the fundamentals of how voters think about elections and candidates.

Conclusion

We began this chapter by illustrating that the Court's past rulings have implicitly assumed the potential impact of campaign finance information on voters' candidate preferences and, presumably, their subsequent voting behavior. While the extant literature on vote choice assumes that voters' preferences are dominated by party identification, our theoretical position is that information about campaign contributions—especially the source of these contributions—might provide voters with important additional information about candidates. As expected, our survey experiments suggest that information about the source of campaign contributions *can* affect the public's support for a candidate. More specifically, if contributions come from special interest groups, Democratic candidates tended to lose support while Republican candidates were (mostly) unaffected. This is consistent with the notion that long-standing ties between the GOP and corporate and professional interest groups were already factored into even first-blush appraisals by voters of Republican candidates.

We were less sanguine with respect to the possibility that voters' candidate preferences would shift with information about how much money a candidate had raised. This skepticism proved warranted, as our evidence indicated that enormous contribution amounts did not affect (i.e., decrease) support for the candidate. This is not to say that information about how much a candidate has raised never had an effect. Rather, the potential impact of contribution amount seems to be dependent on funding source, the candidate's party, and (to a lesser degree) the voter's party.

Beyond the general findings, we were struck by two other results. First, partisans were often more influenced by information about their own candidate than about the candidate of the opposing party. On the one hand, partisans are heavily predisposed to reject the other party's candidate, so additional negative information failed to move the dial very much. On the other hand, information about where their candidate gets her funding can decrease what would otherwise be a high level of support.

The other noteworthy result is that voters apparently expected Republican candidates to have raised money from corporations and special interest groups and were therefore less likely to "punish" them. This is consistent with the broader theoretical notion that disclosure must provide "new" information to be useful to voters; campaign contribution information must go beyond what they expect of partisan (and nonpartisan) candidates.

Once again, the sum of our analysis is that the Court sometimes gets it right and sometimes gets it wrong. We do not mean this as a facile, off-the-cuff comment about the Court's jurisprudence. Rather, our contention about the hit-and-miss nature of the Court's behavioral model is perhaps the most consistent and worthwhile theme to our project. Indeed, we think the collective results presented in the previous chapters justify our claim that it is eminently important to more carefully identify and empirically test the specific assumptions that the Supreme Court has advanced to justify legislation and regulation that, in its own words, stifles speech. In light of our findings, however, one might reasonably ask if we wish to go further: Would we argue that the Court's behavioral model is sufficiently "off" as to make existing campaign finance regulation "wrong"? In the final chapter, we turn to what our results mean for how the Court should proceed and the future of campaign finance laws and regulations in the United States.

7
Whither Campaign Finance Jurisprudence?

In its landmark 1976 *Buckley v. Valeo* decision, the U.S. Supreme Court established the modern legal framework for campaign finance in the United States. Most notably, the decision forevermore put the regulation of campaign finance explicitly in tension with First Amendment speech rights. The tension was complicated by the Court's acceptance of a compelling government interest—the mitigation of corruption, real or perceived—as allowable grounds for upholding laws limiting money in politics, laws that would otherwise be found unconstitutional.

In laying out its argument for why corruption mitigation is sufficiently compelling to warrant intrusion on First Amendment speech rights, the Court advanced a nuanced behavioral model ultimately linking campaign contribution limits to political participation, the foundation of democratic legitimacy. This book explores the empirical veracity of the Court's model, interrogating the degree to which the Court's behavioral assumptions track the beliefs and choices of the American public. As this book demonstrates, the empirical foundations of the Court's corruption teleology are shaky.

At the heart of the Court's argument reside three major claims that sequentially and dependently link the passage of campaign finance laws to political participation:

1. Campaign finance laws lower perceptions of political corruption;
2. lower perceptions of corruption raise trust in government; and
3. greater trust in government raises political participation.

These links establish the behavioral model used by the *Buckley* Court to justify upholding, most notably, laws limiting contribution limits.

The evidence presented in the preceding chapters for these and related behavioral claims is mixed, with particularly weak support for claims that political participation, the sine qua non of democracy, is improved by limiting

The Appearance of Corruption. Daron R. Shaw, Brian E. Roberts, and Mijeong Baek, Oxford University Press (2021).
© Oxford University Press. DOI: 10.1093/oso/9780197548417.003.0007

money in politics. In fact, as shown in Chapter 5, heightened perceptions of corruption are associated with *elevated* political participation.

We view these findings as call for renewed conversation about and empirical examination of the pillars supporting the foundation of modern campaign finance regulation. That our findings hold up in a post–*Citizens United* world is particularly striking.

What to Make of the *Citizens United* Case?

As we consider the implications of our research, we think it important to re-examine the impact of one of the most controversial Supreme Court decisions of this young century. Understanding the degree to which the 2010 *Citizens United* decision changed political beliefs and behavior in the United States is an important objective of a book focused on perceptions of political corruption. *Citizens United v. Federal Election Commission* (2010) elicited far more public reaction than the substantively more important *Buckley v. Valeo* (1976), even though it did little more than restate the principles established in *Buckley*.

The unprecedented attention to the *Citizens United* decision started at the top.[1] Less than a week after the Court's opinion was released, President Obama took the occasion of his first State of the Union address, with six Supreme Court justices in the audience, to call out the decision, saying it "reversed a century of law," would "open the floodgates for special interests," and called on Congress to close them.[2] Even more than ten years after the decision, *Citizens United* remains a touchstone of American politics, attacked as it was by every leading candidate in the 2020 Democratic presidential primaries.

Remarkably, the basic conclusion of this book, that the *Buckley* Court's behavioral model is empirically suspect, largely holds despite the unprecedented salience of campaign finance in public and elite discourse following the 2010 *Citizens United* decision. Little in the post–*Citizens United* record suggests the *Buckley* Court's behavioral model finally acquired legs. This is an important observation because the limited extant empirical research addressing components of the Court's model all predate *Citizens United* and also fail to support the Court's behavioral assumptions. If the truly remarkable attention to campaign finance issues raised by the *Citizens United* decision cannot breathe life into a model built on perceptions of political corruption, it is not clear what could.

More specifically, one of the more interesting pre- and post-*Citizen United* findings is that knowledge of campaign finance laws and behavior evidenced no significant changes, where one might have expected the volume of discussion and media coverage to have better informed the public's understanding of baseline campaign finance numbers (see Chapter 2). Another interesting twist are the post-*Citizen United* findings linking campaign finance knowledge and perceptions of corruption, to wit, that better understanding of the post-*Citizen United* campaign finance landscape (e.g., more accurate knowledge of Super PACs) is associated with *lower* perceptions of corruption.

A mainstay of pre-*Citizen United* public opinion was that campaign finance never rose to the top, or anywhere near the top, of any survey ranking important issues facing the country. As discussed in Chapter 3, *Citizens United* did little to change that. Although campaign finance reform—a key set of provisions in For the People Act of 2019 (H.R. 1)—remains a centerpiece of elite discourse, it still eludes broader public concern.

The post-*Citizen United* world does exhibit greater perceptions of political corruption, a fact confirmed by both our own and ANES surveys. What fails to change, however, is the weak to nonexistent linkage between perceptions of political corruption and campaign finance measures documented in prior research, including the scale of campaign expenditures and, closer to the immediate concerns of the Court, variation in the stringency of campaign finance laws.

As discussed in Chapter 3, a couple of issues do vary across the pre- and post-*Citizen United* divide. One, which may raise eyebrows among journalists, is that pre-*Citizen United* evidence of news media consumption correlating positively with perceptions of corruption vanishes in the post-*Citizen United* world. A different characterization of these results is that factors other than news media consumption now better explain variation in perceived corruption. A second thing to emerge is a new relationship between identification with the political parties and perceptions of corruption. The more partisan a survey respondent—regardless of party—the *less* likely the respondent is to perceive political corruption; pre-*Citizen United* there was a notable partisan asymmetry, with Republicans somewhat more likely to think the political process corrupt.

Reform in the Post–Citizens United World

A necessary condition for upholding the constitutionality of a law limiting money in politics is that it holds the promise of mitigating corruption, real or apparent. Nothing in the empirical records, before or after *Citizens United*, suggests that existing campaign finance restrictions, at either the federal or state level, realize that goal. In other words, the logic chain of the *Buckley* Court's corruption teleology seemingly breaks at the first link. The rest of the Court's model fares no better.

Much of the damage done to the Court's model rests with the inability of either campaign finance laws or the amount of money in politics to explain variation in any of the key variables: perceived corruption, trust in government, and political participation. It is one thing to find generic evidence of relationships between corruption, trust, and participation, but it turns out to be an entirely different challenge to place money in politics in any meaningful role in those relationships.

Americans remain very cynical about both the role of money in American politics and the willingness and ability of elected officials to deal with it. The post–*Citizens United* world is not only one with a heightened sense of money in politics but also one with rising concerns about income inequality and its translation to political power. None of this new context, however, has improved the performance of the Court's model, one rooted in the behavioral response to the perceived corruption of money in politics.

Given that every elected official is (by definition) elected under existing campaign finance laws, voters are understandably cynical about the political will to pursue true campaign finance reform; no laws to date have discernably slowed either the flow of money into politics or the reelection rates of incumbent politicians.[3] Political scandals occasionally prompt legislative action, but, the public wonders, to what effect?[4]

Dan Lowenstein, in his famous article, "On Campaign Finance Reform: The Root of All Evil Is Deeply Rooted," cites social scientists' mismeasurement of corruption by attacking their reluctant conclusion that because campaign contributions for the most part do not influence congressional votes, there is no empirical basis for claiming money influences political outcomes (Lowenstein, 1989). In similar fashion, the mismeasurement of the key variables in the *Buckley* Court's model cannot be dismissed as a possible explanation for the null findings to date. That said, both the work in this book and in kindred research consider multiple measures of the key variables, none of which yields support for the Court's argument. Convinced as we are of our main take on the problematic nature of the model advanced in *Buckley*, it would be a singular contribution of this book should it prompt broader and more concerted efforts to test the Court's argument.

* * *

One might ask whether, in light of our findings, we think the Court should overturn key elements of *Buckley* in some future case, most notably laws limiting individual contribution limits. The short answer is "not necessarily." Although the data are thus far relatively clear and consistent on the flaws riddling the Court's behavioral model, post–*Citizens United* research is only beginning to inform (and confirm) these questions (Primo and Milyo, 2020). The rapidly changing modern campaign finance landscape, particularly with the emergence of Super PACs in the wake of *SpeechNow.org v. FEC* (2010) and the relaxation of aggregate contribution limits following the 2014 *McCutcheon v. FEC* decision—not to mention the scale and prominence of recent self-financed campaigns—may yet, after more than several decades, vindicate the *Buckley* Court's behavioral model. Nothing suggests this is happening. The vigilance of additional empirical analysis, however, is not just welcome but also necessary.

Social Science and Supreme Court Jurisprudence

Social science has had an uneasy relationship with the Supreme Court. Beginning with *Brown v. Board of Education of Topeka* (1954) through contemporary debates over partisan gerrymandering, the Court has listened to but too often dismissed social science. In recent years, federal courts have been unevenly attentive to social science research. As noted earlier, federal districts courts have alternately dismissed and accepted scholarly research on the effects of photo-identification requirements for voting.[5] On the other hand, it was not so long ago that Supreme Court Justice Anthony Kennedy plaintively asked social scientists to offer a standard for adjudicating the fairness of partisan redistricting plans:

> Because there are yet no agreed upon substantive principles of fairness in districting, we have no basis on which to define clear, manageable,

> and politically neutral standards for measuring the particular burden a given partisan classification imposes on representational rights. Suitable standards for measuring this burden, however, are critical to our intervention. Absent sure guidance, the results from one gerrymandering case to the next would likely be disparate and inconsistent.[6]

Of course, with respect to *Buckley*, the potential problem is not really inconsistency. Indeed, with respect to an informed consideration of the efficacy of campaign finance limits, the Court's assumed connection between regulation and beneficent attitudes and behaviors makes for mostly consistent, if misguided, jurisprudence.

At the time of its *Buckley* decision, the Court had no recourse to systematic empirical evidence to inform its behavioral model, citing only limited anecdotal accounts and impressions in support of its logic. To the Court's credit, in the wake of the decision, its behavioral model was not the target of criticism; to most it passed the sniff test. Over time, however, elements of it were questioned in the popular press—for example, Samples (2008) and Smith (2009)—and, more systematically in the few but determined efforts of social scientists investigating the behavioral claims.

The extent to which this book updates and reaffirms findings of a suspect behavioral model cuts both ways in legal and policy debates. Given that the Court entertains corruption mitigation as the one and only compelling government interest in upholding campaign finance limits that otherwise infringe on First Amendment speech rights, the failure of the Court's supporting logic to survive empirical scrutiny argues in favor of dismantling existing limits altogether. On the other hand, the same findings may inspire renewed efforts to have the Court adopt alternative compelling interests.[7] The challenge for such proposals will again rest with their implied behavioral models, particularly to the extent they derive impetus from political participation.

The question for social scientists is whether anybody cares. The more searching question is whether they should care.

Appendices

APPENDIX 2.1

Sampling and Weighting Methodology for U.S. National Surveys

We conducted five unique national surveys for this study.

- The 2009 survey consisted of a single wave of 2,100 respondents and was conducted October 13–22, 2009. We sometimes refer to the 2009 survey as "2008" because instrumentation referred to the 2008 campaign and election.
- The 2012 survey consisted of pre- and post-election waves of 1,000 respondents. The pre-election survey was conducted September 24–November 5, 2012. The post-election survey was conducted November 7–December 14, 2012. The 2012 survey was part of the 2012 Cooperative Congressional Election Study.
- The 2013 survey consisted of a single wave of 2,000 respondents and was conducted October 24–31, 2013.
- The 2016 modules consisted of pre- and post-election waves of 1,000 respondents each. The pre-election surveys were conducted September 28–November 7, 2016. The post-election surveys were conducted November 9–December 14, 2016. The 2016 surveys were part of the 2016 Cooperative Congressional Election Study.

All surveys were conducted online by Polimetrix/YouGov. The methodology used by Polimetrix/YouGov is described later.

Survey Panel Data

The PollingPoint panel, a proprietary opt-in survey panel, is made up of 1.6 million U.S. residents who have agreed to participate in YouGov/Polimetrix's Web surveys. At any given time, YouGov/Polimetrix maintains a minimum of five recruitment campaigns based on salient current events. Panel members are recruited by several methods and on a variety of topics to help ensure diversity in the panel population. Recruiting methods include Web advertising campaigns (public surveys), permission-based email campaigns, partner-sponsored solicitations, telephone-to-Web recruitment (RDD based sampling), and mail-to-Web recruitment (voter registration–based sampling).

The primary method of recruitment for the PollingPoint Panel is Web advertising campaigns that appear based on keyword searches. In practice, a search in Google may prompt an active PollingPoint advertisement soliciting opinion on the search topic. After the brief survey respondents are invited to join the PollingPoint panel to receive and participate in additional surveys. After a double opt-in procedure, where respondents must confirm their consent by responding to an email, the database checks to ensure the newly recruited panelist is in fact new and that the address information provided is valid.

Additionally, YouGov/Polimetrix augments their panel with difficult to recruit respondents by soliciting panelists in telephone and mail surveys. For example, in the fall and winter of 2006, YouGov/Polimetrix completed telephone interviews using RDD sampling and invited respondents to join the online panel. Respondents provided a working email where they could confirm their consent and request to receive online survey invitations. YouGov/Polimetrix also employed registration-based sampling, inviting respondents to complete a pre-election survey online. After that survey, respondents were invited to become PollingPoint members and receive additional survey invitations at their email address.

Sampling and Sample Matching

Sample matching is a methodology for selection of "representative" samples from non-randomly selected pools of respondents. It is ideally suited for Web access panels but could also be used for other types of surveys, such as phone surveys. Sample matching starts with an enumeration of the target population. For general population studies, the target population is all adults and can be enumerated using the decennial Census or a high-quality survey, such as the American Community Survey. In other contexts, this is known as the sampling frame, though, unlike conventional sampling, the sample is not drawn from the frame.

Traditional sampling, then, selects individuals from the sampling frame at random for participation in the study. This may not be feasible or economical as the contact information, especially email addresses, is not available for all individuals in the frame and refusals to participate increase the costs of sampling in this way.

Sample selection using the matching methodology is a two-stage process. First, a random sample is drawn from the target population. We call this sample the target sample. Details on how the target sample is drawn are provided later, but the essential idea is that this sample is a true probability sample and thus representative of the frame from which it was drawn.

Second, for each member of the target sample, we select one or more matching members from our pool of opt-in respondents. This is called the matched sample. Matching is accomplished using a large set of variables that are available in consumer and voter databases for both the target population and the opt-in panel.

The purpose of matching is to find an available respondent who is as similar as possible to the selected member of the target sample. The result is a sample of respondents who have the same measured characteristics as the target sample. Under certain conditions, described later, the matched sample will have comparable properties to a true random sample. That is, the matched sample mimics the characteristics of the target sample. It is, as far as we can tell, "representative" of the target population (because it is like the target sample).

When choosing the matched sample, it is necessary to find the closest matching respondent in the panel of opt-ins to each member of the target sample. Polimetrix employs the proximity matching method to find the closest matching respondent. For each variable used for matching, we define a distance function, d(x,y), which describes how "close" the values x and y are on an attribute. The overall distance between a member of the target sample and a member of the panel is a weighted sum of the individual distance functions on each attribute. The weights can be adjusted for each study based on which variables are thought to be important for that study, though, for the most part, we have not found the matching procedure to be sensitive to small adjustments of the weights. A large weight, on the other hand, forces the algorithm toward an exact match on that dimension.

Sampling Frame and Target Sample

YouGov/Polimetrix constructed sampling frames of U.S. residents from the 2006, 2010, and 2014 American Community Surveys (ACS), including data on age, race, gender, education, and party identification. The frames were constructed by stratified sampling from the full ACS samples with selection within strata by weighted sampling with replacements (using the person weights on the public use file). Data on party identification was matched from the 2004–2008 National Annenberg Election Studies. The target samples were drawn from U.S. residents in the sampling frames and were selected by stratification by age, race, gender, education, and by simple random sampling within strata.

Weighting

Because matching is approximate, rather than exact, and response rates vary by group, the sample of completed interviews normally shows tiny amounts of imbalance that can be corrected by post-stratification weighting.

Raking, first proposed by Deming and Stephan (1940), adjusts an initial set of weights to match a known set of population marginals, using a method of iterative proportional fitting (see Bishop, Fienberg, and Holland, 1975 for details). In this procedure, the weights are adjusted sequentially to match the marginal distribution of each weight variable. The process proceeds until all marginals are matched. It does not require any information about the joint distribution of the variables (though, if these data are available and believed to be important, they can be employed by defining a marginal distribution involving a cross-classification of two variables).

We calculated post-stratification weights by raking the completed interviews to known marginals for the general U.S. population from the 2006, 2010, and 2014 American Community Surveys for the following variables: age, race, gender, and education.

APPENDIX 2.2

Campaign Finance Reform and Regulation in the States, 2006–2016

State	Corporate regulations	Campaign regulations	Individual limits	State Party limits	PAC limits	Corporate limits	Union limits	Summary measure
Alaska	High	Yes	Yes	Yes	Yes	Prohibited	Prohibited	7
Alabama	High	Yes	No	No	No	No	No	0
Arkansas	Medium	Yes	Yes	Yes	Yes	Yes	Yes	5
Arizona	High	No	Yes	Yes	Yes	Prohibited	Prohibited	7
California	Medium	No	Yes	No	Yes	Yes	Yes	5
Colorado	High	Yes	Yes	Yes	Yes	Prohibited	Yes	6
Connecticut	High	Yes	Yes	Yes	Yes	Prohibited	Prohibited	7
Delaware	Medium	No	Yes	Yes	Yes	Yes	Yes	5
Florida	Medium	No	Yes	Yes	Yes	Yes	Yes	5
Georgia	Medium	No	Yes	Yes	Yes	Yes	Yes	5
Hawaii	Medium	No	Yes	Yes	Yes	Yes	Yes	5
Iowa	High	Yes	No	No	No	Prohibited	No	2
Idaho	Medium	No	Yes	Yes	Yes	Yes	Yes	5
Illinois	Low	No	Yes	No	Yes	Yes	Yes	4
Indiana	Medium	No	No	No	No	Yes	Yes	2
Kansas	Medium	No	Yes	No	Yes	Yes	Yes	4
Kentucky	High	Yes	Yes	No	Yes	Prohibited	Yes	5
Louisiana*	Medium	No	Yes	No	Yes	Yes	Yes	4
Massachusetts	High	Yes	Yes	Yes	Yes	Prohibited	Yes	6
Maryland	Medium	No	Yes	Yes	Yes	Yes	Yes	5
Maine	Medium	No	Yes	Yes	Yes	Yes	Yes	5
Michigan	High	Yes	Yes	Yes	Yes	Prohibited	Prohibited	7

State	Corporate regulations	Campaign regulations	Individual limits	State Party limits	PAC limits	Corporate limits	Union limits	Summary measure
Minnesota	High	Yes	Yes	Yes	Yes	Prohibited	Yes	6
Missouri	Low	No	No	No	No	No	No	0
Mississippi	Medium	No	No	No	No	Yes	No	1
Montana	High	Yes	Yes	Yes	Yes	Prohibited	Prohibited	7
North Carolina	High	Yes	Yes	No	Yes	Prohibited	Prohibited	6
North Dakota	High	No	No	No	No	Prohibited	Prohibited	4
Nebraska	Medium	No	No	No	No	No	No	0
New Hampshire	Medium	No	Yes	Yes	Yes	Yes	Prohibited	6
New Jersey*	Medium	No	Yes	No	Yes	Yes	Yes	4
New Mexico	Low	No	Yes	Yes	Yes	Yes	Yes	5
Nevada	Medium	No	Yes	Yes	Yes	Yes	Yes	5
New York	Medium	Yes	Yes	No	Yes	Yes	Yes	4
Ohio	High	Yes	Yes	Yes	Yes	Prohibited	Prohibited	7
Oklahoma	High	Yes	Yes	No	Yes	Prohibited	Prohibited	6
Oregon	Low	No	No	No	No	No	No	0
Pennsylvania	High	Yes	No	No	No	Prohibited	Prohibited	4
Rhode Island	High	Yes	Yes	Yes	Yes	Prohibited	Prohibited	7
South Carolina	Medium	No	Yes	Yes	Yes	Yes	Yes	5
South Dakota	High	Yes	Yes	No	No	Prohibited	Prohibited	5
Tennessee	High	Yes	Yes	Yes	Yes	Yes	Yes	5
Texas	High	Yes	No	No	No	Prohibited	Prohibited	4
Utah	Low	No	No	No	No	No	No	0
Virginia*	Low	No	No	No	No	No	No	0
Vermont	Medium	No	Yes	No	Yes	Yes	Yes	4
Washington	Medium	No	Yes	Yes	Yes	Yes	Yes	5
Wisconsin	High	Yes	Yes	Yes	Yes	Prohibited	Prohibited	7
West Virginia	High	Yes	Yes	Yes	Yes	Prohibited	Yes	6
Wyoming	High	Yes	Yes	No	Yes	Prohibited	Prohibited	6

* Data from relevant election year: 2005, 2009, and 2013.

Notes: "Corporate regulations" is based on outside assessments of the overall level of regulation. "Campaign regulations" refers to whether the state limits or prohibits independent expenditures from the general treasury. Data on campaign finance regulation are from National Council of State Legislatures.

APPENDIX 2.3

Campaign Spending in the States, 2006–2016 (in millions)

State	2016 Pop.	2016 Spend.	2014 Spend.	2012 Spend.	2010 Spend.	2008 Spend.	2006 Spend.
Alaska	0.71	$16.61	$47.95	$7.91	$21.47	$12.00	$14.58
Alabama	4.83	$16.13	$69.85	$16.26	$122.21	$17.30	$95.07
Arkansas	2.96	$35.74	$76.10	$31.12	$60.58	$10.63	$29.88
Arizona	6.63	$90.64	$68.48	$65.94	$90.52	$55.66	$50.43
California	38.33	$824.63	$553.88	$756.70	$837.17	$635.41	$762.37
Colorado	5.27	$128.01	$132.70	$43.76	$71.97	$82.68	$37.68
Connecticut	3.60	$28.70	$51.74	$132.36	$140.71	$12.08	$23.33
Delaware	0.93	$10.72	$12.94	$15.64	$23.22	$12.98	$9.87
Florida	19.55	$262.63	$291.81	$212.12	$414.31	$88.83	$203.17
Georgia	9.99	$68.29	$131.57	$54.75	$116.25	$27.89	$100.69
Hawaii	1.40	$13.95	$31.98	$25.04	$22.24	$6.23	$10.86
Iowa	3.09	$67.26	$86.09	$57.70	$78.28	$33.53	$51.07
Idaho	1.61	$13.83	$22.22	$13.51	$19.50	$4.96	$13.86
Illinois	12.88	$349.63	$305.40	$187.88	$261.49	$92.36	$305.40
Indiana	6.57	$118.52	$46.28	$96.73	$62.39	$75.24	$46.28
Kansas	2.89	$32.57	$45.48	$22.36	$39.80	$12.99	$20.84
Kentucky	4.40	$43.05	$78.50	$29.22	$47.52	$16.12	$13.24
Louisiana	4.63	$40.95	$85.57	$21.15	$68.96	$7.30	$103.03
Massachusetts	6.69	$103.38	$128.67	$147.01	$136.35	$35.22	$110.58
Maryland	5.93	$54.36	$87.26	$142.34	$82.68	$9.70	$73.96
Maine	1.33	$32.64	$38.86	$30.94	$32.22	$15.26	$17.02

State	2016 Pop.	2016 Spend.	2014 Spend.	2012 Spend.	2010 Spend.	2008 Spend.	2006 Spend.
Michigan	9.90	$62.95	$138.67	$267.15	$121.61	$46.66	$128.45
Minnesota	5.42	$66.15	$94.25	$115.09	$82.59	$23.05	$55.10
Missouri	6.04	$216.29	$57.88	$150.83	$93.90	$102.69	$85.01
Mississippi	2.99	$5.47	$45.74	$18.24	$39.55	$3.28	$56.88
Montana	1.02	$34.00	$22.66	$40.79	$6.63	$13.94	$3.92
North Carolina	9.85	$162.19	$112.38	$108.06	$87.20	$95.46	$40.41
North Dakota	0.72	$19.45	$18.46	$30.42	$14.76	$7.40	$3.95
Nebraska	1.87	$17.34	$44.75	$27.58	$12.05	$6.22	$19.20
New Hampshire	1.32	$54.98	$46.79	$22.27	$40.06	$7.88	$9.51
New Jersey	8.90	$91.40	$91.40	$51.72	$91.93	$6.39	$128.45
New Mexico	2.09	$22.89	$40.55	$35.18	$43.38	$12.36	$30.28
Nevada	2.79	$91.29	$53.97	$47.68	$101.77	$21.72	$55.08
New York	19.65	$188.07	$248.39	$179.64	$293.95	$101.55	$169.76
Ohio	11.57	$139.28	$172.22	$216.51	$233.54	$172.70	$163.83
Oklahoma	3.85	$50.76	$58.69	$29.21	$60.47	$22.21	$40.75
Oregon	3.93	$132.47	$128.88	$79.40	$94.42	$52.58	$67.19
Pennsylvania	12.77	$202.87	$220.17	$168.47	$242.41	$119.62	$142.07
Rhode Island	1.05	$13.41	$30.20	$24.06	$21.39	$4.53	$37.88
South Carolina	4.77	$33.67	$58.24	$32.62	$67.51	$25.64	$38.69
South Dakota	0.84	$27.89	$21.50	$12.39	$27.79	$11.51	$20.19
Tennessee	6.50	$36.84	$59.17	$56.52	$75.69	$21.33	$25.81
Texas	26.45	$173.43	$318.78	$291.12	$299.35	$118.00	$186.57
Utah	2.90	$34.45	$18.34	$34.37	$18.49	$12.17	$7.99
Virginia	8.26	$136.01	$136.01	$70.55	$112.83	$8.62	$89.78
Vermont	0.63	$17.60	$5.29	$13.60	$12.81	$3.89	$4.65
Washington	6.97	$119.88	$71.70	$149.50	$142.45	$75.79	$41.70
Wisconsin	5.74	$103.28	$99.94	$125.21	$94.61	$17.29	$39.45
West Virginia	1.85	$31.86	$28.47	$33.36	$25.78	$14.53	$8.54
Wyoming	0.58	$4.60	$8.30	$7.19	$6.79	$1.31	$4.28

* Data from relevant election year: 2013, 2009, and 2005.
Notes: Campaign spending figures are total statewide expenditures and come from Follow the Money, https://followthemoney.org.

APPENDIX 2.4

Descriptive Statistics for Key Variables, 2016

	Range	Mean	Std. Dev.
Political participation	0 (no acts)–5 (5+ acts)	1.88	1.89
Turnout (self-reported)	0 (no)–1 (yes)	0.65	0.48
Political interest	1 (low)–5 (high)	4.05	1.28
Presidential approval	1 (strongly approve)–4 (strongly disapprove)	2.59	1.22
Congressional approval	1 (strongly approve)–4 (strongly disapprove)	3.01	0.87
TV use	0 (no)–1 (yes)	0.72	0.45
Newspaper use	0 (no)–1 (yes)	0.45	0.50
Social media use	0 (no)–1 (yes)	0.69	0.46
Economy	1 (much better)–5 (much worse)	3.13	1.04
Male	0 (no)–1 (yes)	0.48	0.50
African American	0 (no)–1 (yes)	0.11	0.32
Latino	0 (no)–1 (yes)	0.10	0.30
Under 30 years of age	0 (no)–1 (yes)	0.11	0.31
65 years of age and older	0 (no)–1 (yes)	0.09	0.29
College degree or more	0 (no)–1 (yes)	0.27	0.44
High school degree or less	0 (no)–1 (yes)	0.40	0.49
Democrat	0 (no)–1 (yes)	0.44	0.50
Republican	0 (no)–1 (yes)	0.37	0.48
Union household	0 (no)–1 (yes)	0.16	0.30
Church attendance	0 (infrequently)–1 (frequently)	0.23	0.42
Catholic	0 (no)–1 (yes)	0.20	0.40
Jewish	0 (no)–1 (yes)	0.03	0.16
Summary measure of perceived corruption	0 (low)–8 (high)	5.51	1.92
Trust in the federal government	0 (low)–10 (high)	4.17	2.83
Summary of knowledge of restrictions on special interests in campaigns	0 (low)–3 (high)	0.82	0.79
Summary of knowledge of campaign spending	0 (low)–8 (high)	2.68	2.05

	Range	Mean	Std. Dev.
Summary measure of limits on individuals, parties, PACs, corporations, unions	0 (no limits)–7 (maximal limits)	4.39	1.91
Statewide corporate regulatory environment	1 (minimal limits)–3 (maximal limits)	2.31	0.68
Statewide prohibition or limit on independent expenditures	1 (no limits)–2 (limits)	1.47	0.50
Average total candidate and committee expenditures per capita, 2006–2016	\$1.00–\$28.29	\$13.25	\$4.25
Statewide population based on 2016 Census projections (in millions)	0.58–38.33	12.87	10.24

Source: University of Texas Modules for the 2016 Cooperative Congressional Election Study.

For the 2016 survey, the political participation measure consists of fourteen distinct "yes/no" items ("part 1" to "part 14") asking about participation in the period from 2012 to 2016. These measures were simply added together, with the resultant 0–14 scale recoded into a 0–5, where the 5 category includes 5+ acts.

We use two separate campaign finance knowledge variables for analysis. The first is an additive summary measure, made up of the nine items focusing on individual contribution limits, spending, and disclosure. The second variable is also an additive summary measure, but it is made up of the three items on restrictions on special interests spending in campaigns.

To assess general perceptions of corruption, we combine two survey items: (1) how honest and ethical is the average member of Congress, and (2) how serious a problem is corruption? Both items are scored 1–5, with 1 representing less corruption and 5 representing more corruption. We combine the items into an additive, nine-category (2–10, which we rescore to range from 0–8) measure of perceived corruption.

"State corporate regulatory environment" is scored either 1 ("low"), 2 ("medium"), or 3 ("high").[1] "State limit or prohibition of independent expenditures" is scored either 1 ("no limits") or 2 ("limits").[2] The summary measure of limits on individuals, parties, PACs, corporations, and unions ranges from 0 to 7 (see Appendix 2.2). The average per capita statewide spending by candidate campaign committees over the 2006–2016 election cycles is used to measure campaign spending (see Appendix 2.3).

Political trust comes from a single measure in which respondents are asked to rate their trust in the federal government on a 0–10 scale.

APPENDIX 2.5

Descriptive Statistics for Key Variables, 2009

Variable	Range	Mean	Std. Dev.
Political participation	0 (0 acts)–5 (5+ acts)	2.31	1.79
Turnout (self-reported)	0–1	0.75	0.43
Political interest	1 (never)–5 (all of the time)	3.71	1.26
Media consumption	0 (minimal) –10 (maximal)	4.20	2.42
Political knowledge	0 (no correct)–4 (4 correct)	2.28	1.27
Male	0 (no)–1 (yes)	0.48	0.50
African American	0 (no)–1 (yes)	0.11	0.31
Latino	0 (no)–1 (yes)	0.13	0.33
Under 30 years of age	0 (no)–1 (yes)	0.22	0.41
65 years of age and over	0 (no)–1 (yes)	0.12	0.33
High school degree or less	0 (no)–1 (yes)	0.46	0.50
College educated or more	0 (no)–1 (yes)	0.25	0.43
Republican	0 (no)–1 (yes)	0.35	0.48
Democratic	0 (no)–1 (yes)	0.41	0.49
Summary measure of perceived corruption	0.83 (low)–10.0 (high)	6.90	1.87
Summary measure of campaign finance knowledge	0 (none correct)–4 (4 correct)	0.57	0.77
Summary measure of limits on individuals, parties, PACs, corporations, unions	0 (no limits)–7 (maximal limits)	4.60	1.77
Statewide corporate regulatory environment	1 (minimal limits)–3 (maximal limits)	2.30	0.69
Statewide prohibition or limit on independent expenditures	1 (no limits)–2 (limits)	1.47	0.50
Average total candidate and committee expenditures per capita, 2008	\$1.00–\$23.65	\$9.06	\$5.14
Statewide population based on 2010 Census (in millions)	0.59–39.14	13.10	11.16

Source: University of Texas Money in Politics Survey (Shaw and Roberts, 2009).

For the 2009 survey analysis, the political participation measure is an additive scale comprised of nine 0–1 (no–yes) items (Q101_1 to Q101_9), ranging from "discussing politics with other," to "vote in a primary election," to "march in a protest," to "sign a petition." The resultant 0–9 scale is transformed to a 1–10 scale for purposes of presentational clarity.

The political knowledge scale is based on the total number of correct scores across four factual items concerning American politics.

The campaign finance knowledge scale is the total number of correct scores across four factual items concerning federal election campaign finance.

The political corruption measure is an additive scale of four items: (1) salience of federal government corruption (Q70), (2) attitudes on how corrupt the federal government is (Q67), (3) attitudes on how often politicians are influenced by campaign contributions (Q64), and (4) how often politicians solicit contributions from corporations and interest groups (Q65). Each item is scaled 0–3, and the resultant 0–12 scale is transformed to a 0–10 scale for purposes of presentational clarity.

The news media consumption measure is an additive scale comprised of eight 0–4 scaled items (ranging from "never" use the media source to "every day") that gauge how often a respondent uses the news media source. The resultant 0–28 scale is transformed to a 0–10 scale for purposes of presentational clarity.

"State corporate regulatory environment" is scored either 1 ("low"), 2 ("medium"), or 3 ("high").[1] "State limit or prohibition of independent expenditures" is scored either 1 ("no limits") or 2 ("limits").[2] The summary measure of limits on individuals, parties, PACs, corporations, and unions ranges from 0 to 7. Total per capita statewide spending by candidate campaign committees over the 2007–2008 election cycle ranges from a low of $1.03 to a high of $26.90.

Finally, our measure of perceived corruption is based on four items:

1. "How often do politicians vote based on what their contributors want?" (Q64)
2. "How often do politicians appeal to wealthy but reluctant contributors?" (Q65)
3. "How ethical is the Congress?" (Q72)
4. "How salient is the issue of political corruption?" (Q70)

We re-scale these items so that each is arrayed on a 0–2.5 scale and then add them. The result is a 0–10 scale of perceived corruption.

Notes

Chapter 1

1. The Supreme Court is not alone in placing political participation at the heart of democracy. See, for example, Verba and Nie (1972); Verba, Schlozman, and Brady (1995); Leighley and Nagler (2013).
2. Early work, especially by Jeffery Milyo and David Primo, and pioneering articles by Nathaniel Persily and Kelli Lammie, and Beth Ann Rosenson raised questions about the Court's behavioral assumptions.
3. While the Supreme Court has addressed contribution limits, it has only been in the context of permissible lower limits—not something addressed explicitly in the *Buckley* decision—without consideration of the basic principle supporting contribution limits per se. See Nixon v. Shrink Missouri Government PAC, 528 U.S. 377 (2000); Randall v. Sorrell, 548 U.S. 230 (2006); Zimmerman v. Austin, No. 16-51366 (5th Cir. 2018)—denied a writ of certiorari by the Supreme Court—and Thompson v. Hebdon, No. 19–122 (2019), in which the Supreme Court vacated a ruling by Ninth U.S. Circuit Court of Appeals upholding the State of Alaska's contribution limits, sending the case back to the Ninth Circuit for reconsideration of the First Amendment implications of the state's law.
4. Burgess Everett and Glenn Thrush, "McConnell Throws Down the Gauntlet: No Scalia Replacement under Obama," Politico, February 13, 2006, https://www.politico.com/story/2016/02/mitch-mcconnell-antonin-scalia-supreme-court-nomination-219248.
5. Hillary Clinton publicly signaled she would select a nominee to fill the Scalia vacancy who would support overturning the *Citizens United* decision; Matea Gold and Anne Gearan, "Hillary Clinton's litmus test for Supreme Court nominees: a pledge to overturn Citizens United," *Washington Post*, May 14, 2015, https://www.washingtonpost.com/news/post-politics/wp/2015/05/14/hillary-clintons-litmus-test-for-supreme-court-nominees-a-pledge-to-overturn-citizens-united/.
6. Brett Kavanaugh, who replaced retiring Supreme Court Justice Anthony Kennedy on October 8, 2018, is not expected to change the direction of the Court's recent campaign finance decisions. Although a swing vote on many legal issues before the Court, Justice Kennedy, the author of the *Citizens United* decision, was a stalwart supporter of the Roberts Court's efforts to restore stronger First Amendment protections for political speech.
7. The Bipartisan Campaign Reform Act (Pub.L. 107–155, 116 Stat. 81), enacted March 27, 2002. Also known as the McCain-Feingold Act, this law was notable for banning "soft" money—a source of unlimited funds for national political parties—and its efforts to rein in "sham" issue ads through the creation and regulation of a new

category of political spending, electioneering communications. Both soft money and sham issue ads arose as significant issues in the mid to late 1990s.

8. Congress did pass two sets of amendments to the FECA—in 1976 and 1979—designed principally to clarify or clean up the campaign finance statutes to reflect various elements of the *Buckley* decision; they were not major revisions to the law, with none but one of their provisions ever challenged in court. One of the more tangible and perhaps unintentional consequences of the 1979 amendments was sanctioning of the channel by which soft money—unlimited expenditures by political parties for generic party building activities—emerged. This was subsequently eliminated by the 2002 Bipartisan Campaign Reform Act.
9. The amendments were introduced in the Senate as S. 3044 on February 21, 1974, by Senator Howard Cannon (D-NV) and co-sponsor Howard Metzenbaum (D-OH). It was signed by President Ford, becoming Public Law 93-443, October 15, 1974. The amendments included, among other things, stringent contribution and expenditure limits, heightened disclosure requirements, and creation of the Federal Election Commission (see: https://www.congress.gov/bill/93rd-congress/senate-bill/3044).
10. Buckley v. Valeo was originally filed in district court on January 2, 1975, by, among others, Senator James L. Buckley (R-NY) and Eugene McCarthy, former senator from Minnesota. McCarthy's participation is noteworthy because his 1968 campaign to wrest the Democratic presidential nomination from, initially, President Lyndon Johnson, was financed by singularly large contributions from a small number of wealthy donors, led by Howard Stein, the late chairman of the Dreyfus Corporation. The 1974 FECA Amendments would make similarly financed insurgent campaigns all but impossible.
11. Federal Election Commission v. Wisconsin Right to Life, Inc., 551 U.S. 449 (2007). This case was an "as applied" challenge to provisions of the 2002 BCRA that banned corporations, including incorporated nonprofit corporations such as Wisconsin Right to Life, Inc. from funding electioneering communications, a new category of political expenditure created by the legislation. In its opinion, the Supreme Court significantly limited the scope of electioneering communications and in so doing broke a long string of post-*Buckley* Court decisions broadening the reach of campaign finance regulation, most notably the 2003 McConnell v. FEC decision that upheld all but a few minor provisions of the BCRA.
12. As noted, 2016 marked the fortieth anniversary of the *Buckley* decision and was cause for considerable retrospection. See, for instance, Allard (2016), Hellman and Schultz (2016).
13. A simple Google search for "money equals speech" yields thousands of results.
14. If political communication costs reach the point they no longer financially burden political speech, the Court has, by not equating money and speech, provided ample room to decouple money and speech. It is worth noting, then, that contemporary mass political communication does not resemble the world of 1974; there are far more communication channels available, "mass" communication has increasingly given way to highly individualized (targeted) appeals, and technology has driven the marginal cost of some mass communication vanishingly close to zero. In light

of these new realities, particularly the declining marginal cost argument, some have called for the Court to reexamine its First Amendment concerns relating to money in politics. These arguments, however, are belied by the scale of expenditures in contemporary federal elections, most of which continue to pay for political communication.

15. The appellees mounted several arguments for treating the regulation of money in politics as anything but an incidental First Amendment issue. The principal counterargument was that campaign finance laws primarily regulate conduct, not speech, with analogies made to the upholding of laws banning draft cards over First Amendment objections (BeVier, 1994; Sullivan, 1996). The *Buckley* Court dismissed this argument, even though it had been accepted by the U.S. Court of Appeals, noting that the Supreme Court "has never suggested that the dependence of a communication on the expenditure of money operates itself to introduce a nonspeech element or to reduce the exacting scrutiny required by the First Amendment" (p. 16). A second line of argument sought to have the FECA limits treated as "the reasonable time, place, and manner regulations, which do not discriminate among speakers or ideas, in order to further an important governmental interest unrelated to the restriction of communication" (p. 18). The Court dismissed this argument, finding the impact of FECA restrictions on the volume of political speech to be the overriding consideration: "The critical difference between this case and those time, place, and manner cases is that the present Act's contribution and expenditure limitations impose direct quantity restrictions on political communication and association by persons, groups, candidates, and political parties in addition to any reasonable time, place, and manner regulations otherwise imposed" (p. 18).
16. Getting the Court to establish a First Amendment argument was a key goal of the *Buckley* appellants (Winter, 1997).
17. Earlier Supreme Court cases, e.g., United States v. CIO, 335 U.S. 106 (1948) and Pipefitters. v. United States, 407 U.S. 385 (1972), reference the First Amendment implications of campaign finance laws—e.g., the 1925 Federal Corrupt Practice Act—but stop well short of rooting all consideration of such laws in the Bill of Rights.
18. See Fallon (2006), Siegel (2006).
19. In addition to advancing a compelling government interest, an otherwise constitutionally suspect law or policy must be "narrowly tailored" and be the most effective—least constitutionally invasive—means of realizing the government's interest.
20. The reference to CSC v. Letter Carriers in the quote should not be mistaken as an appeal by the *Buckley* Court to precedent for including the appearance of corruption as a compelling state interest. The reference is to a downstream state interest—"confidence in the system of representative Government"—that, as discussed later in the chapter, is an important plank in the Court's corruption teleology.
21. More broadly, appeals to appearances in the law are common (Samaha, 2012).
22. The issue of whether the courts do or should consider "real harm" is taken up by La Pierre (2000), who criticizes the apparent lack of concern (and lack of evidence) in campaign finance cases for real harm (in this case, of actual or perceived corruption). Bruce La Pierre argued for the appellants in Shrink Missouri v. Adams where the issue of "real harm" was taken up by the Eighth Circuit.

23. Recent cases have drawn attention to lower court splits over what constitutes the foundation of perceived corruption, particularly in the wake of recent Supreme Court decisions—e.g., *Citizens United* and *McCutcheon*—that restored the operative definition of corruption to the quid pro quo standard articulated in *Buckley*. The lower court split largely hinges on whether patterns of actual quid pro quo corruption must exist before laws limiting the appearance of corruption meet the threshold of addressing a compelling state interest. For a discussion of the lower court split, see amicus brief submitted by the Public Policy Legal Institute in Zimmerman v. City of Austin in support of a writ of certiorari to the Supreme Court.
24. Justice Stewart famously used the phrase, "I know it when I see it" in reference to a description of hardcore pornography in Jacobellis v. Ohio, 378 U.S. 184 (1964).
25. In Shrink Missouri v. Adams, 5 F. Supp. 2d 734 (E.D. Mo. 1998), the district court suggests that public opinion surveys are not necessary to establish the appearance of corruption, deference to the experience of legislators is sufficient:

    > *The Court does not believe that polling the citizenry is required in order to demonstrate that the integrity of a state's election process is facing a perceived threat. As the recipients of campaign contributions, members of the legislature are uniquely qualified to gauge whether allowing those contributions to go unchecked endangers our democratic system of government, and, if so, to prescribe an appropriate remedy therefor.* (P. 738)

    Deference to legislators is a prominent theme in *Buckley*, a fact noted by the Eighth Circuit its Shrink Missouri v. Adams decision (161 F.3d 519, at 37):

    > *See 424 U.S. at 27, 28, 30, 96 S.Ct. 612 (Congress "could legitimately conclude" that avoiding the appearance of corruption is essential to maintaining confidence in government; Congress "was surely entitled to conclude" that disclosure limitations alone would not adequately combat corruption and its appearance; Congress "was justified in concluding that the interest in safeguarding against the appearance of impropriety requires that the opportunity for abuse inherent in the process of raising large monetary contributions be eliminated.").*

26. Measurement issues abound in survey data, including those associated with question wording, question ordering, and response options (see, for example, Asher, 2016; Bardes and Oldendick, 2015). Adding significantly to such complications, as discussed in the next section, are the multiple definitions of corruption accepted over time by the Court in the context of campaign finance.
27. There are still further questions to ask. Does the potential effectiveness of a law—the degree to which it mitigates corruption—matter? Would a law with high effectiveness be upheld if a relatively small number of people perceived there to be corruption? Would a law with low likely effectiveness nonetheless be upheld if an overwhelming percentage of Americans perceived money to be corrupting the political process? The latter would seem to be the model we have been living with, as it accounts for the coexistence of persistent and broad perceptions of corruption with deep skepticism that current laws and regulations are the least bit effective (See Chapter 3).
28. Bribery of public officials is defined in 18 U.S. Code §201. This law has not itself escaped recent scrutiny, particularly as it relates to what constitutes an official act

subject to illegal influence (bribery). Responding in 2016 to a Writ of Certiorari in the case of McDonnell v. United States (136 S. Ct. 2355) the Supreme Court vacated the conviction of former Virginia Governor Robert McDonnell and his wife, Maureen McDonnell, narrowing the definition of an official act by noting that things such as "setting up a meeting, talking to another official, or organizing an event—without more—does not fit that definition of 'official act'" (p. 2).

29. The *Austin* Court understood that it could not uphold the Michigan law banning corporate independent expenditures using the *Buckley* Court's quid pro quo definition of corruption and, more important, how that definition factored into its decision to ban limits on independent expenditures found in the 1974 FECA Amendments. See discussion later in the chapter on the *Buckley* Court's use of quid pro quo corruption in assessing contribution and expenditure limits.
30. 572 US _ (2014), 134 S. Ct. 1434, 4.
31. The importance of the Court's (re)invoking of the quid pro quo definition of corruption is one of the truly underappreciated aspects of the Citizens United v. FEC decision. It shut down a proven strategy for expanding the scope of campaign finance regulation; the *Austin* court recognized that it could not reach a decision upholding a ban on corporate independent expenditures without an expanded definition of corruption.
32. For examples of proposed state interests see, Post (2014), Alexander (2005), and Strauss (2016).
33. For a discussion of measuring attitudes toward corruption and governmental trust, see Hetherington (2006); Anderson and Tverdova (2003).
34. FECA 74.
35. The Supreme Court recently turned away the latest effort when it denied a writ of certiorari—declined to hear—Laura Holmes, et al. v. FEC, a case seeking to change campaign contribution limits by permitting individuals to aggregate contributions to a candidate that they currently must split across different elections (e.g., a primary and general election). The case was remanded to the original district court for further consideration of possible First Amendment issues.
36. Seeking to further clarify this definition, the *Buckley* opinion added examples in the now famous footnote 52 of qualifying language: "vote for," "elect," "support," "cast your ballot for," "Smith for Congress," "vote against," "defeat," "reject." These became known as the "magic words" and were treated as bright lines for determining whether an ad involved express advocacy. This issue was at the heart of the soft money ban in the 2002 BCRA, which targeted so-called sham issue ads, which stopped (just) short of express advocacy.
37. Disclosure statutes represented some of the earliest federal campaign finance reforms, emerging from Progressive Era concerns about the corrupting influence of money in politics. Samuel McCall (R-MA) introduced the first disclosure bill in 1906 (a year before the passage of the Tillman Act banning corporate campaign contributions). Although this first bill failed, subsequent efforts in 1910 (c.392, 36 Stat. 822) and again in 1911 (§2, 37 Stat. 26) brought to life the first meaningful federal campaign finance disclosure laws (Mutch, 1988: pp. 8–16).

38. The *Buckley* Court cites the extremity of the threats described in NAACP v. Alabama, 357 U.S. 449 (1958) in establishing a disclosure exemption threshold.
39. Using spatial modeling techniques, researchers have demonstrated the ability to use campaign finance information to place candidates on a "political spectrum" (McCarty and Poole, 1998; Bonica, 2014). Whether voters have the wherewithal to do something equivalent is an open question.
40. Chief Justice Roberts in oral argument of Beverly R. Gill, et al. v. William Whitford, et al., No. 16-1161, on October 3, 2017.
41. Political scientists have weighed in on several campaign finance cases, perhaps most notably in McConnell v. FEC (2003), where different sets provided expert testimony at the district court trial (see earlier discussion) and submitted an amicus brief to the Supreme Court supporting the soft money ban in Title I of the 2002 BCRA; none of this was referenced in the Supreme Court's decision.
42. Although Chief Justice Earl Warren's *Brown* decision has been described as "a remarkable culmination of the legal realist project of taming abstract legal propositions with the whip of social science" (Brewer, 1998: p. 1553), there was considerable concern about the motivation—lending scientific legitimacy to a controversial legal decision—and efficacy of introducing the social science research found in the decision's famous footnote 11 (Mody, 2002). Subsequent criticisms of the research design and methods and of the cited works along with still arguably unsettled science on the question of school segregation and student performance are given as inherent risks in the courts' reliance on social science; risks that have only been inflamed by recent evidence of the irreproducibility of significant numbers of peer reviewed research.
43. Fuller (1934).
44. The first use of social science as a source of "legislative facts" came with the introduction of what subsequently became known as a "Brandeis brief" in Muller v. Oregon, 208 U.S. 412 (1908), named after a 100-plus page brief replete with social science research related to working conditions submitted by future Supreme Court Justice Louis Brandeis. Credit for the compilation of the voluminous research record in the brief belongs in large measure to Josephine Clara Goldmark, Brandeis' sister-in-law and legal activist. The *Muller* brief is legally notable because the findings were not introduced as evidence in the original lower court trial, but as part of the appeal to the Supreme Court. As such, the findings in the brief could not be considered part of the factual record of the case. Nonetheless, the brief is widely acknowledged to have influenced the Supreme Court's decision by providing valuable contextual information.
45. See Monahan and Walker (1986); Faigman (1989, 1991).
46. Most efforts to find a causal pathway from money to votes falter when congressional vote models adequately account for constituent interests, suggesting that most corporate PAC money supports members of Congress already predisposed, by dint of constituent preferences, to vote a particular way.
47. The lack of systematic evidence of a relationship between corporate PAC contributions and legislative outcomes has led scholars to search elsewhere for evidence that corporations, through their PACs, are rationally investing in politics.

Dan Lowenstein (1989) makes the general point that most of this research is looking in the wrong place for evidence of money's influence, that the damage is done, and buried, well before a final vote on a bill takes place. In that spirit, Hall and Wayman (1990) look elsewhere in the legislative process—preferential congressional committee activity—for the influence of campaign contributions. McChesney (1987, 1997) argues that through a process of rent extraction politicians are able to extort contributions from corporate interests in exchange for nothing more than preserving the (rent-laden) status quo. Interestingly, the rent extraction argument is precisely what was used by the Committee for Economic Development—a prominent business interest group—in its 2003 amicus brief urging the Supreme Court to uphold the BCRA ban on soft money in McConnell v. FEC (2003). See https://campaignlegal.org/sites/default/files/ecdevamicus.pdf

48. Starting with the 1910 Federal Corrupt Practices Act (2 U.S.C. Section 241), federal law has compelled disclosure of campaign finances in one form or another for well over one hundred years. However, until the Federal Election Commission began distributing data in the late 1970s, campaign finance reports were stored deep in the U.S. Capitol and effectively inaccessible to all but the most intrepid social scientists; the early efforts by Louise Overacker (1932) and Alexander Heard (1956, 1960) are rare exceptions.
49. The role of perceptions in suspect behavioral models advanced in election-related court decisions is not limited to the domain of campaign finance. In Frank v. Walker, 768 F.3d 744 (7th Cir. 2014) the Seventh Circuit decision references Ansolabehere and Persily (2008), noting their finding that

    > *perceptions of voter-impersonation fraud are unrelated to the strictness of a state's voter ID law. This suggests that these laws do not reduce such fraud, for if they did one would expect perceptions of its prevalence to change. The study also undermines the suggestion in the* [lower court] *panel's opinion (offered without supporting evidence) that requiring a photo ID in order to be allowed to vote increases voters' confidence in the honesty of the election, and thus increases turnout.*

50. The lower court arguments in McConnell v. FEC (2003) both for and against, made extensive use of public opinion data, but largely to talk past each other. Evidence that large majorities of the public believe money is a corrupting influence in American politics was not challenged. Neither was equally compelling evidence by the plaintiffs that the American public does not place campaign finance reform anywhere near the top of their concerns, that the public is profoundly unaware of campaign finance laws, and that there is little to no faith in the efficacy of campaign finance regulations.
51. The Court requires further consideration of how narrowly tailored the law is and that there does not exist some less constitutionally threatening alternative.
52. Measurement of corruption is an issue (Alt and Lassen, 2003).
53. A $10,000 limited carve out for state and local parties known as "Levin funds" included in an amendment by Senator Carl Levin to the 2002 Bipartisan Campaign Finance Act represents the last vestige of soft money in American politics.
54. After largely dismissing any possible impact of campaign finance legislation on average perceptions of corruption, Persily and Lammie (2004) estimate a multivariate

model seeking to explain individual variation in perceived corruption. As we discuss at more length in Chapter 3, they fail to find a role for money in politics in their model.

55. See Werner (2011); Werner and Coleman (2014); Klumpp, Mialon, and Williams, (2016).
56. In addition to variation in enforcement of seemingly comparable laws (e.g., contribution limits), states vary in the speed at which they adapt their laws to reflect state and federal court decisions. Although approximately half the states limited or prohibited corporate independent expenditures prior to the *Citizens United* decision, very few (if any) have explicitly changed either their laws or regulations to match.
57. The 2010 *Citizens United* decision rendered unconstitutional bans on corporate independent expenditures in twenty-four states. Arizona Free Enterprise Club v. Bennett, 564 U.S. 721 (2011) significantly constrains the range of public funding options available to states.
58. A positive relationship between the political efficacy—a concept related to, but considered distinct from, trust (Craig, Niemi, and Silver, 1990)—and participation has empirical support (Milbrath, 1965; Easton and Dennis, 1967; Verba and Nie, 1972; Finkel, 1987; Verba, Schlozman, and Brady, 1995).
59. For specific empirical results showing the effects of corruption on participation see Mishler and Rose (2001); Anderson and Tverdova (2003); and Uslaner (2001).
60. The relationship between political efficacy and trust—and how to measure them—is a subject of considerable debate within political science (Craig, Niemi, and Silver, 1990).
61. A larger literature considers voter reactions to specific charges of corruption (broadly defined) and generally finds that voters punished the accused (Peters and Welch, 1980; Welch and Hibbing, 1997).
62. The inability of public funding systems to limit independent spending, particularly in the wake of Arizona Free Enterprise v. Bennett (2011), makes it very difficult to evaluate any narrow claims regarding such systems and turnout.
63. The effects of negative advertising have been contested (Lau et al., 1999). The finding of significant negative effect of negative advertising on turnout by Ansolabehere and Iyengar (1995) has been challenged by Finkel and Geer (1998). Negative advertising has acquired new interest with the rise of Super PACs, which spend most of their money on negative advertising (Miller, 2017).
64. *Citizens United* has prompted a wide range of new questions related to campaign finance. See, e.g., Brewer, Lambe, and Jones (2017); Klumpp, Mialon, and Williams (2016); Bowler and Donovan (2015); La Raja and Schaffner, (2014); Werner and Coleman (2014); Coates (2012); and Werner (2011).

Chapter 2

1. The ANES surveys are face-to-face (FTF), although since 2008 the FTF survey has been supplemented with an online, web-based survey. The 2012 and 2016 ANES surveys also include online interviews that parallel the traditional face-to-face format.

The universe includes citizen adults. As noted in the text, sample sizes are typically around 2,000 respondents. The ANES also conducted midterm election surveys from 1954 through 2002. Details are available at http://www.electionstudies.org/.

2. A more complete description of the survey methodologies is presented in Appendix 2.1.
3. It is worth pointing out that even if we wanted to test local effects, we do not have sufficiently granular geographic locational information for our respondents to match them to appropriate circumstances. As for national effects, since the survey is of all Americans there is no variation in spending or regulatory environment at the national level.
4. See Annenberg Civics Knowledge Survey (2017).
5. Consider, for example, the creation of popular websites such as "followthemoney.org" and "opensecrets.org" that publish reports as well raw contribution and expenditure data in a searchable, user-friendly format.
6. "Dark money" refers to funds given to nonprofit organizations—including 501(c)(4) (social welfare), 501(c)(5) (unions), and 501(c)(6) (trade association) groups—that can receive unlimited donations from corporations, individuals, and unions and can spend funds to influence elections, but are not required to disclose their donors.
7. The regulatory and legal environment was remarkably stable over this decade-plus time period, allowing us to use the same underlying data for our 2009–2016 analyses.
8. The underlying data on statewide campaign finance reforms and regulations are presented in Appendix 2.2.

Chapter 3

1. Both Alt and Lassen (2003) and Rosenson (2009) rely on Boylan and Long's survey of statehouse reporters to measure statewide corruption attitudes. See Cordis and Milyo (2013) for a critique.
2. As noted, Primo and Milyo (2020) argue that Americans are skeptical about the efficacy of campaign finance reform, but the conventional wisdom holds that support for campaign finance reform is indicative of a belief that such reform will help curb corruption.
3. The only corruption examples referenced in the *Buckley* decision relate to the all too real post-1972 election Watergate revelations cited in the earlier Court of Appeals *Buckley* opinion (171 U.S. App. D.C., at 190–191, and nn. 36–38, 519 F. 2d, at 839–840, and nn. 36–38). The Court offers no examples of perceived corruption, claiming only that such corruption is "inherent in a system permitting unlimited financial contributions" (p. 28).
4. Although we are obviously not fans of corruption, we have a healthy respect and admiration for excellent nicknames.
5. The obvious rebuttal is the unknowable counterfactual that perceptions of corruption would have, but for the passage of the BCRA, been even greater. The burden of proof lies elsewhere.

6. See Appendix 2.1 for details.
7. Diagnostic assessments of the summary variable—correlations with each other, correlations with ratings of who has power, and factor analyses of these measures—indicate that it is strong measure of corruption. It has the added attraction of having been asked on both of our 2016 national surveys, yielding 2,000 respondents.
8. Summary statistics on these variables are presented in Appendix 2.4. The campaign finance spending measure is a per capita estimate of statewide expenditures in a given cycle, based on data from the Campaign Finance Institute, as presented at followthemoney.org.
9. As suggested, previous studies either did not offer fully specified multivariate models of the sort we are estimating here (i.e., Persily and Lammie, 2004) or focused on a different estimation strategy (employing instrumental variables) and a different dependent variable (i.e., Rosenson, 2009).
10. The main difference is that the correlation between statewide population and perceived corruption remains positive but is no longer statistically significant at the 0.05 level. By contrast, the relationship between greater campaign finance regulation and perceived corruption remains statistically significant at the 0.01 level.
11. We measure party identification by asking about the direction of identification. We then ask identifiers about the strength of their association, while non-identifiers are asked about whether they lean closer to one side or the other. This creates a 7-point scale: strong Democrats, not so strong Democrats, leaning Democrats, independents, leaning Republicans, not so strong Republicans, strong Republicans. Following the work of Keith et al. (1991) and Petrocik (1974), we treat strong, not so strong, and leaning identifiers as partisans.
12. See Appendix 2.5 for variable descriptions and statistics.
13. The amicus brief submitted by the Committee for Economic Development (a business group) in McConnell v. FEC strongly supported the BCRA soft money ban—eliminating a means by which corporations could contribute unlimited amounts to national parties—precisely because they felt politicians engaged in "a corrupt soft money shakedown" in which corporations donate to "avoid retribution in the form of adverse governmental action on issues that directly affect solicited businesses corporate soft money." McChesney (1987) modeled this behavior and labeled the practice "rent extraction."
14. Lobbyists as a source of significant campaign contributions are probably misunderstood by most survey respondents. Lobbyists, as individuals, are limited by federal contribution limits like everybody else, but as "bundlers"—publicly disclosed facilitators of large numbers of coordinated individual contributions by others—they can serve as conduits for sometimes large amounts of campaign contributions.
15. One additional, small observation is worth offering. It does not appear that respondents distinguish between lobbyists and Super PACs. Conversely, they do seem to distinguish between these groups and campaign contributors. The notion that Americans distinguish between and amongst sources of campaign contributions is something we consider later in this project.

16. Given that contributions per year to a candidate from PACs and parties are limited to $5,000 and, in 2009, only $2,400 from individuals ($2,700 in 2016), Congress clearly erred on the side of caution in setting these limits.
17. It's doubtful that existing disclosure rules governing outside groups are fully understood by the general public; all PACS, including Super PACs must fully disclose both the sources of their funds and how they are spent. Current disclosure policy debates center on the limited disclosure rules governing social welfare organizations—more commonly referred to as 501(c)4s— which are able to fund independent expenditures without having to disclose publicly the names of donors unless their contributions were explicitly designated (earmarked) for specific independent expenditures. In 2018 the D.C. District Court in CREW v. FEC (16–259) struck down the FEC rules and required the FEC to issue new regulations broadening donor disclosure to include those who give to the organization for the purpose of influencing a federal election or give for the purpose of funding the organization's independent expenditures, whether tied to a specific candidate or not. New rules are yet to appear but, pending the issuance of new rules, the FEC offers guidance consistent with the District Court decision (see: https://www.fec.gov/updates/fec-provides-guidance-following-us-district-court-decision-crew-v-fec-316-f-supp-3d-349-ddc-2018/).
18. Every Congress sees the introduction of scores of bills seeking to reform campaign finance in one way or another. None of any consequence passes, suggesting something of a mismatch between congressional and public preferences. Most dramatically, the first bill introduced in the House in the 116th Congress—HR 1 (aka, the For the People Act of 2019)—was replete with dramatic proposals for changes to federal campaign finance law, including significant new disclosure rules—so significant that the ACLU responded with a 13-page letter decrying the proposed laws' threat to First Amendment rights—and a proposal for public funding of congressional elections; HR 1 was never destined to see the light of day, but it served as a useful prop for any number of 2020 candidates and at least one party platform. What the public fails to appreciate is that every member of Congress was elected, by definition, under existing campaign finance law; having cracked that code, there is predictably little appetite to change it.
19. Although Clinton did not mention campaign finance reform explicitly in the debates, she did call for overturning *Citizens United* in two of them, adding that she would make support for such a move a "litmus test" for any Supreme Court nominee. Another reason for her reticence might be that Trump had aggressively "used" the existing campaign finance system as a businessman, while Clinton had raked in enormous amounts of cash from dozens of special interest groups in 2008 and 2016. This point was made repeatedly by the one presidential candidate who did focus on campaign finance reform in 2016, Democrat Bernie Sanders (I-VT). We should also point out that in her convention speech Clinton did say, "and we will pass a constitutional amendment to overturn *Citizens United*!"
20. Frenzel offered this quote at a December 1997 dinner sponsored by the University of Texas at Austin's Government Department. Frenzel spoke alongside long-time

colleague J. J. "Jake" Pickle (D-TX). Perhaps his comment was more time dependent than we heretofore assumed.

21. Campaign spending figures are in the millions of dollars and are based on total statewide expenditure estimates from the Campaign Finance Institute accessed at https://www.followthemoney.org/ on June 7, 2017. Per capita estimates are based on population figures from the U.S. Census.
22. As noted, one might also object to using a state-level variable for an individual-level data set. Typically, multilevel data require the calculation of robust clustered standard errors and the estimation of a fixed effects or hierarchical model. We have, in fact, calculated robust clustered standard errors for our fixed-effects model, and the significance estimates for the effects associated with the predictor variables are diminished. The effect is not substantial, however, and the substantive interpretation of the models is not fundamentally altered.

Chapter 4

1. As noted in Chapter 3, the Court never directly asserts a linkage between campaign spending and perceptions of corruption in *Buckley*. As also noted earlier, however, campaign spending is a proxy (albeit, an imperfect one) for the total amount of money in politics and thus might plausibly be expected by those following the Court's logic to affect perceived corruption.
2. This is often ascertained by asking, "How confident are you that the federal government will do the right thing?" Gallup asks, "Now I'd like to ask you several questions about our governmental system. First, how much trust and confidence do you have in our federal government in Washington when it comes to handling [international problems/domestic problems]—a great deal, a fair amount, not very much, or none at all?"
3. The internal efficacy questions include items such as "Do you agree or disagree with the following statement: 'Sometimes politics and government seem so complicated that a person like me can't really understand what's going on'?" and "Do you agree or disagree with the following statement: 'People like me don't have any say about what the government does'?" The primary external efficacy question is "Do you agree or disagree with the following statement: 'Public officials don't care much what people like me think'?"
4. Both the absolute level of trust and the trend are corroborated by polling data from other sources. For example, according to the Pew Research Poll conducted in April 2017, only 20% of Americans trust the government in Washington to do the right thing "just about always" or "most of the time" (Pew Research, 2017).
5. The zero-order correlation coefficients between the "trust" and "crooked" items of the American National Election Studies Cumulative Survey, 1958–2016 are statistically significant.
6. Exploratory tests of the relationship between perceived corruption and trust in government reveal that using ANES data raises some serious methodological issues

(some of which are discussed in a slightly different context in this chapter). On the whole, however, the relationships suggested by 2SLS based on CCES data from 2016 are mostly consistent with those gleaned from the time-series analyses of 1952–2016 cumulative file data from the ANES.

7. In pre-tests on college undergraduate students, the zero-order correlation between our scaled measure of trust correlates and the ANES measure is about 0.35.
8. The specific variables included in the trust model are presidential and congressional job evaluations, sex, race, ethnicity, age, education, media use, partisanship, evaluations of the national economy, knowledge of campaign finance laws, state-level average statewide per capita campaign expenditure by candidates and committees, and statewide population (see Appendix 2.4 for summary statistics on the predictor variables).
9. Given the use of state-level spending and population data, we performed an additional analysis adding state fixed effects and then calculated robust clustered standard errors for the predictor variables. As expected, the underlying relationships were unaffected, but their magnitudes were slightly diminished. Most notably, the positive correlation between statewide campaign spending and decreased trust is statistically significant at the 0.05 (but not the 0.01) level.
10. The main test we rely on is the Hausman test (or Durbin-Wu-Hausman test), an augmented regression test for endogeneity. The results show that the OLS residuals are highly correlated with the disturbance term, thus prompting us to explore a 2SLS solution.
11. As a statistical matter, the 2SLS model suggests that regulation does *not* explain trust directly. But our primary interest here is on testing the specific claim by the Court that regulation affects trust *indirectly* (by positively influencing perceived corruption).

Chapter 5

1. As noted in Chapters 3 and 4, another methodological issue facing our study is that estimating the effects of campaign spending and regulatory environments on individuals requires mixing state- and individual-level data. This requires an estimation strategy that accounts for the hierarchical nature of the data, otherwise the clustering of responses at the state level can produce biased estimates of effects and (more importantly) an overstatement of statistical significance. As with our previous analyses, we re-estimated all models in this chapter with clustered standard errors as a check on the straightforward least squares models. No substantive differences occurred, although the statistical significance of many relationships decreased. Given the absence of any meaningful differences, we report the more traditional least squares standard errors.
2. Political party committees include the Republican National Committee (RNC), the Democratic National Committee (DNC), the National Republican Senate Committee (NRSC), the Democratic Senate Campaign Committee (DSCC), the National Republican Congressional Committee (NRCC), and the Democratic Congressional Campaign Committee (DCCC).

3. This includes ten retrospective assessments of participation over the past four years: Have you given money to a candidate, campaign, or party; attended a political rally or meeting; participated in a political rally or protest; discussed politics with friends or family; contacted elected representatives; contacted newspaper or magazine editors for political causes; signed a petition; voted in a primary election; volunteered for a political campaign; or other? The measure also includes four retrospective assessments of participation over the past year: Have you attended a local meeting; put up a political sign; worked for a candidate or campaign; donated money to a candidate?
4. Full descriptions and summary statistics for key dependent and independent variables from the 2016 and 2009 survey data sets are offered in Appendices 2.4 and 2.5, respectively.
5. Bear in mind, our summary measure of political participation excludes voting.
6. See Appendix 2.5 for descriptions and summary statistics for key 2009 variables. Note that we refer to the participation and turnout models estimated from our 2009 survey as "2008 models" in this chapter because they ask about behavior in the 2008 election.
7. Besides missing governmental trust, the 2009 survey did not include the sort of exhaustive battery of items on campaign finance knowledge, nor did it have the same corruption questions.
8. The inclusion of state-level measures induces us to once again re-estimate the 2008 models with robust clustered standard errors, as a check on the more traditional OLS and logistic regression models. In both cases, the RCSEs somewhat reduce the estimated significance of the attendant relationships but produce no meaningful substantive differences in the model. We therefore report the coefficients and standard errors.
9. See Table 5.4 for a summary of key variable effects across time.
10. Items on religious affiliation, church attendance, and union membership were not asked in the 2009 instrument.

Chapter 6

1. The informational role of campaign finance information has been long featured in theoretical models (Ingberman, 1992; Coate, 2012; Ashworth, 2006). Researchers have also demonstrated the ability to recover the ideological positions of candidates using campaign contribution information (McCarty and Poole, 1998; Bonica, 2013), but these impressive results do not speak to the effect such information has on voter behavior.
2. The negative manifestation of this is "guilt by association." Despite that political consultants commonly attempt to prod this in campaigns (e.g., Republican efforts to tie Barack Obama to Reverend Jeremiah Wright and William Ayers in 2008, and Democratic efforts to tie Mitt Romney to Senator Larry Craig in 2012), there is surprisingly little systematic empirical evidence that voters downgrade candidates based on their less well-regarded associates.

3. Although Chris Jones is an androgynous name, the candidate is identified as "he" in the news story.
4. The story was based on an actual Associated Press report, Kimberly Hefling, "Some Incumbent Senators Seem to Get No Respect," *USA Today*, July 26, 2009, http://www.usatoday.com/news/washington/2009-07-25-senators-primarychallenge_N.htm.
5. When examining treatment effects by party identification, cell sizes average approximately thirty-five cases.
6. Indeed, we use a scaled measure of perceived corruption as an independent variable in predicting vote choice in our multivariate models.
7. McCutcheon v. Federal Election Commission, 572 U.S. 185 (2014) overturned aggregate contribution limits but left in place limits on contributions to individual candidates established under the 2002 BCRA.
8. Because of federal campaign contribution limits, neither an individual nor a PAC can make either a $50K or a $20M contribution to a candidate in a given election cycle. Multiple donors from a particular industry, however, can coordinate contributions to a PAC or they can "bundle" their individual contributions to signal a common (e.g., industry) affiliation. As with any experiment, there is always the question of external validity. Our treatment consists of substantial contributions from a narrow range of specific sources, contributions that may strike the informed observer as rare. There is, however, ample evidence—both in the literature and in our own data—that voters know next to nothing about the particulars of campaign contributions and that news media greatly and systematically exaggerate the magnitude of campaign contributions (see, e.g., Ansolabehere, Snowberg, and Snyder, 2005). We expand on how generalizable our study is later on.
9. These allow us to ascertain the impact of receiving contributions from well-regarded versus noxious groups. Of course, contributions from corporations cannot come directly from their treasuries, rather they must come from affiliated political action committees, through which no corporate money can flow. Note also that we are not directly measuring perceived corruption. Rather, we gauge whether information about "extreme" campaign contributions affects voters.
10. The most notable example is the saga of the solar energy company Solyndra. A report from the Inspector General's office, after more than four years of investigation, concluded that Solyndra officials used inaccurate information to mislead the Department of Energy in its application for a $535 million loan guarantee. The report also found that there were shortcomings in the Department of Energy's process of managing and approving the loan guarantee to Solyndra.
11. Although we do not directly measure mobilization with a turnout variable, we assume that greater enthusiasm by in-partisans toward their candidate correlates with a higher turnout probability.
12. This effect, however, is only for the Democratic candidate—when Republican Jones gets $20M in contributions from green energy companies, he does about the same as in the $50K condition.

13. The other example is when a Republican candidate received big money from friends and acquaintances or trial lawyers—his support increased but the shift was not statistically significant at the 0.10 level.
14. These results reflect expressed rather than revealed preferences. Furthermore, it is at least possible that Democrats are relatively willing to state that they would punish their own candidates for taking money from undesirable sources, but these voters may not actually follow through on that threat when casting their actual ballot.
15. The differences in support for green energy versus other funding sources are statistically significant ($p < 0.01$).
16. More specifically, we offer controls for the respondent's party identification (Republican, independent, and Democrat), age, education, income, union household status (2009 only), gender, and general political knowledge.
17. We experimented with different interaction terms and models. In the end, we decided that simple multiplicative interaction term in which contribution source information was turned "on" or "off" based on the candidate's party was the best way to estimate the underlying relationship.
18. The interaction coefficients should be judged against the baseline category: Jones is an independent candidate who has received $50K from friends and acquaintances. For the three-way interaction term, the baseline category is slightly different: it would be a non-Democratic candidate who has received $50K from the tobacco industry or friends and acquaintances.
19. We did not ask a union household item in the 2013 survey, so it is not included in the 2013 model.

Chapter 7

1. Perhaps the most over-the-top reaction came from MSNBC commentator Keith Olbermann on the night of the decision, when he declared *Citizens United* to have overtaken Dred Scott v. Sandford (1857) as the worst Supreme Court decision in U.S. history; Olbermann's televised diatribe against the Court's opinion carried on for more than eleven minutes.
2. The television audience was treated to a view of Justice Samuel Alito seemingly mouthing the words "not true," in likely response to the president's reference to a century of law having been overturned. The president was, in fact, a bit off on his history; corporate (and union) independent expenditures, the political money liberated by *Citizens United*, were first banned in the 1947 Taft-Hartley Act.
3. The campaign finance, as well as others, aspect of the 2016 elections were anomalous in ways that political scientists are only just beginning to understand, notably including breakdowns in relationships between campaign spending and votes received (Magleby, 2019). Nothing in the public opinion record, however, suggests any lessening of perceived corruption resulting from questions raised by the 2016 election.
4. LaRaja (2008) argues that substantive changes to campaign finance laws result primarily from inter- and intra-party conflicts arising from emergent fundraising disparities.

5. See, Frank v. Walker (2014) and Veasey v. Abbott, No. 14–41127 (5th Cir. 2016).
6. Vieth v. Jubelirer (02–1580) 541 U.S. 267 (2004) 241 F. Supp. 2d 478, affirmed.
7. Notable among those calling for the Court to broaden its view is Robert Post, former dean of the Yale Law School, who argues for enhanced electoral integrity as the new standard by which campaign finance limits should be judged constitutional (Post, 2014).

Appendix 2.4

1. Data on statewide corporate regulatory environment come from the National Council on State Legislatures (NCSL).
2. Data on campaign spending come from the Federal Election Commission (FEC).

Appendix 2.5

1. Data on statewide corporate regulatory environment come from the National Council on State Legislatures (NCSL).
2. Data on campaign spending come from the Federal Election Commission (FEC).

Court Cases Cited

Arizona Free Enterprise Club v. Bennett, 564 U.S. 721 (2011)
Austin v. Michigan Chamber of Commerce, 494 U.S. 652 (1990)
Brown v. Board of Education of Topeka, 347 U.S. 483 (1954)
Buckley vs. Valeo, 424 U.S. 1 (1976)
Citizens United v. Federal Election Commission, 558 U.S. 310 (2010)
CREW v. FEC, No.16–259 (2018)
CSC v. Letter Carriers, 413 U.S. 548 (1973)
Dred Scott v. Sandford, 60 U.S. 393 (1857)
FEC v. Wisconsin Right to Life, 551 U.S. 449 (2007)
Frank v. Walker, 768 F.3d 744 (7th Cir. 2014)
Gill v. Whitford, No. 16–1161 (2017)
Holmes v. Federal Election Commission, 17–1297 (2017)
Jacobellis v. Ohio, 378 U.S. 184 (1964)
McConnell v. Federal Election Commission, 540 U.S. 93 (2003)
McCutcheon v. Federal Election Commission, 572 U.S. 185 (2014)
McDonnell v. United States, 136 S. Ct. 2355 (2016)
Muller v. Oregon, 208 U.S. 412 (1908)
NAACP v. Alabama, 357 U.S. 449 (1958)
Nixon v. Shrink Missouri Government PAC, 528 U.S. 377 (1999)
Pipefitters. v. United States, 407 U.S. 385 (1972)
Randall v. Sorrell, 548 U.S. 230 (2006)
Shrink Missouri v. Adams, 5 F. Supp. 2d 734 (E.D. Mo. 1998)
SpeechNow.org v. Federal Election Commission, No. 08–5223 (2010)
Thompson v. Hebdon, No. 19–122 (2019)
United States v. CIO, 335 U.S. 106 (1948)
Veasey v. Abbott, No. 14–41127 (5th Cir. 2016)
Vieth v. Jubelirer, 541 U.S. 267 (2004)
Zimmerman v. Austin, No. 16–51366 (5th Cir. 2018)

References

Abramowitz, Alan. (1988). "Explaining Senate Election Outcomes." *American Political Science Review* 82(2): 385–403.

Abramson, Paul R., and Ada W. Finifter. (1981). "On the Meaning of Political Trust: New Evidence from Items Introduced in 1978." *American Journal of Political Science* 25: 297–307.

Alexander, Mark C. (2005). "Let Them Do Their Jobs: The Compelling Government Interest in Protecting the Time of Candidates and Elected Officials." *Loyola University Chicago Law Journal* 37(4): 669–722.

Allard, Nicholas W. (2016). "A Landmark Decision Turns Forty: A Conversation on *Buckley v. Valeo*." *Journal of Law and Policy* 25(1): 11–30.

Alt, James E., and David Dreyer Lassen. (2003). "The Political Economy of Institutions and Corruption in American States." *Journal of Theoretical Politics* 15(3): 341–65.

The American National Election Studies. (2020). These materials are based on work supported by the National Science Foundation under grant numbers SES 1444721, 2014–2017, the University of Michigan, and Stanford University (www.electionstudies.org).

Anderson, Christopher J., and Yuliya V. Tverdova. (2003). "Corruption, Political Allegiances, and Attitudes toward Government in Contemporary Democracies." *American Journal of Political Science* 47(1): 91–109.

Annenberg Civics Knowledge Survey. (2017). "Americans Are Poorly Informed about Basic Constitutional Decisions." Annenberg School of Public Policy. https://www.annenbergpublicpolicycenter.org/americans-are-poorly-informed-about-basic-constitutional-provisions/.

Ansolabehere, Stephen, and Alan Gerber. (1994). "The Mismeasure of Campaign Spending: Evidence from the 1990 U.S. House Elections." *Journal of Politics* 56(4): 1106–18.

Ansolabehere, Stephen, and Shanto Iyengar. (1995). *Going Negative: How Political Advertisements Shrink and Polarize the Electorate*. New York, NY: Free Press.

Ansolabehere, Stephen, Erik C. Snowberg, and James M. Snyder. (2005). "Unrepresentative Information: The Case of Newspaper Reporting on Campaign Finance." *Public Opinion Quarterly* 69(2): 213–31.

Ansolabehere Stephen, James M. Snyder, and Eric C. Snowberg. (2005). "Statistical Bias in Newspaper Reporting: The Case of Campaign Finance." *Public Opinion Quarterly* 69(2): 213–31.

Asher, Herb. (2016). *Polling and the Public: What Every Citizen Should Know*. 9th ed. Washington, DC: Congressional Quarterly Press.

Ashworth, Scott. (2006). "Campaign Finance and Voter Welfare with Entrenched Incumbents." *American Political Science Review* 100(1): 55–68.

The Associated Press. (2001). *The Freedom Forum Survey*.

Bardes, Barbara A., and Robert W. Oldendick. (2016). *Public Opinion: Measuring the American Mind*. 5th ed. Plymouth, UK: Rowman and Littlefield.

Barnes, Samuel H., and Max Kaase. (1979). *Political Action: Mass Participation in Five Western Societies*. Beverly Hills, CA/London: Sage.

Berelson, Bernard, Paul Lazarsfeld, and William McPhee. (1954). *Voting: A Study of Opinion Formation in a Presidential Campaign*. Chicago, IL: University of Chicago Press.

BeVier, Lillian R. (1994). "Campaign Finance Reform: Specious Arguments, Intractable Dilemmas." *Columbia Law Review* 94(4): 1258–80.

Bishop, Yvonne M. M., Stephen E. Fienberg, and Paul W. Holland. (1975). *Discrete Multivariate Analysis: Theory and Practice*. Cambridge, MA: MIT Press.

Blais, André. (2006). "What Affects Voter Turnout?" *Annual Review of Political Science* 9(1): 111–25.

Blass, Abby, Brian Roberts, and Daron Shaw. (2012). "Corruption, Political Participation, and Appetite for Reform: Americans' Assessment of the Role of Money in Politics." *Election Law Journal* 11(4): 380–98.

Bonica, Adam. (2013). "Ideology and Interests in the Political Marketplace." *American Journal of Political Science* 57(2): 294–311.

Bonica, Adam. (2014). "Mapping the Ideological Marketplace." *American Journal of Political Science* 58(2): 367–86.

Bowler, Shaun, and Todd Donovan. (2015). "Campaign Money, Congress, and Perceptions of Corruption." *American Politics Research* 44(2): 272–95.

Bowler, Shaun, and Gary M. Segura. (2011). *The Future is Ours: Minority Politics, Political Behavior, and the Multiracial Era of American Politics*. Washington, D.C. Congressional Quarterly Press.

Boylan, Richard T., and Cheryl X. Long. (2003). "Measuring Public Corruption in the American States: A Survey of State House Reporters." *State Politics & Policy Quarterly* 3(4): 420–38.

Brewer, Paul R., Jennifer L. Lambe, and Philip Edward Jones. (2017). "The Foundations of U.S. Public Opinion about Campaign Finance in the Post-*Citizens United* Era." *Election Law Journal* 16(1): 183–95.

Brewer, Scott. (1998). "Scientific Expert Testimony and Intellectual Due Process." *Yale Law Review* 107: 1535–53.

Bronars, Stephen G., and John R. Lott, Jr. (1997). "Do Campaign Donations Alter How a Politician Votes? Or, Do Donors Support Candidates Who Value the Same Things That They Do?" *Journal of Law and Economics* 40(2): 317–50.

Burke, Thomas F. (1997). "The Concept of Corruption in Campaign Finance Law." *Constitutional Commentary* 14(1): 127–49.

Campbell, Angus, Philip E. Converse, Warren E. Miller, and Donald E. Stokes. (1960). *The American Voter*. Chicago, IL: University of Chicago Press.

Chang, Eric CC, and Yun-han Chu. (2006). "Corruption and Trust: Exceptionalism in Asian Democracies?" *Journal of Politics* 68(2): 259–71.

Chanley, Virginia A., Thomas J. Rudolph, and Wendy M. Rahn. (2000). "The Origins and Consequences of Public Trust in Government: A Time Series Analysis." *Public Opinion Quarterly* 64(3): 239–56.

Citrin, Jack. (1974). "Comment: The Political Relevance of Trust in Government." *American Political Science Review* 68(3): 973–88.

Citrin, Jack, and Donald Philip Green. (1986). "Presidential Leadership and the Resurgence of Trust in Government." *British Journal of Political Science* 16(4): 431–53.

Coates, John C., IV. (2012). "Corporate Politics, Governance, and Value Before and after *Citizens United*." *Journal of Empirical Legal Studies* 9(4): 657–96.

Coleman, John J., and Paul F. Manna. (2000). "Congressional Campaign Spending and the Quality of Democracy." *Journal of Politics* 62(3): 757–89.

The Cooperative Congressional Election Study. (2012). *University of Texas Modules for the Cooperative Congressional Election Study.*

The Cooperative Congressional Election Study. (2016). *University of Texas Modules for the Cooperative Congressional Election Study.*

Cordis, Adriana, and Jeff Milyo. (2013). "Do State Campaign Finance Reforms Reduce Public Corruption?" Working Paper 13–09. Mercatus Center, George Mason University.

Corrado, Anthony, Thomas E. Mann, and Trevor Potter, eds. (2003). *Inside the Campaign Finance Battle: Court Testimony on the New Reforms.* Washington DC: Brookings Institution Press.

Craig, Stephen C., Richard G. Niemi, and Glenn E. Silver. (1990). "Political Efficacy and Trust: A Report on the NES Pilot Study Items." *Political Behavior* 12(3): 289–314.

Davis, Kenneth Culp. (1942). "An Approach to Problems of Evidence in the Administrative Process." *Harvard Law Review* 55(3): 364–425.

Delli Carpini, Michael X., and Scott Keeter. (1996). *What Americans Know about Politics and Why It Matters.* New Haven, CT: Yale University Press.

Deming, W. Edwards, and Frederick F. Stephan. (1940). "On Least Square Adjustment of a Frequency Table When the Expected Marginal Totals Are Known." *Annals of Mathematical Statistics* 11(4): 427–44.

Dowling, Conor M., and Michael G. Miller. (2014). *Super PAC!: Money, Elections, and Voters after Citizens United.* New York, NY: Routledge.

Downs, Anthony. (1957). "An Economic Theory of Political Action in a Democracy." *Journal of Political Economy* 65(2): 135–50.

Easton, David, and Jack Dennis. (1967). "The Child's Acquisition of Regime Norms: Political Efficacy." *American Political Science Review* 61(1): 25–38.

Enelow, James, and Melvin J. Hinich. (1984). *The Spatial Theory of Voting: An Introduction.* Cambridge University Press.

Epley, Nicholas, and David Dunning. (2000). "Feeling 'Holier than Thou': Are Self-Serving Assessments Produced by Errors in Self- or Social Prediction?" *Journal of Personality and Social Psychology* 79(6): 861–75.

Faigman, David L. (1989). "To Have and Have Not: Assessing the Value of Social Science to the Law as Science and Policy." *Emory Law Journal* 38: 1005–96.

Faigman, David L. (1991). "'Normative Constitutional Fact-Finding': Exploring the Empirical Component of Constitutional Interpretation." *University of Pennsylvania Law Review* 139(3): 541–613.

Fallon Jr, Richard H. (2006). "Strict Judicial Scrutiny." *UCLA Law Review* 54: 1267–337.

Finkel, Steven E. (1987). "The Effects of Participation on Political Efficacy and Political Support: Evidence from a West German Panel." *Journal of Politics* 49(2): 441–64.

Finkel, Steven E., and John G. Geer. (1998). "A Spot Check: Casting Doubt on the Demobilizing Effect of Attack Advertising." *American Journal of Political Science* 42(2): 573–95.

Freedman, Paul, Michael Franz, and Kenneth Goldstein. (2004). "Campaign Advertising and Democratic Citizenship." *American Journal of Political Science* 48(4): 723–41.

Frendreis, John P., and Richard W. Waterman. (1985). "PAC Contributions and Legislative Behavior: Senate Voting on Trucking Deregulation." *Social Science Quarterly* 66(2): 401–12.

Fuller, Lon L. (1934). "American Legal Realism." *University of Pennsylvania Law Review and American Law Register* 82(5): 429–62.

Gadarian, Shana Kushner, and Bethany Albertson. (2014). "Anxiety, Immigration, and the Search for Information." *Political Psychology* 35(2): 133–64.

Gold, Matea, and Anu Narayanswamy. (2016). "The New Gilded Age: Close to Half of All Super PAC Money Comes From 50 Donors." April 15, 2016. https://www.washingtonpost.com/politics/the-new-gilded-age-close-to-half-of-all-super-pac-money-comes-from-50-donors/2016/04/15/63dc363c-01b4-11e6-9d36-33d198ea26c5_story.html.

Green, Donald Philip, and Jonathan S. Krasno. (1988). "Salvation for the Spendthrift Incumbent: Reestimating the Effects of Campaign Spending in House Elections." *American Journal of Political Science* 32(4): 884–907.

Hall, Richard L., and Frank W. Wayman. (1990). "Buying Time: Moneyed Interests and the Mobilization of Bias in Congressional Committees." *American Political Science Review* 84(3): 797–820.

Hasen, Richard L. (2011a). "*Citizens United* and the Illusion of Coherence." *Michigan Law Review* 109(4): 581–623.

Hasen, Richard L. (2011b). "The Nine Lives of *Buckley v. Valeo*." In *First Amendment Stories*, edited by Richard W. Garnett and Andrew Koppelman. New York, NY: Foundation Press.

Hasen, Richard L. (2016). *Plutocrats United: Campaign Money, the Supreme Court, and the Distortion of American Elections*. New Haven, CT: Yale University Press.

Hasen, Richard L. (2018). *The Justice of Contradictions: Antonin Scalia and the Politics of Disruption*. New Haven, CT: Yale University Press.

Hayes, Danny. (2006). "Beyond the Horse Race: The Content and Consequence of Issue News in American Elections." Doctoral Dissertation, the University of Texas at Austin.

Heard, Alexander. (1956). *Money in Politics*. New York, NY: Public Affairs Committee.

Heard, Alexander. (1960). *The Costs of Democracy*. Chapel Hill: University of North Carolina Press.

Hellman, Deborah, and David Schultz. (2016). "Special Issue on Campaign Finance." *University of Pennsylvania Law Review Online* 164: 207–93.

Herrnson, Paul S. (2009). "The Roles of Party Organizations, Party-Connected Committees, and Party Allies in Elections." *Journal of Politics* 71(4): 1207–24.

Hetherington, Marc J. (1998). "The Political Relevance of Political Trust." *American Political Science Review* 92(4): 791–808.

Hetherington, Marc J. (1999). "The Effect of Political Trust on the Presidential Vote, 1968–96." *American Political Science Review* 93(2): 311–26.

Hetherington, Marc J. (2006). *Why Trust Matters: Declining Political Trust and the Demise of Political Liberalism*. Princeton, NJ: Princeton University Press.

Hetherington, Marc J., and Jason A. Husser. (2012). "How Trust Matters: The Changing Political Relevance of Political Trust." *American Journal of Political Science* 56(2): 312–25.

Huber, Gregory A., and Kevin Arceneaux. (2007). "Identifying the Persuasive Effects of Presidential Advertising." *American Journal of Political Science* 51(4): 957–77.

Imai, Kosuke. (2005). "Do Get-Out-the-Vote Calls Reduce Turnout? The Importance of Statistical Methods for Field Experiments." *American Political Science Review* 99(2): 283–300.

Ingberman, Daniel E. (1992). "Incumbent Reputations and Ideological Campaign Contributions in Spatial Competition." *Mathematical and Computer Modelling* 16(8): 147–69.

Issacharoff, Samuel. (2010). "On Political Corruption." *Harvard Law Review* 124: 118–42.

Jacobson, Gary C. (1978). "The Effects of Campaign Spending in Congressional Elections." *American Political Science Review* 72(2): 467–91.

Johnston, Michael. (1983). "Corruption and Political Culture in America: An Empirical Perspective." *Publius: The Journal of Federalism* 13(1): 19–39.

Keith, Bruce E., David B. Magelby, Candice J. Nelson, Elizabeth Orr, and Mark C. Westlye. (1991). *The Myth of the Independent Voter*. Berkeley: University of California Press.

Kelly, Kristin J. (2016). "Political Quid Pro Quo and the Impact of Perceptions of Corruption on Democratic Behavior." *Election Law Journal* 15(2): 160–74.

Klumpp, Tilman, Hugo M. Mialon, and Michael A. Williams. (2016). "The Business of American Democracy: *Citizens United*, Independent Spending, and Elections." *Journal of Law and Economics* 59(1): 1–43.

Kostadinova, Tatiana. (2009). "Abstain or Rebel: Corruption Perceptions and Voting in East European Elections." *Politics and Policy* 37(4): 691–714.

Kraus, Jeffrey. (2006). "Campaign Finance Reform Reconsidered: New York City's Public Finance Program after Fifteen Years." *The Forum* 3(4):.

La Pierre, D. Bruce. (2000). "Campaign Contribution Limits: Pandering to Public Fears about 'Big Money' and Protecting Incumbents." *Administrative Law Review* 52(2): 687–741.

La Raja, Raymond J. (2008). *Small Change: Money, Political Parties, and Campaign Finance Reform*. Ann Arbor: University of Michigan Press.

La Raja, Raymond J., and Brian F. Schaffner. (2014). "The Effects of Campaign Finance Spending Bans on Electoral Outcomes: Evidence from the States about the Potential Impact of *Citizens United* v. *FEC*." *Electoral Studies* 33: 102–14.

Lau, Richard R., Lee Sigelman, Caroline Heldman, and Paul Babbitt. (1999). "The Effects of Negative Political Advertisements: A Meta-Analytic Assessment." *American Political Science Review* 93(4): 851–75.

Lee, Jae Kook, Jihyang Choi, Chensoo Kim, and Yonghwan Kim. (2014). "Social Media, Network Heterogeneity, and Opinion Polarization." *Journal of Communication* 64(4): 702–22.

Leighley, Jan E., and Jonathan Nagler. (2013). *Who Votes Now?: Demographics, Issues, Inequality, and Turnout in the United States*. Princeton, NJ: Princeton University Press.

Levitt, Steven D. (1994). "Using Repeat Challengers to Estimate the Effect of Campaign Spending on Election Outcomes in the U.S. House." *Journal of Political Economy* 102(4): 777–98.

Lewis-Beck, Michael S., Helmut Norpoth, William G. Jacoby, and Herbert F. Weisberg. (2008). *The American Voter Revisited*. Ann Arbor: University of Michigan Press.

Lipset, Seymore M., and William Schneider. (1983). "The Decline of Confidence in American Institutions." *Political Science Quarterly* 98(3): 379–402.

Lodge, Milton, Marco R. Steenbergen, and Shawn Brau. (1995). "The Responsive Voter: Campaign Information and the Dynamics of Candidate Evaluation." *American Political Science Review* 89(2): 309–26.

Lowenstein, Daniel Hays. (1989). "On Campaign Finance Reform: The Root of All Evil Is Deeply Rooted." *Hofstra Law Review* 18(2): 301–67.

Lupia, Arthur. (1994). "Shortcuts versus Encyclopedias: Information and Voting Behavior in California Insurance Reform Elections." *American Political Science Review* 88(1): 63–76.

Magleby, David B., ed. (2019). *Financing the 2016 Elections*. Washington, DC: Brookings Institution.

McCann, James A., and Jorge I. Dominguez. (1998). "Mexicans React to Electoral Fraud and Political Corruption: An Assessment of Public Opinion and Voting Behavior." *Electoral Studies* 17(4): 483–503.

McCarty, Nolan M., and Keith T Poole. (1998). "An Empirical Spatial Model of Congressional Campaigns." *Political Analysis* 7(1): 1–30.

McChesney, Fred S. (1987). "Rent Extraction and Rent Creation in the Economic Theory of Regulation." *Journal of Legal Studies* 16(1): 101–18.

McChesney, Fred S. (1997). *Money for Nothing: Politicians, Rent Extraction and Political Extortion*. Cambridge, MA: Harvard University Press.

McDonald, Michael. (2020). *U.S. Election Project*. http://www.electproject.org/

Mellman, Mark, and Richard Wirthlin. (2003). "Public Views of Party Soft Money." In *Inside the Campaign Finance Battle*, eds. Anthony Corrado, Thomas E. Mann, and Trevor Potter. Washington, DC: Brookings Institution Press.

Mensah, Yaw M. (2014). "An Analysis of the Effect of Culture and Religion on Perceived Corruption in a Global Context." *Journal of Business Ethics* 121(2): 255–82.

Milbrath, Lester W. (1965). *Political Participation: How and Why Do People Get Involved in Politics?* Chicago, IL: Rand McNally College.

Miller, Arthur H. (1974). "Political Issues and Trust in Government: 1964–1970." *American Political Science Review* 68(3): 951–72.

Miller, Kenneth. (2017). "Cooperative Media Spending in Senate Campaigns Post–*Citizens United*." *The Forum* 15(2): 269–89.

Milyo, Jeffrey, David M. Primo, and Matthew J. Jacobsmeier. (2011). "Does Public Financing of State Election Campaigns Increase Voter Turnout?" In *Public Financing in American Elections*, edited by Costas Panagopoulos. Philadelphia, PA: Temple University Press.

Mishler, William, and Richard Rose. (2001). "What Are the Origins of Political Trust? Testing Institutional and Cultural Theories in Post-Communist Societies." *Comparative Political Studies* 34(1): 30–62.

Mody, Sanjay. (2002). "Brown Footnote Eleven in Historical Context: Social Science and the Supreme Court's Quest for Legitimacy." *Stanford Law Review* 54(4): 793–829.

Monahan, John, and Laurens Walker. (1986). "Social Authority: Obtaining, Evaluating, and Establishing Social Science in Law." *University of Pennsylvania Law Review* 134(3): 477–517.

Montinola, Gabriella R., and Robert W. Jackman. (2002). "Sources of Corruption: A Cross-Country Study." *British Journal of Political Science* 32(1): 147–70.

Morris, Stephen D., and Joseph L. Klesner. (2010). "Corruption and Trust: Theoretical Considerations and Evidence from Mexico." *Comparative Political Studies* 43(10): 1258–85.

Mutch, Robert E. (1988). *Campaigns, Congress, and the Courts: The Making of Federal Campaign Finance Law*. New York, NY: Praeger.

NBC/Wall Street Journal. (2016). *May 2016 U.S. National Survey*.

Newsweek. (2011). *American Citizenship Survey*. As cited in Andrew Romano, "How Ignorant are Americans?" (March 20, 2011). https://www.newsweek.com/how-ignorant-are-americans-66053

Olsson, Sofia. (2014). "Corruption and Political Participation: A Multilevel Analysis." Working Paper Series 12th ser.: 1-53. Quality of Government Institute, University of Gothenburg.

Overacker, Louise. (1932). *Money in Elections*. New York, NY: Macmillan.

Persily, Nathaniel, and Kelli Lammie. (2004). "Perceptions of Corruption and Campaign Finance: When Public Opinion Determines Constitutional Law." *University of Pennsylvania Law Review* 153(1): 119–80.

Peters, John G., and Susan Welch. (1980). "The Effects of Charges of Corruption on Voting Behavior in Congressional Elections." *American Political Science Review* 74(3): 697–708.

Petrocik, John R. (1974). "An Analysis of the Intransitivities in the Index of Party Identification." *Political Methodology* 1: 13–47.

Petrocik, John R. (1996). "Issue Ownership in Presidential Elections with a 1980 Case Study." *American Journal of Political Science* 40(3): 825–50.

Pew Research. (2017). "Public Trust in Government, 1958–2017." http://www.people-press.org/2017/05/03/public-trust-in-government-1958-2017/.

Piven, Francis Fox, and Richard A. Cloward. (2000). *Why Americans Still Don't Vote: And Why Politicians Want It That Way*. Boston, MA: Beacon Press.

Polsby, Daniel D. (1976). "*Buckley v. Valeo*: The Special Nature of Political Speech." *Supreme Court Review* 1976: 1–43.

Popkin, Samuel L. (1991). *The Reasoning Voter*. Chicago, IL: University of Chicago Press.

Post, Robert C. (2014). *Citizens Divided: Campaign Finance Reform and the Constitution*. Cambridge, MA: Harvard University Press.

Primo, David M. (2002). "Public Opinion and Campaign Finance: Reformers versus Reality." *The Independent Review* 7(2): 207–19.

Primo, David M. (2003). "Campaign Contributions, the Appearance of Corruption, and Trust in Government." In *Inside the Campaign Finance Battle*, edited by Anthony Corrado, Thomas E. Mann, and Trevor Potter. Washington, DC: Brookings Institution Press.

Primo, David M., and Jeffery Milyo. (2006). "Campaign Finance Laws and Political Efficacy: Evidence from the States." *Election Law Journal* 5(1): 23–39.

Primo, David, and Jeffrey Milyo. 2020. *Campaign Finance and American Democracy: What the Public Really Thinks and Why It Matters*. Chicago: Chicago University Press.

Redlawsk, David P., Andrew J. W. Civettini, and Karen M. Emmerson. (2010). "The Affective Tipping Point: Do Motivated Reasoners Ever 'Get It'?" *Political Psychology* 31(4): 563–93.

Rose-Ackerman, Susan. (1999). *Corruption and Government: Causes, Consequences and Reform*. Cambridge: Cambridge University Press.

Rosenson, Beth Ann. (2009). "The Effect of Political Reform Measures on Perceptions of Corruption." *Election Law Journal* 8(1): 31–46.

Rosenstone, Steven J., and John Mark Hansen. (1993). *Mobilization, Participation, and Democracy in America*. New York, NY: Macmillan.

Samaha, Adam M. (2012). "Regulation for the Sake of Appearance." *Harvard Law Review.* 125(7): 1563–638.

Sances, Michael W. (2013). "Is Money in Politics Harming Trust in Government? Evidence from Two Survey Experiments." *Election Law Journal* 12(1): 53–73.

Samples, John. (2008). *The Fallacy of Campaign Finance Reform.* Chicago, IL: University of Chicago Press.

Shapiro, Robert. (2003). "Public Attitudes toward Campaign Finance Practice and Reform." In *Inside the Campaign Finance Battle*, edited by Anthony Corrado, Thomas E. Mann, and Trevor Potter. Washington, DC: Brookings Institution Press.

Shaw, Daron R., and Brian D. Roberts. (2009). *University of Texas Money and Politics Survey.*

Shaw, Daron R., and Brian D. Roberts. (2013). *University of Texas Money and Politics Survey.*

Siegel, Stephen A. (2006). "The Origin of the Compelling State Interest Test and Strict Scrutiny." *American Journal of Legal History* 48(4): 355–407.

Silver, Brian D., Barbara A. Anderson, and Paul R. Abramson. (1986). "Who Overreports Voting?" *American Political Science Review* 80(2): 613–24.

Simpser, Alberto. (2005). "Making Votes Not Count: Strategic Incentives for Electoral Corruption." Doctoral Dissertation, Stanford University.

Smith, Bradley A. (2009). *Unfree Speech: The Folly of Campaign Finance Reform.* Princeton, NJ: Princeton University Press.

Snyder, Mark. (1974). "Self-Monitoring of Expressive Behavior." *Journal of Personality and Social Psychology* 30(4): 526–37.

Stockemer, Daniel. (2013). "Corruption and Turnout in Presidential Elections—A Macro-Level Quantitative Analysis." *Politics and Policy* 41(2): 191–214.

Stockemer, Daniel, and Patricia Calca. (2012). "Presidentialism and Voter Turnout in Legislative Elections." *Parliamentary Affairs* 67(3): 561–83.

Stockemer, Daniel, Bernadette LaMontagne, and Lyle Scruggs. (2013). "Bribes and Ballots: The Impact of Corruption on Voter Turnout in Democracies." *International Political Science Review* 34(1): 74–90.

Stratmann, Thomas. (1991). "What Do Campaign Contributions Buy? Deciphering Causal Effects of Money and Votes." *Southern Economic Journal* 57(3): 606–620.

Strauss, David A. (2016). "The Equality Taboo." *University of Chicago Legal Forum*, vol. 2015, article 15.

Sullivan, Kathleen M. (1996). "Political Money and Freedom of Speech." *UC Davis Law Review* 30: 663–90.

Taber, Charles S., and Lodge, Milton. (2006). "Motivated Skepticism in the Evaluation of Political Beliefs." *Political Science* 50(3): 755–769.

Tocqueville, Alexis de. (1838). *Democracy in America.* New York: G. Dearborn & Co.

Tversky, Amos, and Daniel Kahneman. (1974). "Judgment under Uncertainty: Heuristics and Biases." *Science* 185(4157): 1124–31.

Uslaner, Eric M. (2001). "Corruption, Inequality and the Rule of Law: The Bulging Pocket Makes the Easy Life." In *The Handbook on Social Capital,* edited by Gert Tinggaard-Svendsen and Gunnar Lind Haase Svendsen. London: Edward Elgar.

Verba, Sidney, and Norman H. Nie. (1972). *Participation in America.* New York, NY: Harper & Row.

Verba, Sidney, Kay Lehman Schlozman, and Henry E. Brady. (1995). *Voice and Equality: Civic Voluntarism in American Politics*. Cambridge, MA/London: Harvard University Press.

Warren, Mark E. (2013) . "The Meaning of Corruption in Democracies." In *The Routledge International Handbook of Political Corruption*, edited by Paul M. Heywood. Albington, England: Routledge.

Weintraub, Ellen L. (2004). "Perspectives on Corruption." *Election Law Journal* 3(2): 354–59.

Welch, Susan, and John R. Hibbing. (1997). "The Effects of Charges of Corruption on Voting Behavior in Congressional Elections, 1982–1990." *Journal of Politics* 59(1): 226–39.

Welch, William P. (1982). "Campaign Contributions and Legislative Voting: Milk Money and Dairy Price Supports." *Western Political Quarterly* 35(4): 478–95.

Werner, Timothy. (2011). "The Sound, the Fury, and the Nonevent: Business Power and Market Reactions to the *Citizens United* Decision." *American Politics Research* 39(1): 118–41.

Werner, Timothy, and John J. Coleman. (2014). "*Citizens United*, Independent Expenditures, and Agency Costs: Reexamining the Political Economy of State Antitakeover Statutes." *Journal of Law, Economics, and Organization* 31(1): 127–59.

Winter, Ralph K. (1997). "The History and Theory of *Buckley v. Valeo*." *Journal of Law and Policy* 6(1): 93–109.

Wright, John R. (1985). "PACs, Contributions, and Roll Calls: An Organizational Perspective." *American Political Science Review* 79(2): 400–14.

Index

For the benefit of digital users, indexed terms that span two pages (e.g., 52– 53) may, on occasion, appear on only one of those pages.

Note: Tables and figures indicated by an italic *t* and *f* following the para ID.